MESTIZO

The History, Culture and Politics of the Mexican and the Chicano

The Emerging Mestizo-Americans

Arnoldo Carlos Vento

University Press of America,® Inc.
Lanham • New York • Oxford

Copyright © 1998 by
University Press of America,® Inc.
4720 Boston Way
Lanham, Maryland 20706

12 Hid's Copse Rd.
Cummor Hill, Oxford OX2 9JJ

Library of Congress Cataloging-in-Publication Data

Vento, Arnoldo C.
Mestizo : the history, culture, and politics of the Mexican and the
Chicano : the emerging Mestizo-Americans / Arnoldo Carlos Vento.
p. cm.
Includes bibliographical references and index.
1. Mexican Americans— History. 2. Mestizos—United States—
History. 3. Mexican Americans—Ethnic identity. 4. Mestizos—
United States—Ethnic identity. 5. Mexcian Americans—Politics
and government. 6. Mestizos—United States—Politics and
government. I. Title.
E184.M5V42   1997   305.868'72073—dc21   97-37402 CIP

ISBN 0-7618-0919-8 (cloth: alk. ppr.)
ISBN 0-7618-0920-1 (pbk: alk. ppr.)

CONTENTS

PART I   ROOTS, COLONIALISM
**   AND CONFLICT (300 A.D.--1890)**

CHAPTER I PRE-COLUMBIAN CULTURES OF AMERICA
I THE CLASSICAL PERIOD:THE RISE OF GREAT CIVILIZATIONS

II THE POST-CLASSIC PERIOD:THE TOLTEKAH CONFEDERATION

            (1) Chicano Cultural Background
            (2) European Racial Legacy
            (3) Socio-Economic Classifications
            (4) The Treaty of Guadalupe Hidalgo
            (5) The Chicano Movement
            (6) Chicano Characteristics
            (8) Assimilation & Imitation
            (10) The Mexican and *Mexicanidad*
            (11) The Chicano/Chicana & *Chicanidad*
            (12) The New *Mestizajicanidad*

CHAPTER IV   THE CLASH OF TWO CULTURES
            (1) The Background: English-American &
                Spanish Colonialism
            (2) Culture and the Hegemonic Process
            (3) Religious Intolerance, Expansionism
                and Exploitation
            (4) Cultural/Religious Bias and Colonial
                Literature
            (5) Attitudes towards Mexicans and Native-
                Americans

PART II   THE XX CENTURY MESTIZO/ CHICANO

CHAPTER V   MEXICAN/ CHICANO ADAPTATION,
RACISM & RESISTANCE

PREFACE

During the mid eighties, after teaching and compiling a variety of cross-disciplinary materials for my courses in the essay on the Mexican and the Chicano, a plan to develop a cross-disciplinary text was brought to fruition. Concerned with the socio-political, cultural and religious background to the various cultures affecting the Mexican and Chicano, research was completed after a number of years in the following areas: (1) Pre-Columbian cultures, particularly Aztec or Anahuakano nations forming the Confederation of Anauak., (2) Medieval Europe, Bizantium and Islam, (3) Colonial and twentieth century Mexico, and (4) The United States Mexican and /or Chicano, from 1848 to the present.

While there are some chapters that present highly detailed research, the overall intent is to create an introductory text to the study of *La Raza*, its cultural, political and religious heritage from the Native-American past to the North American present. One of the concerns is the question of identity, which has been, for some time, an issue with Mestizos of Hispanic and amerigenous heritages on both sides of the border. Thus, identity becomes a central issue in addition to the insider/ outsider labels that change from time to time. Moreover, the important issue of gender is discussed as it affects Chicanas and Latinas both in Mexico and the United States. At the core of discussion is the ideology and philosophy of Western culture vis a vis ancient autocthonous civilizations with their universal principles and world view in addition to possible alternatives for a new society as we enter the twenty first century.

Chapter I lays the foundation for the Mexican and Chicano Mestizo. Its main objective is to present an autocthonous perspective relative to their world outlook, their philosophy and metaphysics. This position is different from the traditional Western /European interpretation of Pre-Conquest society and culture. Discussion ranges from the Classic Cultures to the Post Classic Renaissance of the Confederation of Anauak. Particular attention is placed on the differences between Western / European culture and Pre-Columbian civilization and some of the guiding principles of pre-Conquest native peoples.

Chapter II is concerned with the effect and impact of European/ Spanish culture and religion on existing native cultures. The Medieval religious and political legacy , especially as it relates to the Spanish and the *Sanctum Officium* are outlined in detail. Moreover, Colonial myths established by the *Gachupin/ Criollo* of New Spain about Aztecs is presented in detail, ranging from the Colonial myth of polytheism to human sacrifice.

Chapter III probes into Mexican counter hegemony, the self criticism of the twentieth century, and the problem of identity . Essayists range from Antonio Caso to Roger Batra. In addition to the themes of *Mestizaje* and *Mexicanidad,* the second part of the chapter discusses the cultural and political background of the Chicano/ Tejano/ Mexican-American. It moves from a discussion of Chicanidad to the new *Mestizajicanidad.*

Chapter IV analyzes the clash of two cultures within the parameters of the United States . This chapter explore the myths established by the dominant culture and its historical and political negative impact on native and peoples of color. Hegemony, hispanophobia and expansionism are analyzed vis a vis the Spanish-speaking population in the United States.

Chapter V looks into the Mexican/ Chicano adaptation and resistance to racism, the various organizations that formed in the twenties, thirties and forties to cope with racial discrimination against the Spanish-speaking in different levels of society.

Chapter VI brings into focus Chicano mobilization and organization in the sixties and seventies. The role of César Chávez,

Reies López Tijerina, Rodolfo Corky Gonzáles and Angel Gutiérrez are perused as well as the role of *La Raza Unida* Party.

Chapter VII brings to light the positive effects of the Chicano Movement as seen in the Chicano academic, cultural and literary achievements. Discussed are Chicano Studies programs, Student organizations, Chicano presses, literary and artistic festivals and prose fiction. Luis Valdez' contribution to theater and Ricardo Sánchez' in poetry are discussed in greater detail.

Chapter VIII presents the cultural inheritance, the question of identity and gender awareness . It begins with Chicano dialects, humor, Curanderismo, Tejano music, Chicano cinema and moves into an analysis of *Chicanismo* and *Mestizajicanidad*. The last part of the Chapter is dedicated to the Chicana/ Latina. It presents the stereotypes , the Western models and the new Mestiza-American, in addition to their accomplishments in culture, politics and literature.

In short, it presents a critical insider's view from a cross-disciplinary perspective of the problems affecting the fastest growing ethnic group in the United States. The issues discussed here are but a point of departure for future discussion of what promises to be the most important group that will impact U.S. society in the twenty first century.

Arnoldo Carlos Vento
University of Texas at Austin

ACKNOWLEDGMENTS

Mestizo as a text was conceived in the late eighties. The objective was to present a multi-disciplinary view of the Mexican and Chicano. Much work has gone into bringing together the eight chapters, front and end matter. First, I am indebted to the few who contributed with technical assistance in the initial stages of the writing of the text: They are: Kay Sammons for the initial chapters concerned with the pre-Columbian cultures and Colonial Mexico and Betty Guzmán for the chapters analyzing Chicano culture and identity. Similarly, I would like to extend my gratitude to Beatriz Ramírez Vento for assisting with the Bibliography and Jean Lord Vento for her meticulous proof-reading of the final draft.

This text brings together twenty two images of the Mexican and Chicano's cultural and political heritage. With the exception of the photos of Selena provided by her father Abraham Quintanilla and the Austin Chicano protest photos of the seventies by Allan Pogue, the rest were photographed from a variety of sources by this writer. I would like to express my sincere thanks and gratitude to those that extended permission to reprint the photos used for this book: they include Pauline Kibbe and the University of New Mexico Press (p.174), Stan Steiner and Harper Colophon Books (p.209), La Raza Publications (p.284), Barrio Bilingual Communications (p.248), Mr. Gilbert García of San Juan, Texas (p.144), Mrs. Teresa Sánchez and Rikard Sánchez (p.245), Cecilia Preciado Burciaga (p.125), Mr. Abraham Quintanilla and Q Productions (p.273), Mr. Allan Pogue (pp.217, 288), Dr.Ramón de León and artist Diane Edwards (p.269), Herschel Manuel and The University of Texas (p.193), and Dorset Press, Mirolav Hroch and Anna Skybova (pp.41,72)

Finally, I would be remiss if I did not extend thanks to the Center for Mexican-American Studies and Prof. David Montejano at the University of Texas-Austin for his assistance and encouragement which has contributed much to the total effort of producing this work.

PART I

ROOTS, COLONIALISM AND CONFLICT

CHAPTER I

PRE-COLUMBIAN CULTURES OF MEXICO

I. THE CLASSICAL PERIOD: THE RISE OF GREAT CIVILIZATIONS
INTRODUCTION

The golden age of Mexico, the florescence era known as the Classic Period, is a time when great civilizations with arts and sciences reach their highest refinement. This Classic span is generally thought to cover between A.D.300-900. Literacy begins very early; dates were recorded in terms of the 52-year Calendar Round and in the Gulf Coast the Long Count was used. From the Olmec period, now a crystallized complete pantheon shared by all Mexicans, surface abstract representations of Rain, Fire, Sun and Moon in sculpture and paintings. These were not gods per se but manifestations of the Great Spirit Force; thus they paid homage to them since they were basic forces affecting everyday life.

Care must be taken not to place particular characteristics on a people simply because such a notion may have taken place, e.g., warfare. It is doubtful that any civilization in the world flourished without some type of military defense. This, however, does not make a nation warlike nor imperialistic. The notions of militarism were introduced by the Spanish, who projected this into their writings as participants of a war machine and an imperialistic European tradition. On the other hand, it must be remembered that not all tribes were peaceful; many, for different reasons, represent the attacks that have befallen high civilizations as was the case with *Tollan* (Tula). The early Mexican Amerigenous cultures raised numerous buildings, decorated with beautiful frescos. They produced pottery and figurines in unbelievable quantity and covered everything with sculptures. Farming continued now with new irrigation methods; there is also the intensification of sharp social cleavages throughout Mexico and the consolidation of the ruling groups. It has been assumed that the mode of government was theocratic and to some extent religious as a way of looking at the cosmos but not in superstitious, medieval ways of the European; rather, it was viewed as a science in view that the priests were also the astronomers and scientists. Neither did the scientists-priests have total power; they were an integral part of the educational system along with other important rulers of government.

THE URBAN CIVILIZATION OF *TEOTIHUÁKAN*

Teotihuákan was perhaps the greatest city of all ancient Mexico. Even *Moktekuzoma Xokoyotzin* made pilgrimages there during late Aztec times. Memories of its greatness have been kept after the Conquest. Here in symbol, the forces came together to give light to the New Sun (age), the Fifth Sun. Governments were established, the lords or ruler-scientist-priests were "wise men, knowers of occult things, possessors of the traditions". The pyramids were said to have been built as a resting place for the great lords; these were built by giants who lived in those days.[1]

The metropolis covered nine square miles and was fully urbanized about the time of Christ on a grid plan consistently oriented 15 degrees, 25 minutes east of true north[2] The city was laid out in quarters with the major axis running north to south for a distance of four miles. The Pyramids of the Sun and Moon measure 225 meters long and as little as 70 meters high. Of interest is a cave underneath the Pyramid of the Sun that was discovered by accident in 1971. The cave is a natural lava tube running 100 meters in an easterly direction six meters beneath the pyramid, in from a stairway on its main axis, reaching a multi-chambered terminus shaped something like a four-leaf clover.[3]

Teotihuákan, by the sixth century, will reach a population of 200,000 at its maximum, making it the sixth largest city in the world. The city was cosmopolitan; in the west there was a Oaxacan ward; in the east a ward for businessmen from lowland Veracruz and Mayan areas. The palace compounds were residences of the lords of the city. Typical of what a palace layout might be, the palace of *Xolalpan* was a rectangular complex of about forty five rooms and seven forecourts; these border four platforms, which are arranged around a central court. The court was depressed below the general ground level and was open to the sky, with a small altar in the center. Air and light were admitted through a roof and rainwater could be drained off. Doorways were rectangular and covered by a cloth. The walls of palaces were adorned by magnificent frescos. The most famous is at *Tepantitla*, where a large fresco in blue, red, yellow and brown covers an entire wall representing a paradise ambiance of *Tlalokan* or the symbol of rain and its creative beauty.

In the *Teotihuákan* pantheon, there are many representations in sculpture of the forces of the Great Spirit; *Tlalok*--Rain Force; *Ketzalkóatl*--a creative force associated with intelligence, *Metzli*--representation of the Moon Force and *Xipe Totek*--symbol of the annual renewal of vegetation. Particularly common are the stone effigy incense burners in the form of the Ancient Fire Force, *Huehuetéotl.* Additionally, a colossal statue is found of *Chalchiuhtlikue*, representing the "feminine" aspect of the Rain Force, related to *Tlalok*. Early Classic *Teotihuákan* culture is characterized by the cylindrical pottery vase with three slab-shaped feet, a fitted lid and handles in the shape of a bird. Other characteristic forms in clay include vessels shaped like a flower, large polychrome incense burners, mold-made figurines of men and representations of transcendental forces. Obsidian chipping reached new heights of elaboration with the production of spear and dart points as well as human effigies. The *Teotihuákan* state controlled great deposits of green obsidian; over 350 obsidian workshops existed near present-day Pachuca, Hidalgo alone. Bone needles and bodkins testify to the manufacture of clothing and basketry. Paintings reveal that men wore loincloth and/or a type of kilt with sandals and women, the pull-over *huipil* and underskirt.

Writing existed both for ritual and administrative use as witnessed on the pottery and in the frescos. It is known that the bar and dot numeration (used later by Toltecs and Aztecs) was used in the 260-day count (almanac year). Diet consisted of small-cobbed maize, common and runner beans, squashes, pumpkins, husk tomatoes, prickly pear cactus, avocados, amaranth and a large variety of wild plants. The important food animals were deer, rabbits, turkeys, wild ducks and geese. Irrigation systems were in use and there is evidence of a chinampa or "floating garden" cultivation.

Its success is also linked to its long-distance trade and influence, even in regions as remote from the capital as the Gulf Coast, Oaxaca and the Maya area. *Teotihuákan* art has been found in the highlands of Guatemala and in Tikal. Who were these people? The origin is in question from Totonac to Otomí to Popoloca. What is clear are the affinities between *Teotihuákan* and Toltec-Aztec sacred and secular features, i.e., the *Uto-Azteka-Metzikak* features. The city will meet its end by A.D.700 through deliberate burning and destruction. Archeologically, tombs after A.D. 600 no longer stock refined products of *Teotihuákan*. Some $_6$suggest internal crisis or long-term political and economic malaise; however, the cyclical idea of birth and rebirth inherent in $_7$pre-Columbian cultures is probably a more plausible explanation. Severe climactic changes associated with the$_8$calendar may also have played a role in the desertion of the city.

CACAXTLA AND XOCHIKALKO--THE MAYAN LINK

After the disintegration of the *Teotihuákan* empire in A.D.700, there appears to be a more active interrelationship with the Maya and the highland Mexican. *Cacaxtla* is one of a number of hilltop sites in the Puebla--Tlaxcala border area that was controlled by "the people of the region of the rubber" and the "people of the land of calabashes"$_9$ The latter had an important trading town controlled by the Putun-speaking Maya, seafaring merchants whose commercial interest ranged from the Olmec country through the entire coast of the Yucatán Peninsula as far as the shore of Honduras. The murals of *Cacaxtla* are thoroughly Maya but the flat-roofed architecture is not and there are similarities to the coeval palaces of *Xochicalco* and the later Tula. The artwork is highly symbolic with eagle, jaguar, serpent, maize, bird and sea animals juxtaposed for meaning at metaphysical levels as interpreted by the sage scientist-priests. *Xochicalco* similarly shares this connection, founded about A.D. 700, it had extensive foreign contacts with the Maya area, Zapotec, Mixtec, Oaxaca and Classic Central Veracruz. Near the ceremonial plaza and not far from the Temple of the Feathered Serpent is a cave transformed as an underground observatory with a man-made tube to the surface where for two days of the year a beam$_{10}$ of sunlight penetrates the shaft to the observatory floor. Moreover, *Xochicalco's* ball court with its Maya-like I-shape has the same dimensions as the ball court at Tula of the Toltecs centuries later.

THE CLASSIC VERACRUZ CIVILIZATION

A large number of finely carved stone objects found in the Gulf Coastal plain in its own unique style characterize Classic Veracruz. Some are elongated, others "yoke"-shaped, cylindrical or headdress designs. An important center lying five miles southwest of Papantla is *El Tajin*; its nucleus covers about 60 hectares but subsidiary ruins are scattered over several thousand hectares. Occupied in the Early Classic, its peak activity was towards the close of the late Classic (A.D.600-900). Most impressive is the Pyramid of the Niches, a four-sided structure with unusual symmetry with the solar days (365) on the sides and inside is a duplicate pyramid of the outer one. Relief panels exhibit winged dancers, eagle-like warriors, ceremonial ball court rituals and bar-and-dot numerals with day glyphs testifying to the literacy of this civilization.

Death and sacrifice has been greatly misunderstood by Westerners. It begins with the superstitious colonial chroniclers and clerics and is echoed by art historians and modern researchers of pre-Columbian peoples. Death and sacrifice are associated with the spirit and not the body as was the case with medieval Europeans. Death means rebirth; it is constant in nature and in our actions as human beings; it is not to be looked at from a literal sense, but rather from a transcendental metaphysical framework. Sacrifice requires fasting, meditation, and giving in prayer and ritual. Blood letting (not leading to physical but spiritual transformation [death]) from particular spiritual zones was a type of$_{12}$ sacrifice alluded to in El Tajin as well as other high civilizations.

An exuberant style of pottery from Central Veracruz named *Remojadas* pottery reveals much ethnographic formation of this period. Figures cast in clay molds with paint are subjects, both male and female, animal and human: infantile boys and girls with laughing faces and filed teeth; ballplayers, lovers or friends in swings, warriors, symbolic representations of forces, i.e., death, rain, light. Most notable is pottery showing the use of wheels and the understanding of its principle albeit in clay figurines.

The end of *El Tajin* was by fire, similar to *Teotihuákan*. Common tradition suggests that it was conquered by Chichimec nomadic barbarians from the highlands circa A.D.1300.

CLASSIC MONTE ALBAN

The civilization of Monte Alban in the Valley of Oaxaca during Classic times was the product of Zapotecan-speaking peoples. Oaxaca was sufficiently isolated during the Classic Period and its people were left to themselves to populate their own territory, building site after site. By the close of the Early Classic (Monte Alban III), there were no less than 200 sites in the Valley of Oaxaca. The buildings have architecture in common with *Teotihuákan*, stuccoed and beautifully painted. It contained large plazas, stairways, ball courts and grandstands. In the subterranean parts of pyramids, 170 tombs have been discovered. They contain elaborate chambers, fine frescos, hieroglyphs, and clay urns. The style is characteristic of *Teotihuákan* and the pantheon of symbolic representations of forces are shared with the Mexican peoples: Rain Force (*Cocijo*), the Maize Energy (*Pitao Cozobi*), the Life Force (*Ketzalkóatl*), the Old Fire Force (*Huehuetéotl*) and possibly the feminine aspect of the Rain Force, (*Chalchiuhtlikue*). Although there are no surviving codices, glyphs appear everywhere in sculptured relief, on funerary urns and walls, both at the principle site and at other Monte Alban centers. By A.D. 700, the capital was largely abandoned with no signs of conflagration.

THE CLASSIC COLLAPSE

When Teotihuákan disintegrated in the seventh century, the unifying force in Mesoamerica was gone, and with it, widespread inter-regional trade. The Late Classic saw increasing fractionalization, each culture moving along its own lines. By A.D. 800, the powerful but never unified Mayan city-states began to disintegrate. However, the Putun or master traders (Olmec-Xicallanca) appear to have prospered during these times as they are in contact with both the Central Mexicans and declining Maya rulers. No one is certain regarding the identifying factor for the collapse. Some point to an agricultural collapse (due to a climactic change), some to pressure from the barbarians form the north. In the end, it is more probable that multiple forces came together cyclically to announce the end of these civilizations but only to bring forth new ones in the Post-Classic Period.

II. THE POST-CLASSIC PERIOD: THE TOLTEKAH CONFEDERATION

After A.D. 900 a new mode of organized life emerged. The salient characteristic is the emphasis on defense, probably because of the constant threat of northern nomadic barbaric tribes. It is not that the intellectual[13] hierarchy of the older cultures was relegated to inferior status, but a new need for defense brought about the formation of military orders, not in a material but in a spiritual sense; thus, the sacred forces symbolized by the jaguar and eagle now were part of a sacred duty, i.e., the defense of a culture, a nation. The introduction of metallurgy appears to have taken place at the beginning of the Post-Classic Period. Casts of metal objects, almost entirely of copper, appear on the West Coast of the Republic with form and technique similar to Peru and Ecuador, suggesting trade with the Andean area along the Pacific Coast. In the realm of jewelry, the craftsmanship of the Mexican goldsmith reached heights of great artistry.

THE NORTHERN NOMADS: THE *"TEO-CHICHIMEKAH"*

A number of nomadic hunters carrying bows and arrows inhabiting the desert wastelands beyond the northern limits of Mesoamerican farming began to migrate southward, bringing pressure on the newly developing states. These northerners were called *Chichimekah* and, according to Sahagún, the wildest of all were the *Teo-Chichimekah*, who lived in animal skins, subsisting on wild fruits, roots, seeds and meat of small animals. Among them was a more civilized group called *Tamime-Cichimekah*, who had acculturated somewhat with their neighbors to the south. Together, they were the heirs of ancient cultures: the Uto-Aztecan-speaking *Zakatekah* and Tepehuan, the Guachichil of unknown affiliation and the Pame. In general, the northerners, like all desert culture tribes, were quite peaceful, particularly when conditions were relatively good. When, however, the reverse was true, the nomads, driven to desperation and starvation, pushed south into regions occupied by tillers of the soil, raiding the outposts of civilization. This would account for the great Chichimec invasions which took place in the Post-Classic Period.

TOLLAN AND THE *TOLTEKAHS*

The Toltecs (the artificers), composed in the beginning of disparate tribal elements, built a civilization that became the highest in arts and sciences. From their capital, *Tollan*, they ruled much of Northern and Central Mexico as well as parts of the Guatemalan highlands and most of the Yucatán Peninsula. Among the Toltec groups included the *Toltekah-Chichimekah* and the *Nonoalka*, who, according to some scholars, were sculptors and artisans from Puebla and the Gulf Coast brought in to construct the monuments of *Tollan*. Led by the legendary *Mixkóatl* (Serpent of the Cloudy Milky way) known as a patron of hunting after his death,[14] the *Toltekah-Chichimekah*, by A.D. 908 had entered civilized Mexico at the southern extension of the Sierra Madre Occidental, passing through what now comprises northern Xalisco and southern Zacatecas. Much of their history is registered from post-Conquest contradictory accounts, but according to the generally accepted scheme of Jiménez-Moreno, *Mixkóatl* and his people first settled at a place in the Valley of Mexico called *Colhuákan*. It was Jiménez-Moreno who observed that even Sahagún was not infallible. Since he depended upon what common informants told him, we can never be sure that they did not sometimes follow the time-honored custom[15] of telling their interlocutor what they guessed he wanted to hear.

Culhuákan, from *Culhua* or *Colhua*, derives from *kolli*, meaning grandfather; thus, *Culhuákan* is "the place of those who have ancestors". This name became associated with the Toltec urban dwellers of the Valley of Mexico as distinct from the successive waves of *Toltekah-Chichimekah* after the fall of *Tollan Xikokotitlan*. The fall of *Tollan* covered a period of some two generations.[16] People were leaving by A.D. 1122 or 50 years before the departure of *Topiltzin Ketzalkóatl*. According to Nigel Davies, it is more likely that *Topiltzin* is headed for the Valley of Mexico than Mayaland, whose communications by then had been severed. *Huemak*, his rival, followed quickly in his wake, and in 1178 left *Tollan* for Chapultepec, where he perished. The *Nonoalcas* also departed, led by *Xelhua* and other rulers, eventually reaching the *Cozkatlan-Teotitlan-Tehuákan* area after settling *Huakechula, Izukar* and other places on their route. *Ixtlilxochitl* mentions the Toltecs dispersing in many other direction: Xiuhucoac (toward Huasteca), Guatemala, Tehuantepec, Totontepec (coast of Oaxaca), Tecolutla (Gulf Coast) and Campeche.

The *Memorial Breve* names the Culhuas among the original migrants to Central Mesoamerica who came out of Chicomostok; it also calls them Chichimecs. Six cities were subject to *Kulhuákan* when it was *Tollan's* partner: *Xochimilko, Kuitlahuak, Mizkuik, Coyoakan, Maninalko* and *Okuilan*. The *Memorial Breve* insists on the importance of this city and states that a triple alliance of *Tollan, Kulhuákan* and *Otompan* comprised the Toltec Confederation.

Reconstructing the history of the Toltec as well as the Aztec has led to a confusing plethora of contradictions; on the one hand, archeological evidence does not always agree with the written records or conclusions and/or methodology of the investigators. Many of the records are post-Conquest, unreliable or merely allegorical. Thus, the student of Mesoamerica is faced with a multitude of problems which are aggravated by a lack of contemporary versions of events and the limitations of pictorial codices, often misread or misinterpreted.

Moreover, many of the surviving accounts were not compiled in the sixteenth century or soon after contact with the Spaniards, but emanate from later chroniclers more remote from native traditions. One of the most blatant inventions, now Native-American/Colonial mythology, is the creation of a physical *Ketzalkóatl* god, who is immolated in one version or disappears in the east in another; this invention has all the trappings of Western perceptions. On the one hand, we have an anthropomorphic god similar to the Christ figure of Christianity; on the other hand we have the convenient expectation of his return, now, of course, in the shape of the Spaniard entering through the east, i.e., Veracruz. The idea of the destruction of *Ketzalkóatl* is not possible in the pre-Columbian mind-set. It is not a person but a force that is eternal. The historic person alluded to here is *Topiltzin*, born in A.D. 935 or 947, son of

Mexkóatl of *Cohuakan* in the Valley of Mexico (later identified to the confusion of modern scholars with the plumed serpent, symbol of *Ketzalkóatl*). It is clear that the *Ketzalkóatl* referred to historically in Toltec times is a person and an office or title. There is not cosmic connections whatsoever between *Ce-Acatl Topiltzin-Ketzalkóatl* disappearing in *Tlillan Tlapallan* and the symbolic force depicted as a feathered serpent or alluded to as *Tlahuizkalpantekuhtli-Xólotl* (the planet Venus)[20]

It is this historic personage that becomes heir to *Mixkóatl* and his first rule is to transfer the Toltec capital from *Cohuakan* to the ancient *Tollan*. According to tradition, he was a priest-ruler dedicated to the peaceful worship of "the Feathered Serpent", *Ketzalkóatl*. He is depicted as a Christ-like figure, performing fasts and penances. He creates a schism with *Huemak*, associated with the *Nonoalcas* of *Tollan*. Some scholars have come to see a religious conflict, i.e., *Tezkalipoka* with *Huemak* and *Ketzalkóatl* with *Topilzin*. This is not likely since this type of war belongs only to fallible types here on earth; it is not part of the divine scheme of things as might be the case with an ancient angry *Yahweh*. Neither is it an ethnic conflict; rather, it is a political/power struggle between two rulers. The result is the expulsion of *Topiltzin* and his followers circa A.D.987. After this begin the tales, the mythology and the colonial accommodation.

Another concept much in controversy and confusion is the term *Tamoanchan*. Seler sees it in the west as "the house of birth", associated with a goddess living in *Cihuatlampa*, "the mythical west", the Kingdom of Darkness where the sun sinks into the earth.[21] Others see it in the south, the Center of the Earth. Davies argues that there are probably two references; one a mythical reference and the other, an historical place. Due to the many references to *Tamoanchan* in many different contexts, it has come to represent a new but related concept. Linguistically, there are many derivations offered but most probable is the idea of a place of origin where there is richness and abundance, water, cloud and mist. This is the prehistoric place of origin of the Toltecs; it is analogous to *Aztlan* for the Aztecs. With regard to *Tlillan Tlapallan*, associated with *Topiltzin* as his after his expulsion from *Tollan*, there appears to be no consensus as to its meaning. Seler sees it as the Mayaland; Davies sees its significance as the east, the place where the red of the newly-risen sun emerges out of the surrounding darkness[22] Here, again, there is confusion between the legend and the historic event. While there are some that suggest that *Topiltzin* migrated into the east and by inference into Putun territory, i.e., Tabasco, Campeche and the east coast of Yucatán, the symbolic sacred references of black and red associated with *Ketzalkóatl* refer not to environmental descriptions but to written knowledge and perhaps the coming or the return of the Quetzal to Chichén Itzá.[23]

In summation of the aforementioned events, the following chronology outlines the Mexican impact on the Maya: (1) After the disintegration of *Teotihuákan* during the predominantly *Puuc* period in Campeche and Yucatán as well as Late-Classic Maya sites farther inland, "Mexican" or non-Maya influences became manifest particularly in the Tuxtla mountains in southern Veracruz and part of Tabasco as well, (2) Sometime during the ninth century a Putun group (later called Itzás) departed southward and occupied Chichén, (3) Toltecs from the *Nonoalcah* stock came back from *Tollan* to *Nonoalco* in Tabasco and continued their journey to what is now Chichén Itzá. What is not clear is whether they arrived as traders or as invaders. Since trade was paramount since *Teotihuákan* times, one must assume that this was a primary force. War, however, could have broken out but not the type that signifies conquest. What is most likely is the reaching of an accord in which each group lives separately, influences notwithstanding, impacting both cultures. Roys insists that the Toltecs have imported general concepts and attitudes rather than a definite pattern of living and that a Maya aristocracy continued to exist in Yucatán during the Toltec period,[24] 4)Art forms develop as the result of contact for both cultures. While Maya skill is present, there develop new concepts of space and subject attributable to the Toltecs, in addition to religious and ceremonial influence. Too much has been made about conquest, a theme projected in mind and fact by the Spanish and subsequently reiterated by scholars today. Somehow, it is inconceivable to the Western mind that the development of an empire can be made without the violence that Europeans were accustomed to enacting. Confederations of both the *Toltekah* and *Aztekah* nations were the result of a highly developed diplomacy, an established understanding of international law, ethnic and linguistic respect and a sophisticated democratic government of confederated tribes.[25]

The concept of *Toktekáyotl* should be seen from different levels, i.e., intellectual, historical, aesthetic and spiritual: (1) the Toltecs of *Teotihuákan*, the possessors of wisdom and the creators of arts and sciences (stemming from earlier origins), (2) the Early Post-Classic *Toltekahs* of *Tollan-Xikokotitlan*, the developers of a large confederation, (3) the Late Post-Classic Toltecs of Cholula, Tabasco and Yucatán as great artists and craftsmen, the epitome of all that is delicate and refined in Mesoamerica, and (4) the continuation of ancient religious concepts abstracted in stone and paintings opposes the generally accepted view of religious proselytism, a characteristic that is inconsistent with Mesoamerican cultures[26]

THE UNITED STATES SOUTHWEST CONNECTION

As examples of Toltec influence to the north are the sites of Alta Vista and La Quemada in the state of Zacatecas during the Early Post-Classic Period. Contact with Pueblo peoples can be seen at the site of Casas Grandes, Chihuahua. There, the presence of platform temple mounds, an I-shaped ball court and the homage paid to the Feathered Serpent are indicative of its links to Toltec culture. The transmission of these cultural traits still plays a role in the rituals of the Hopi and Zuni. The trading route has been given the modern appellation of The Turquoise Road due to the blue-green turquoise available in the New Mexico area for trade. Similarly, Toltec traits are evident in the Southeastern United States (Alabama, Georgia, Tennessee) where temple mounds and ceremonial plazas, associated pottery and other artifacts, show strong Toltec influence. This suggests two possible scenarios: (1)Trading routes northward were common (as oral history suggests), and (2)The Uto-Aztecan linguistic family have cultural traits in common ranging from the Algonquian tribes to the Midwest (Menomini, Lakota, etc.) to the Southwest (Hopi, Zuni, Pima, etc.).

LATE *ZAPOTEKAN* CULTURE: MITLA

In the Early Post-Classic a new center of *Zapotekan* civilization sprang up in Mitla. Among its inhabitants it was known as *Lyobaa* or "Place of Rest". The architecture of Mitla is of unparalleled beauty; long panels and entire walls are covered with geometric stonework mosaics. Underneath the five groups of palace-like structures are catacombs believed to be the resting place of past holy priests.

In mountainous land in western and northern Oaxaca are the *Mixtekans*. Miraculously, eight *Mixtekan* pre-Hispanic codices have survived the inquisition of the Spanish. They are a combination of pictographic and rebus principles accompanied by dates of the 52-year Calendar Round. The rebus phonetic method was also used later by the *Aztekan* peoples in the Valley of Mexico. The *Mixtekans* were great statesmen as they ruled not only the *Mixtekah* proper but most of the *Zapotekan* territory by Post-Classic times.

Michael Coe cites several dynasties beginning in the Post-Classic Period after the *Mixtekan* power was overthrown in a town called "a Mountain that Opens". Here, the establishment of the first dynasty ruled jointly by *Tilantongo* and *Xipe* bundle. During the second dynasty, when the *Mixtekans* were clearly under the influence of the *Toltekahs*, a young boy called 8 Deer (born in A.D. 1011) son of ruler, became a mighty warrior. In 1045 he made a journey to *Tollan* where he was invested a *Toltekah* nose button,[27] marking the accession to the throne. Expansion of state borders through marriage were an orthodox manner of alliance; 8 Deer marries no less than five times to his alliance wives /"princesses" of other regions. By A.D. 1350 the *Mixtekans* began to expand to the Valley of Oaxaca by the usual method of state marriage, *Mixtekan* royal brides bringing their own retinues to the *Zapotekan* court. They had great wealth and high artistry as they were known as the finest goldsmiths and workers in turquoise mosaic in Mexico. As far north as Cholula, *Mixtekan* artistic influence was felt, resulting in a type of hybrid *Mixtekan*-Pueblan style producing some of the finest manuscripts, sculpture, pottery and turquoise mosaics of latter-day Mexico. By uniting with the *Zapotekahs*, they prevented being vanquished and became one of the few independent nations of Post-Classic Mexico.

THE *PURÉPECHA*: THE TARASCANS

Living in *Michoakan* (The Place of the Masters of Fish), the Tarascans, as a nation, were also never dominated. Much of their history centers on Lake Pátzcuaro in Western Mexico which abounds with fish. Not belonging to the Uto-Aztecan linguistic family, the Tarascan's *Purépecha* language remains a mystery in terms of its origin.[28] By the Late Post-Classic, the Tarascan state was bounded on the south and west by areas under *Aztekah* control and on the north by the *Chichimekahs*. While the majority of the population was ethnically mixed, the small minority of pure Tarascans dominated. Their first capital, Patzcuaro, was founded in A.D. 1325 under their legendary ruler, *Tariakuri*. Eventually, they conquered all of present-day Michoacan. *Ihuátzio*, on the southeastern arm of the lake, became the capital, to be succeeded by *Tzintzúntzan* as the royal seat of power.

Their government was well developed with judges, administrators and counsels; their society enjoyed a variety of functions in occupations: masons, doctors, silversmiths, artists, zoo keepers, military personnel, etc. In terms of the priesthood, celibacy was not practiced in a highly complex religious organization. Rituals included tobacco as homage was paid to the moon, to "grandfather" fire. The ruins of *Tzintzúntzan* have *yácatas* or rectangular stepped pyramids joined by a stepped passageway to a round stepped pyramid. Some have seen similarities to the Incas while others suggest that the Tarascans may have taken over some of the northern *Toltekah* trade routes after the downfall of *Tollan*. They were excellent warriors, great artists and architects with a culture that recalls the civilization of the Andes.

III.THE POST-CLASSIC RENAISSANCE:
    THE CONFEDERATION OF ANAUAK
ROOTS ,EARLY FORMATION AND THE NATURE OF A PEOPLE

Early critical studies of the early *Aztekah-Metzika* migration made in the Thirteenth Century tended toward literal interpretation of the original accounts which were partly symbolic and mythical in nature. During the Nineteenth Century Manuel Orozco y Berra, among others, carried their interpretations to other extremes, treating these sources as merely myth to the degree that *Aztlan* was considered a reflection of *Metziko-Tenochtitlan* in the Valley of Mexico. This position was incredibly held, likewise, by Edward Seler. Davies believes that the question of *Aztlan* should be sought farther afield beyond the pale of Middle American civilization. While most sources agree that the *Azteka-Metzika* visited *Chikomoztok* and *Culhuákan*, some sources confuse the meaning by combining *Aztlan Chikomoztok* and *Aztlan Culhuákan*. It does not mean, as Davies thinks, that they are to be sought in the same area.

Cosmic Energy in Metaphysical Configuration: Mediocrity vs. Elevated Consciousness

Aztlan is described as a place surrounded by water, while *Chikomoztok* is referred to as the rock from which one rises...where there abounds countless wild beasts, bears, tigers and serpents.[33]

I believe that Davies is correct in stating that *Chikomoztok* is a mythical place of departure while *Aztlan* is a place of origin. One needs to add, however, the idea that *Chikomoztok* is not so much a place as it is a time frame in which the various tribes lived. *Yakanini Metzli Kuautemok* (Dr. Juan Luna Cárdenas) was the first to postulate this concept, asserting that it refers to the glaciation period.[34] Dr. Luna Cárdenas, an Aztec native and scholar, breaks down the etymology to mean, "In the age of the multiple caves", a time when man perfected language, pictographs and writing. The long journey from this place probably was not one group but several. While they were referred to as Aztecs since ancient times, there is a point when at least one group will be recognized as *Metzikahs* (Spanish--Mexicas), which some think comes from *metzli*, meaning "moon". I do not accept, however, the romantic and impressionistic notion that they received this name because the moon reflected on the lagoon where they originally lived. Rather, *Metzli* is the name of the clan, ergo, *Metzli* clan is the Moon clan. There are numerous families in the state of Guerrero who can trace their descent to the *Metzli* clan circa 1500s.

It is estimated that the long migration probably lasted from A.D. 1111 to A.D. 1345.[35] It is through pre-cognitive visions by their ruler-sage-priests that they learn of their future, a future with great constructions of temples, ball courts, harvested crops, a word of grandeur with multi-colored cotton, precious stones and splendor. In their migration, they settle in different places, living by agricultural and hunting skills in a specific social/religious structure. Their language is *Aztekah Náhuatl*, the language that predominates from the United States to Central America, and they came with knowledge of astronomy and calendaric calculations. En route they visited *Cuextecatl-Ichocayan* (The Place where the Huaxtec wept) and *Coatlicamac* (In the Mouth of the Serpent). There are apparent splits among the native groups which can further be interpreted symbolically by a tree splitting in two under which the *Aztekah-Metzikah* were sitting. When they reach *Coatepac* or "Hill of the Serpent" near *Tollan* (Spanish--Tula), they celebrate the *Fuego*

Nuevo, which marks a new beginning, a new 52-year cycle in their sacred 260-day calendar.

Friar Sahagún, in his third book, relates the origin of the divinity in a somewhat anthropomorphic form[36] in which *Coatlicue* (Skirt of Serpents) is a devout woman who is the mother of 400 sons and who is impregnated by a ball of feathers. Indignation on the part of the sons and a single sister brings about a plan to slay her, but one turns traitor and forewarns the offspring still in the womb (*Huitzilopochitl*). Thus, *Huitzilopochitl* triumphs over the sister (*Coyolxauhqui*) and orders a river to be dammed to create the conditions of their former home of *Aztlan*. These post-Conquest tales by uneducated informants of Sahagún cannot be taken literally but rather they must be read symbolically. Here there are two central concepts, one of origin and one of propriety and will. The former refers to *Koatlikue* as the dispenser of humanity from its initial origins; the latter refers to the spirit of correctness and will to succeed, i.e., one needs will to succeed but in the path of correct principles. This is the esoteric and symbolic representation of *Huitzilopochitl* and not the common and degenerate interpretation of the "God of War"[37]

These clerical versions (Florentine Codex, Durán, etc.) are, unfortunately, too similar to Biblical accounts, i.e., *Uitzilopochtli*, like Jehovah, leads his people to the promised land. Davies sees a contradiction; he surmises that the original leader (*Huizilopochtli*) was not a deity but a mortal who had died, now a legend, becoming a deity.[38] Alfonso Caso creates the traditional interpretation of rebirth, i.e., the sister and 400 brothers as the moon and the stars with *Huizilopochtli* (sun) wiping them out with the beginning of the day. Thus, he is the Lord of the Daylight Sky associated with blue and with the south.[39] Because of the association of the hummingbird (*huiltzin*) with the departed spirit of warriors, Davies concludes he must be "the God of War", embodying the Mexica will to conquer.[40] Here, the problem is one of association to human deeds; instead, one needs to see it as a symbol, i.e., the struggle between oneself and the consciousness of the ever-present changes and forces. One must find the will to conquer oneself spiritually, not materially. Thus, *Uitzilopochtli* is not the God of War, but a force, a symbol of proper will to overcome changes and subsequent fears, from a spiritual level.

After leaving *Coatepac* in 1168, the *Metzikah* arrive at *Tollan*. By then, *Tollan* is in a state of desolation. They sojourned in *Xaltokan* in the midst of a lagoon. After Xaltokan they came to *Tenayuka* (The Place where Walls are Made), capital now of the nomadic *Chichimekahs* who had occupied the Valley of Mexico after the disintegration of the *Toltekahs*. This town reached its height from A.D.1200 to 1250. In A.D. 1300, the Metzikah arrive in *Chapultépek*. By now, whatever tribes had come into the valley had adopted *Toltekah*[41] high culture. The principle center was still *Kulhuakan*, the surviving *Toltekah* city of the region. It represented as much a renewal as[42] a survival of *Toltekah* civilization, of legitimacy and survival

Two important groups had settled in the valley, the *Acolhua* and the *Tekpanekahs*. The *Acolhua* settled in the region of *Texkoko* along the eastern shore of the lagoon. Their main center was *Koatlichan*; other important centers were *Acolman* and *Huexotla*. Also of great significance[43] of those preceding the *Metzikah* were the *Tekpanekahs*. The *Tekpanekahs* settled to the west of the lagoon, their principle city being *Azcapotzalko* (The Place of Ant Heaps). It was this group that would dominate the *Metzikahs* in the early years. Davies notes with perspicacity that the European chroniclers erred in their labeling of *reyes* or kings in view that it cannot be applied to the governments of Mexico: "frequently the title of ruler is partly elective in nature and, equally, rule tends to be pluralized, with more than one lord for each people."[44]

In the end, they shared the same cultural heritage and the general spiritual[45] pantheon was common to all, including the *Metzikah*. Within the divine dimensions exists the abstract symbol *Ometekuhtli* and *Omecihuatl* within the thirteen dimensions of the cosmos known as *Omeyokan*[46] Their existence underscores the duality principle within all living things; thus, an imitation in rituals and society (two scientist-priests, two merchant leaders, two governing rulers). Since the pre-Columbian civilization was very advanced in mathematics and other natural sciences, numbers became an important factor in everyday life. People carried manual calculators on their wrists and their calendaric understanding of time and space was incredibly accurate. According to Rubén García, the *Aztekahs*, through their cultural/scientific lineage inherited a calendar encompassing 372,400 years and were able to predict[47] eclipses hundreds of years in advance with exact precision. Other numbers important in their cosmic numerology were four (four directions, four ambassadors, etc.) as well as the number five (includes the center of the four directions, a concept familiar to the Chinese). According to Davies, another similarity to Chinese thinking is that the cardinal points are identified with specific colors.[48]

The sacred 260-day calendar formed an integral part of the *Aztekah's* understanding of the cosmos. It is not based on religious principles as usually assumed, but rather on astronomy and scientific understanding of cyclical planetary phenomena. Like other high civilizations of the past (e.g., Chinese), it formed a[49] philosophical/psychological framework around numbers. The *Tonálmatl*, heretofore mentioned, is an instrument that was used by the *Tlamatinimi* or sage scientist-priests to understand the type of personality that would best fit a variety of professions available to the student in a society that was *totally* literate. Post-Conquest information referring to evil (Florentine Codex, II, Chapter 8) by malicious intercalations of ignorant sources and clerics are a good example of psychological projection of medieval Catholicism obsessed with evil and Satan.[50]

THE ARRIVAL TO *CHAPULTÉPEK* AND PROBLEMS OF SETTLEMENT

The arrival of the *Metzikah* to *Chapultepek*, principally is governed by their priest-rulers, the Four Bearers of the Divine Force. It is through visions of *Huizilopochtli* that they await events. Their clans have now risen from the original seven to 15 or 20. Their leaders are sometimes referred to as "captains". Davies cites this phase as a military democracy, although he says it was more theocratic than democratic. Plural rule was in conformity with local traditions but they chose a single leader probably not because of conquest motivations but because at their stage of development, it was necessary. The *Metzitin* (Spanish--Mexica) had no friends and were without an area that they could govern as a nation. To say that they were cast for the role of vassals is to project a European system nonexistent in pre-Columbian Mexico.

According to *Tezozomok*, the *Metzitin* multiplied in number after the fashion of the Sons of Israel in Egypt under King Pharaoh; thus, their neighbors began to be troubled and to make war upon them with the idea of getting rid of them.[51] The *Metzitin* were expelled from *Chapultepek* on two separate occasions. The first assault occurred in 1315; the second in 1319. There are conflicting post-Conquest versions regarding the details of the battles, foes and the aftermath.[52] To be sure the *Metzitin* go to *Kulhuákan* with total humility. In an effort to keep them at a distance but with a watchful eye, the council of *Kulhuákan* decides, after some discussion, to have them establish themselves in *Tizzapan*, a volcanic wasteland infested with snakes and other dangerous reptiles. According to the *Crónica Mexicóyotl*, they not only prospered but roasted and ate all of the reptiles to the amazement of the *Kulhua*. Thereafter, they settled down to cultivate the fields and construct temples and dwellings. Collective rule was restored with their government involving four *Tlamatinimi* or sage priests, *Tenoch* as the foremost among them. Eventually, an alliance is made and the *Metzitin* enter *Kulhuákan* to trade and deal freely. Soon they crossed bloods and became kinsmen. *Wizilo Pochtli*, the historic person, became instrumental in assisting the *Kulhuákans* defend themselves in war against the tribes of *Xochimilko* (Spanish--Xochimilco). The strife that breaks out later with the *Kulhuákans* has several versions, largely gruesome following the pattern of Spanish medieval prejudice and discredit. What is most likely is that the rulers of *Kulhuákan* became threatened by the prowess of the *Metzitin* and warned them that if they did not escape immediately they faced annihilation.[53]

After some struggle, they subsequently escape and go to a place called *Acatzintlan*, where they constructed their ritualistic *temaskalli*.[54] The language of the Codex Ramírez is so brazen and negative that its version of the founding of *Metziko-Tenochtítlan* is simply not deserving of space. Agreement on the origin of the word *Mexico* is nonexistent and the opinions are varied, from "rabbit" to "cactus"; from "springs" to "maguey cacti".[55] A more autocthonous interpretation is by Dr. Juan Luna Cárdenas, who is a native speaker and descendant of *Metzikah-Toltekah* lineage. According to Dr. Luna-Cárdenas, the name was given to a place in honor of a ruler of a particular lineage from where his family derives the name *Meçiti*

(*Metzitin*), later corrupted to *Mexiti*.[56] The word *Metzitli*, in proper *Aztekah Náhuatl* (Lord of the Moon), has the meaning of a character that incarnates the representation of *Metzli* (Moon-Gens. Lunar), i.e., the Clan of the Moon. Thus, *Metziko* is a place of the Clan of the Moon under the totem *Metzitli.Tenochtítlan* means the principle place of *Tenoçkatl*. *Tenoçkatl* was the son of a military head named *Wewe Tenoçkatl* who defended the *Toltekatl* Confederation against the invasion of the northern tribes. He was at that time the supreme head of the *Azteka-Metzika* armies of the Confederation of *Koatépek*, near *Tollan*. Upon his death, his son Tenoçkatl took over and guided the Moon clan to the Valley of Mexico. Proof of this interpretation can be seen in the monolith of *Weyi Teopan* where the correct date of *Ze Toçtli* (One Rabbit) is given, to the appearance of *Wizilo Pochtli* (Spanish--*Huizilopochtli*), and *Tenoçkatl* (the son) is mentioned and the date *Ome Akatl* of the *Fuego Nuevo* (The Sacred Fire of the New Cycle) celebrated a few years after the founding of *Metziko-Tenoçtítlan* is included.

THE FOUNDING OF *METZIKO-TENOCHTÍTLAN*

With regard to the founding of Metziko- Tenochtitilan, the identification of the propitious symbols was not the result of an arbitrary or rational decision. It was the result of visionary phenomena known today as precognitive information acquired through the superconscious level. It is interesting to see scores of researchers think in terms of their own society i.e. rationalist/materialist and then implant it on a society and culture that does not derive from that mold but rather from a metaphysical tradition. It is no wonder that in our society, medical doctors still cannot understand Oriental cosmology or metaphysics. To begin to understand the system of energy flow within the bioplasmic body is to go beyond the material level of understanding of reality.

The pre-Columbian high cultures have much in common with ancient Tibetan and Chinese cultures. To be able to understand their world, scholars first need to release their Western perceptions of reality. Next, they must have a native understanding of their language. And last but most important, they need to use a non-Western, non-Judeo/Christian perception of reality; an understanding into the metaphysical world of pre-Columbian peoples. The latter is difficult since this is the last sacred space that authentic natives are not willing to share with foreigners.[57]

To sum up this point, the long pilgrimage of the *Metzitin Atlanekah* (Men of the Sea) suffered many invasions of unfamiliar tribes although there were tribes of other linguistic nations such as the Tarascan nation that had accompanied them, separating definitively in *Patzakuaro*. Their pilgrimage continues, guided by ruler visionaries. Upon their arrival to the *Valley of Anahuak*, the governing head of *Atzkapotzalko* is *Akolhua*, the forth ruler of the first stage of *Çiçimekah* dynasty.[58] *Akolhua* was ambitious and demanded much from the *Metzitin*. Exhausted by the demands, the *Metzitin* appeal to the ruler of *Tetzikuko* for one of his sons. Not wanting to intervene in view of the ambitious *Akolhua*, he suggests that they go to *Akolhua* directly. In an effort to prevent suspicion, the *Metzitin* divide into two groups; thus, two rulers would be requested. One group settled in what is now the *Zócalo* in México City and what was then called *Metziko-Tenochtitlan* (after a ruler called *Wewe-Tenoçkatl*). Here the third son of *Akolhua* named *Akamapíztli* (he with the face of bamboo) is designated as ruler. The other group is established in what is now *Tlaltelolko* in Mexico City. To this group, the second son *Mixkohuatl* is delegated. Muñoz Angulo sees this as the second of a series of alliances that will be formed leading to various confederations of *Anahuak*. The first alliance in the early formation is the *Aztekah-Metzikah-Tenoçkah*; the second is the *Aztekah-Metzikah-Tlaltelolkah*.[59]

SECOND EPOCH OF FORMATION: GOVERNMENT AND LEADERSHIP

It is important to note that prior to this second epoch in the formation of the *Metzikatl* nation , a type of republican government was comprised of five advisors including women; thus, making it the first government to allow political rights to women. In this case one of the "Presidential" advisors was a woman called *Matlalziuatzin*. It is with *Akamapizli* that the government assumes an elective monarchy. After the death of *Akolhua*, his son *Tezozomok* begins the second stage of the *Çiçimekah* dynasty with its capital now in *Tetzikuko* (Spanish--Texcoco). *Kinatzin Tlaltekatzin* as the eighth ruler, along with *Tezozomok*, were able to defeat the invasions of the kingdoms of *Metztitlan* and *Xaltokan*. *Tezozomok*, however, is threatened by *Kinatzin's* power and slowly attacks him until his death. *Kinatzin's* youngest son *Teçotlatzin* takes over becoming a progressive organizer, stirring jealousy from the monarchy of *Atzkapotzalko-Tenayokan* in the hands of *Tezozomok*. His struggles in defending *Tetzikuko* brings him his death as well as that of his brother *Ixtl Xóchitl*, ninth and tenth rulers, respectively.

Tezozomok, already the great *Çiçimekatl Tekuhtli* of *Atzkapotzalko* and *Tenayokan*, is named ruler of *Tetzikuko* through which he rules with a severe hand. It is only through the diplomatic efforts of the *Metzitin-Tenoçkah* that his successor *Netzalualkóyotl* is pardoned and subsequently taken to Tenochtitlan to be educated in the *Telpochkalli and the Kalmekatl* until reaching mental, emotional and spiritual maturity. The twelfth governing head of the *Çiçimekah* lineage (second stage, *Tetzikuko* as capital) is *Maxtla*, a cruel ambitious successor who produces a war with the *Metzitin-Tenoçkah* (Mexicas of the *Tenoçka*h lineage). He is subsequently defeated allowing *Nezaualkóyotl* to assume the governing head and form part of the Confederation of *Anauak*, thus allied with *Tenochtitlan*. *Nezaualkóyotl*, a noble example, is an architect, a military superior, a legislator, a poet and philosopher. His legacy will be followed prudently by his son, remaining firmly allied with *Tenochtitlan*. The final *Çiçimekah* rulers include *Kakamatzin* who, because of envy of his brother, *Ixtli Xóchitl*, will force a division of land in the nation and who, in a treasonous manner, will ally with the Spanish at the time of the Spanish invasion.

In summation, the *Metzikatl* nation (Mexica--Hispanisized deformation), also known on the coast as *Atlanekah* (sailors) and *Aztlanekah* (men of the beach) in their pilgrimage south to the Valley of Mexico, suffered many invasions by invading tribes, including the Tarascans. They had lived in Nayarit, Xalisco, Michoacán and Guerrero. They were part of the *Tultekatl* lineage. They arrived when *Akolhua* was governing head of *Atzkapotzalko* suffering many hardships. At the beginning in their first epoch after foundation, their governing structure consisted of five governing advisors (four males and one female called *Matlalzinatzin*). In the second epoch there is an elective monarchy in which two governing heads are granted by the *Tetzikuko* capital, i.e., in *Tenochtitlan* (*Akamapíztli*) and in *Tlatelolko* (*Mixkohuatl*). At the beginning the electorate pertained to the administrative body. But the Supreme

Council of Elders, noting the potential of power abuse and self-interest, decided on extending the voting power to the citizens in general, thus preventing social struggles or internal wars. Among the citizens, it was the Elders under the Great Council of Elders that was given the power to elect governance. In this manner the "monarchy" was parliamentary, democratic and elective. The elected governing heads did not have absolute power since it was checked and balanced by the Council of Sages and the Council of Elders. Within the government, they had departments of justice, education, economics, "work", commerce, military and treasury. After the governance of *Akamapixtli* and *Uitzilihuitl*, *Çimalpopoka* governs for a brief time, becoming a victim of internal affairs with the family of *Atzkapotzalko*. Upon hearing the news, the Metzitin reunite the Supreme Council and elects a head from their own tribe. Among the candidates were the highly esteemed *Ilhuikamina* and *Itzkóatl*. It was *Ilhuikamina* that gave his vote of confidence to Itzkóatl and thus began the third governing epoch that was now independent of the *Çiçimekah*. Moreover, it was a time to fortify the defenses due to the threats of *Maxtla*, thirteenth ruler of the *Çiçimekah* dynasty. In a battled headed by the supreme military head Ilhuikamina and assisted by the forces of *Nezaualkóyotl*, the tyrant *Maxtla* was finally defeated. The restoration of *Nezaualkóyotl* to *Tetzikuko* thus became possible to a great degree by the efforts of the *Metztitin*. *Atzkapotzalko* lay in ruins giving way to the building of a new capital and a new city of *Tlakopan*. The *Metzitin* under leadership of *Itzkóatl*, broke new ground in governance, abandoning the old republican and monarchical forms of government and opting for a representative and democratic system. He conceived a peaceful and democratic alliance between *Tetzikuko* (Texcoco) headed by *Ne zauakóyotl* (Nezahualcoyotl), *Tlakopan*, headed by *Totokihuatzin* (*Tekpanekah* tribe) and *Tenochtítlan* (*Itzkóatl*). This is known historically as the Triple Alliance. It is when *Maxtla* (twelfth governing *Çiçimekah* ruler) is defeated that *Ilhuikamina* assumes the rulership of *Koyohuákan*, adding another nation to the existing Triple Alliance, and subsequently forming the Quadruple Alliance, comprised of *Tetzikuko*, *Tlakopan*, *Tenochtítlan* and *Koyohuákan*.

As previously stated, with the fall of *Maxtla*, the twelfth ruler of the *Çiçimekatl* dynasty, the *Metzitin* gained a measure of independence and their town of *Tenochtitlan* rapidly grew into a thriving and prosperous metropolis. According to Muñoz Angulo, this became possible largely through the efforts of the first minister of state, the illustrious diplomat and military genius, *Tlakaelel*. More than once he was offered the highest position of governance and each time he refused, content in guiding the Confederation to social and political development.

After the death of *Itzkóatl* (liberator and organizer of the nation) in 1440 as the first ruler of the third epoch of the development of the *Metzikatl* nation in *Tenochtitlan*, *Moktekuzoma Ilhuikamina* reigns until his death, benefiting from the assistance and advise of *Tlakaelel*. It is at this point that the *Aztin-Tenoçka* (Aztecs from *Tenochtitlan*) swear to defend the national moral code which consisted of not permitting drunkenness, theft, adultery, homosexuality, lies or prostitution. It is also during *Moktekuzoma Ilhuikamina's* reign that construction of a system of dikes begins that stretched 16 kilometers. This was accomplished through the cooperation of the Confederation heads of the Quintuple Alliance of *Tetzikuko*, *Tlakopan*, *Iztapalapan* and *Koyohuákan*. Upon *Moktekuzoma Ilhuikamina's* death in 1468, the young *Axayákatl* is elected at a time when the *Purepecha* (the Tarascans) are planning the extend their domains, giving rise to the great battle of *Tlalximaloyan* (today--Ciudad Hidalgo). Attempting to extend their territory to the sea, they attacked *Akoliman* but were defeated in the environs of *Çapallan* (today--Chapala). It is during these years that the great general and diplomat *Tlakaelel* dies, bringing about a most venerable and solemn funeral. Later, in 1481, *Axayakatl* dies with *Tizok* succeeding him as the ruler of the Confederation. In time, together with Ne *Zuaupilli*, he was able to quell the uprisings near the Gulf of Mexico occurring largely because of commercial reasons. *Tizok*, ironically, dies accidentally during an inundation. Taking his place was the illustrious and intelligent *Ahuizotl*, elected on the thirteenth of April, 1486. During his reign there is progressive Mayan penetration into *Aztin* settlements in *Kuauhtemallan* (today--Guatemala). The *Zapotekah* and *Mixtekah*, likewise, had blocked the passage of the *Aztin* troops and had sacked caravans of *poçtekah* (merchants) en route to Central and South America. *Ahuizotl*, upon learning of these attacks, begins a series of military offenses that marks the possession of the Isthmus of *Tekuantepek, Chiapan,* and *Kuauhtemallan,* unifying, moreover, the *Aztin* of Honduras and Costa Rica, notwithstanding securing the Valley of Oaxaca, establishing an *Aztekah-Tenoçkah* populace.

A peaceful alliance was accorded with the *Zapotekah,* sealed ultimately with the marriage between the ruling *Zapotekah* head and the daughter of *Ahuizotl.* In 1502, there were a rash of social disturbances, attacks on *Aztin* merchants in *Tekuantepek* and *Kuauhtemallan,* which were quickly extinguished by *Ahuizotl.* After these battles and upon returning to *Tenochtitlan, Ahuizotl* falls ill to a sickness acquired during his military campaigns[67] and dies the ninth day of September in 1502.

MOKTEKUZOMA XOKOYOTZIN: THE INVASION OF METZIKO-TENOCHTITLAN

Succeeding *Ahuizotl* was *Moktekuzoma* II, surnamed *Xokoyotzin* (the Younger). *Moktekuzoma Xokoyotzin* was highly cultured, urbane and yet simple in his treatment of others. He was disciplined and responsible in his duties, showing balance and good judgment even when facing danger. When he was elected[68] he had just finished his meditations and was sweeping his room.

The *Otomites* (of Apache origin) in the regions of *Nopallan* and *Ikpaktepek* armed an invasion against the Confederation, probably to test the young ruler. After several *Aztin* families had been killed, *Moktekuzoma Xokoyotzin* took the challenge and quelled the uprising. Shortly thereafter, *Moktekuzoma Xokoyotzin* had to lead a military campaign against the aggressive ruler of the *Mixtekah.* History seldom looks at *Moktekuzoma Xokoyotzin* in this light; rather, he is seen as the ruler who allowed Cortés to take advantage of him, eventually assassinating the *Aztekah* ruler. What is often neglected is the highly advanced diplomatic laws that were in place at the time of the arrival of the Spanish. It was customary to receive ambassadors from other nations and to allow them to rule along side of the existing *Aztekah* ruler for a period of six months. It should also be remembered that co-rulership of the Confederation had been a practice that had its origin since the early days of *Akamapixtli.* It followed the concept of duality in nature; in governance this bi-personal rule had divided the administrative and diplomatic responsibilities between two heads. It is during the

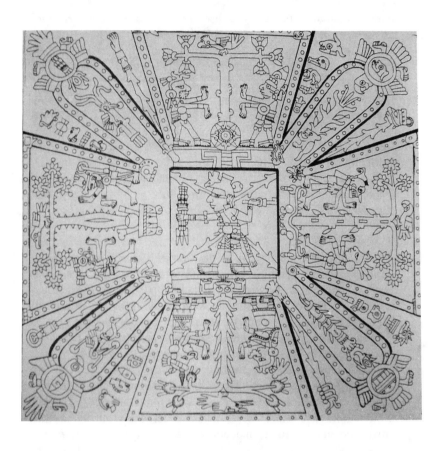

The Concept of Duality within Life and Nature in this Universe

uprising of Cortés and his soldiers (motivated by the gold in the palace of *Axakayatl*) that *Moktekuzoma Xokoyotzin* is assassinated. Subsequently, *Kultlahuiak* is elected to succeed and to defend *Tenochtítlan*, which he accomplishes, defeating Cortés. This is known as the night of victory to the *Aztekahs* and the *noche triste* to the Spanish. A year later, Cortés will ally with the very large tribe of *Tlaxkalla* and together they will systematically attack villages (recruiting warriors) en route to *Metziko-Tenochtítlan*. According to Jorge Gurría Lacroix, there were 460 Spaniards and 524,000 captive natives conscripted for war on hand to attack the capital of the Confederation of *Anauak*, defended by an estimated 12,000 *Aztin* warriors[69] Logistically, the battle favored the attackers in view that *Tenochtítlan* was an island with two causeways and an aqueduct of spring water from *Çapoltepek*. When food and water were cut off from the island, it became a matter of time before the defenders would weaken from starvation and thirst. Incredibly, the island was defended an estimated 72 days.[70]

THE BROKEN TREATY OF AUGUST 22, 1521 AND THE ANATOMY OF A NATION

The last of the defenders of the Confederation of *Anauak* was *Kuautemok*, who was tortured and assassinated by Cortés after a treaty was developed between the Spanish and the Aztekahs. This marks the first broken treaty by the Europeans in the Americas on August 22, 1521. This treaty was drawn by the *Ueyi Tlatokan* (Supreme Council) of the Confederation and called for (1) the safe-guarding of the *Aztin* women in a manner worthy of respect and dignity, (2) the maintenance of *Metzikayotl* or the essence of being *Metzika* (*Mexicanidad*), and cultural beliefs for future generations.[71] Cortés accepted the accord but as soon as he found himself in control of Metziko-Tenochtítlan, he launched a ferocious attack on the native citizenry, destroying monoliths and monuments representative of *Metzikah-Tenoçkah* culture. This ends a highly advanced culture and civilization that had inherited the high principle of human thought from the *Teotihuákan* and *Toltekah* cultures. It includes great works of art, subtle poetry and literature, a positive spiritual/metaphysical framework that was in accord with astronomy and mathematics, an accurate calendaric system unsurpassed by the Western world,[72] a multi-leveled democratic governing system which included women at all levels,[73] an active educational system that guaranteed literacy to all of its citizens,[74] a writing system that was phonetic, numeric, calendaric, pictographic and ideographic, a predictive numeric/psychological profile by which persons could be guided professionally,[75] a scientific understanding of the Supreme Force and its manifestations,[76] a non-materialistic society that obviated possession of things through the cyclical *Fuego Nuevo* celebration,[77] an understanding of evolution in the planetary scheme of things,[78] an advanced knowledge of medicine and surgical procedures,[79] a profound understanding of the interlinking tie between all human beings via *Tloke-Nauake* leading to true fraternity, collaboration and brother/sisterhood, respect for women's rights, respect for other languages and ethnicities via Confederation structures, self-determination as individuals and as confederated tribes, respect for Mother Nature and a deep understanding of its patterns, bringing about ecological balance between man/woman and the natural forces, from which he/she is sustained, the establishment of manual calculators and a highly advanced mathematical system that went beyond the European rectilinear numeric count into curved numeric calculations, open and infinite as well as cyclical and finite, the establishment of a process through which a person could seek *Neltiliztli* (Truth) or the essence and the foundation of things by reaching *In Yoltéotl* (Enlightened Spirit), the creation of botanical gardens that were several miles long, the creation of animal zoos, not as pets but for behavioral study, a positive view of death (cyclical and evolutionary), the development of advanced agronomy (e.g., colored cotton), and the establishment of a moral code that provided a well-balanced and actualized individual.[80]

THE END OF HIGH CULTURE AND THE BEGINNING OF WESTERN HEGEMONY

With the arrival of the Spanish and Western culture came, (1)the vertical and feudal concept of society and the destruction of a democratic and economic communal system, (2)the medieval concept of Might is Right leading to imperialism and exploitation of the weak by the strong, (3)the importation of slavery, (4)the introduction of legalized forced labor (*Casa de Contratación*), (5)*machismo* as a Mediterranean trait, (6)the use and abuse of women with a total disregard for her rights and human dignity,

(7)the introduction of color and race prejudice, (8)the introduction of religions based on fear and damnation, (9)forced holy wars of conversion, (10)religious intolerance, (11)avarice and materialism and (12)the creation of plutocracies.

AZTEKAH EDUCATION AND THE SEARCH FOR *NELTILIZTLI* AND *COHUÁYOTL*

In Aztekah society, self control, good education and social order were very important. Everyone was taught discipline, good behavior and principles. A civilized man was one who could master himself, who had dignity and integrity, a well-developed mind (*in yóllotl*) and spirit (*in ixtli*). To the pre-Columbian *Aztin*, man or woman was not to contemplate on the essences but to achieve an internal possession of the root of things to bring about harmony to the mind and spirit. What was sought was *Neltiliztli*, true words that gave the root and foundation to man or woman on Earth. It was thought that a person could make himself/herself true by establishing a dialogue through the spirit, making the connection with the divine force so that he/she could be transformed, reaching *Yoltéotl* or an enlightened state. This was the most complete act of understanding, an exercise in existential self-affirmation in which will and the self are projected in a positive socio-spiritual framework.[81] This was, in the end, a culture whose high principles and ideals were strongly socialized with the idea of being master of oneself by bringing balance and understanding to the spirit and mind (*in ixtli, in yóllotl*) so that ultimately human kind could live in harmony through the concept of *Cohuáyotl* or community.

ENDNOTES

[1] It is possible that the time frame is inconsistent with the concept and time frame of the giants. Beyond the Biblical references to giants, there are many other cultures and traditions that speak of giants in a prehistoric framework. While Egyptians use pyramids for resting places of the great lords, these had other important functions, i.e., astronomy, metaphysical functions, calendaric functions, etc

[2] Many astronomic explanations have been given for this alignment. To be sure, it is related to astronomy and metaphysical theory of energy.

[3] While post-Conquest tradition point to *Teotihuákan* as the creation of the present "universe", it would appear that the cave had special energy significance, a type of energy vortex in the womb of Mother Earth; this would be reason enough to build the towering Pyramid of the Sun; it follows that the higher-evolved and select lords be in touch spiritually or energetically with outer dimensional forces.

[4] It is interesting to note that among Native Americans of the Uto-Azteca linguistic stock (Lakota, Hopi, etc.), the sacred fire in ceremony is referred to as "grandfather", akin to the *Teotihuákan-Toltekah-Aztekah Wewe* (*Huehue*) meaning "old one" and thus "Grandfather" (Fire Force).

[5] See William Sanders, Jeffrey Parsons, Robert Santley, *The Basin of Mexico: Ecological Process in the Evolution of a Civilization.*

[6] Michael Coe, *Mexico* (New York: Thames and Hudson, 1984), p. 72.

[7] The Aztecs, who fashioned much of their cosmology after the Toltecs and great civilization of *Teotihuákan*, also destroyed all buildings every 52 years (Aztec cyclical "century") to begin anew in another cycle.

[8] It is difficult for most Westerners to imagine leaving possessions and the "economy" behind. In Lakota tradition, Westerners were given all of the material possessions by the native; a position never understood by outsiders.

[9] *Olmeca* for the former and *Xicallanca* for the latter. Cited by chronicler Diego Muñoz Carmargo, referring to their capital as Cholula where the most massive structure in the pre-Columbian world exists, i.e., the great pyramid of Cholula, dedicated to *Ketzalkóatl* (10 hectares and 55 meters in height), complete with palma; in place of a head are seven serpents that

arise form his head. To the Westerner who sees everything from a material/physical standpoint, this represents a severed head, thus human sacrifice (echoes from the colonial clerics). This is a superficial Western view of reality. This stelae is replete with metaphysical symbolism which has to do with astronomy, the spirit, birth and rebirth, all associated with the ball court ritual ceremony. (Were he physically dead, why is he seated so erect and poised?)

[10] No doubt related to astronomy and ritualistic calendar as seen, not only in modern Maya groups but also in Toltec and Aztec tradition.

[11] Too much has been made of human sacrifice by art historians and colonial clerics and subsequently voiced by archeologists, historians and anthropologists. I suspect the problem is one of literal visual perceptions rather than abstract/metaphysical understanding of birth/rebirth cycle of the spirit and not matter. On a stela in Aparicio, Veracruz, a ceremonial ball player *is seated* with a symbolic seven serpent head. It has been suggested that he has been sacrificed (Coe, p. 111). This is based on a relief panel from the northeast wall of the South Ball Court in *El Tajin*, Veracruz. While there appears to be a flint type of instrument by his necklace, there is no concrete evidence that he was killed. Why could it not be a ritual in which "blood letting" is initiated? This ritual has to date been greatly misunderstood as some kind of primitive and painful sacrifice. With regard to the seven-headed ball player, if one is to go on impressions, why is his body alive and seated and not limp and dead? The author makes reference to snakes which bring to mind evil imagery in the Western Judaic/Christian religious symbology. The problem here is that serpents do not symbolize evil or death in the pre-Columbian metaphysical scheme of things. Rather than death or evil, it represents cosmic energy, a connection to higher dimensions, i.e., beyond the third dimensional plane in which we operate. With respect to the relief panel in which there appears an "underworld" dimensional representation on the side, if one is to go to the extent of assuming death to be taking place, then it is possible it may fall under the venerable category of heroic death, distinct from the banal rituals described by revisionist inquisitional clerics responsible for the writing of history during the censored colonial period.

[12] Linda Schele has studied the Maya extensively. She alludes to the practice of blood letting by lords as a form of sacrifice. What comes across, however, is the physical sacrifice, similar to flagellation, both characteristic of medieval European Roman Catholic practice. Rather it should be seen as a technique which transforms energy, a method that brings about higher consciousness much like acupuncture spiritual points. In this regard they were centuries ahead of current medical understanding of the human body. The Sundance of the Lakota is somewhat parallel.

Westerners, however, are horrified in view of their physical material interpretation, as opposed to the spiritual/metaphysical/symbolic reference by the Lakota people.
[13] Michael Coe. Position by the author; also suggests its possible disappearance, when in actuality, the high civilization of *Tollan* (Toltec capital) reached the zenith in arts and sciences the knowledge of which was due largely through the transmission of Teotihuákan knowledge and practices. See *La Casa de Jade*, by Dr. Juan Luna Cárdenas for an appreciation of intellectual and scientific hierarchy and achievement in the Toltec state.
[14] In the *Toltekah-Aztekah* tradition there are various names that are given to a person at varying stages of maturity. The last name given is related to an attribute that the person is able to dominate; here, the skill as a hunter was probably the test that as a young boy, *Mixkóatl* was able to dominate.
[15] Nigel Davies, *The Toltec Heritage: From the Fall of Tula to the Rise of Tenochtítlan* (University of Oklahoma Press: Norman, 1980). Citing Davies: "Sahagún lends added force to statements in other sources depicting Quetzalcoatl as a benevolent deity who shuddered at the mere thought of human sacrifice. According to parallel versions of the story, Quetzalcoatl, like his Peruvian counterpart, Viracocha, traveled through the land dressed rather as a Dominican friar and conducted a kind of preaching tour, healing the sick and summoning the people to repentance. But Viracocha in his original form was a sun deity and Quetzalcoatl both as creator and god of fertility was connected to agriculture. Both were, therefore, typical ancient American deific forces, and their pitiless nature was quite alien to those Christian or European virtues with which they were credited by Spanish chroniclers."(p.20) The same has occurred with Andean pre-Columbian research. John Murra in his *Formaciones económicas y políticas del mundo andino* (pp. 279-80) insists: "It becomes necessary to transform casual reading of the chroniclers into a rigorous examination; only by a persistent analysis of the primary sources will it be possible to find a substitute for those outmoded methods of arbitrary accumulation of reports of questionable value. Such rigorous criteria was used by Maria Rostworowski who was able to make a sound case for the hypothesis that Cuzco was governed by *two* rulers at a time, notwithstanding the insistence of the Hispanized written documents on the presence of a single and supreme Inca." The Aztec oral tradition speaks of two rulers, one political, one administrative as well. See María del Carmen Nieva, *Mexicáyotl* (México: Editorial Orión, 1980).
[16] Nigel Davies, *The Toltec Heritage*, p. 5.
[17] See, *Historia tolteca-chichimeca* (Mexico: Robredo, 1947), p. 151.

[18] Chimalpain, *Memorial Breve*, p. 20, *Acerca de la fundación de la ciudad de Culhuacan*, Trans. Walter Lehmann, Stuttgart, 1958. It should be pointed out that Chikomoztoc is not a place as is interpreted during colonial times and seconded by scholars in pre-Columbian culture; rather, it refers to a time frame, i.e., the glaciation period when man had to live in caves, paint glyphs on the walls and develop their own form of writing.

[19] An example of later writers include *Ixlilxóchitl* and Torquemada who provide valuable information of the ancient past but who, likewise, add to the confusion by adding new mythology of their own to supplement the old. Torquemada thus lists not merely Romans and Carthaginians but even the Irish as possible ancestors of the Toltecs!

[20] To understand the symbology of the Feathered Serpent, one must understand the metaphysical significance behind the Quetzal and the Serpent; in no way can they be seen in physical or material ways.

[21] Edward Seler, *Codex Borgia I*, p. 155.

[22] Davies, p. 181.

[23] Among the *Aztekah Tlamatinimi*, the codices bearing higher knowledge of the sages were always written in black and red. The fusion of *Ketzalkóatl* and *Kukulkan* has been seen as a new Jerusalem but likewise I would like to add as a reinforcement of previous *Teotihuákan* influences.

[24] Roys, Ralfph L., "Native Empires in Yucatán", in *RMEA*, vol. XX, pp. 155-78.

[25] See Juan Luna Cárdenas, *La Casa de Jade, Prehistoria de America*. His four-part video series originating out of the University of Texas--Austin explains an authentic Aztec perspective on government, education, etc., of Aztec civilization.

[26] Davies, Nigel, *The Toltecs: Until the Fall of Tula* (Norman: University of Oklahoma Press, 1977), p. 417.

[27] Michael Coe, p. 140. Author suggests by either 4 Jaguar (a king) or 8 Death (a priest). It would only be proper for a priest to perform this ritual. The codex pictograph appears to show 8 *Mazatl* (8 Deer) and 8 *Miquiztli* (8 Death) as identities through its corresponding calendaric/pictographic glyphs. Moreover, glyphs of *Echekatl* and *Kozkaquantli* signify peace, honesty and spirituality.

[28] See the *Relación de Michoacán*, an early Spanish translation of one or more documents in Tarascan.

[29] Michael Coe (*Mexico*) believes that these traits are more South American than Mesoamerican.

[30] Representative of literal interpretations were Francisco Xavier Clarijero, *Historia antigua de México* (Mexico: Porrua, 1964) and Mariano Veytia, *Historia antigua de Mexico* (Mexico: Editorial Leyenda, 1944) (2 vols.).

[31] See Manuel Orozco y Berra, *Historia antigua de la Conquista de Mexico*, 4 vols. (Mexico: Porrua, 1960) and Edward Seler, *Gesammte Abhandlungen zur Amerikanischen*, Sprachund Altertumskunde (Austria: Druck und Verlaysanstaldt, 1969).

[32] Davies brings up an interesting Western idea on how the clerics' imaginations were easily moved via their own Biblical background and much to the chagrin of the natives. See Fray Diego Durán, *Historia de las Indias de la Nueva España e Islas de la Tierra Firme*, 2 vols. (Mexico: Porrua, 1967).

[33] See the *Crónica Mexicayotl*, written in part by Alvarado Tezozómoc (Mexico: Imprenta Universitaria, 1949).

[34] Juan Luna Cárdenas, *Prehistoria de América* (Mexico: U.Tl. I Aztekatl, 1947), pp. 17-18.

[35] This is according to Prof. Wigberto Jiménez Moreno, *"Diferentes principios del año entre diversos pueblos del Valle de México y su consecuencias para la cronología prehispánica"*, in *México Antiguo*, vol. IX (1961), pp. 137-52.

[36] Fray Bernardino de Sahagún from the *Florintine Codex III*, Chapter I.

[37] *Yakanini Metzli Kuautemok* (Dr. Juan Luna Cárdenas) in a series of private seminars to his followers/collaborators, understudies, speaking of *Kosmosofia* and specifically of the *Tezkalipokas* in their different color representations, referred to the *Tezkalipoka azul* (blue) as *Uilzilopoçitl*, meaning "fine correct thought". From private pamphlet, *Ilhuikayotl o Kosmosofia* (*¿Conoce Ud. la ciencia suprema?*) (Mexico: Central Kosmosofia de Anahuak N.D.)

[38] Davies, *The Aztecs*, p. 17. Another source cited is *Memorial Breve*, p. 22, Cristóbal del Castillo, *Fragmentos sobre la obra general sobre historia de los mexicanos* (Florence: Landi, 1968), pp. 58-59.

[39] Alfonso Caso, *La Religión de los Aztecas* (1945), p. 16.

[40] Davies draws a parallel with the Israelite god, *Yahweh*, who starts out as a wind and weather deity, converted to a God of War. *The Aztecs: A History*, p. 315.

[41] Ibid. Davies suggests that *Culhua* probably derives from the *Aztekah-Nahuatl* word *Colli* or "grandfather", denoting people with forefathers, i.e., high descent.

[42] Davies, p. 22.

[43] Davies suggests the Tepanecs as having Otomí connections, revering the Otomí deity *Otontecuhtli*.

[44] Davies, *History*, p. 23.

[45] Of the ancient symbolic forces, *Tlalok* (Spanish--Tlaloc) (rain) shares the main temple (later in *Tenochtítlan*) with *Witzil Poçitl* (Spanish--

Huitzilopochitl) (*El joven Armado defendiente*) and *Ketzalkóatl* (Spanish--Quetzalcóatl) (symbolic of agronomy, wisdom and the planet Venus). Among the female abstractions in sculpture and stone include *Koalikue* (Spanish--*Coatlicue*) (She of the Skirt of Serpents), *Tlazolteotl* (Lady of "Catharsis"), *Chalchiuhtlikue* (She of the Jade Skirt), *Xilonen* (Young Lady of Maize), *Omecihuatl* (Two Lady), *Xochiketzal* (Spanish--Xochiquetzal) (Precious Quetzal-like Flower).

[46] *Omeyokan* has often been seen as heaven and *Mictlan* as hell. Since this Judeo-Christian concept does not exist in the philosophical/religious framework of the pre-Columbian peoples, it is inappropriate and incorrect. Since it is not a moral question of punishment or rewards, i.e., medieval Catholicism, it must be seen as the place of the highest and purest energy in its total form with *Mictlan*, in a descending scale, as a place where energy, to the contrary, is incomplete.

[47] See Gral. Rubén García, *La Malinche* and Juan Luna Cárdenas, *La Matemática de los Aztekas* (Mexico: Editorial U.Tl. I. Aztekatl). Michael Coe refers to the exactitude of calculations after the completion of a 104-year cycle. *Mexico*, p. 161.

[48] Davies, *History*, p. 25.

[49] Let us not forget that Pythagoras, the father of mathematics, algebra, geometry, etc., for the Greeks, learned it in the East during his ten-year stay there. He introduced this scientific knowledge, including numerology, to the Greeks and Western man. All assumptions regarding fatalism of this numerological system are totally false. To the contrary, it provides twenty psychological profiles of humans (males and females). It is through this that one can better understand his potential and propensities in the various professions: areas that are creative, areas that are mathematical, areas revolving around healing and medicine, spiritual areas, administrative/governing leadership characteristics, etc. The *Tlamatinimi* guided the student as he progressed through the educational system, i.e., *Kuikalli, Telpochkalli, Kalmekah, Teyokalli*. From video interview of *Yakanini Metzli Kuautemok* (Dr. Juan Luna Cárdenas) Department of Spanish and Portuguese, University of Texas--Austin (Producer--Prof. Arnoldo Carlos Vento).

[50] Above and beyond the fanaticism of the Inquisitional system employed in all of colonial Native America (now Latin America), the symbols for the clashing European and pre-Columbian peoples are decidedly opposite in meaning. *Miquiztli* or death is not seen as fearing or evil; neither is a serpent or vulture seen as evil or negative. In the end, the authentic and autocthonous high cultures of pre-Columbian America were positive in nature at all levels; it was medieval Catholicism and the European vertical concept of contradictions, negatives and inequities. Ironically, all of the

accusations by the Spanish of the Aztecs are an exact picture of their society and culture (barbarism, imperialism, religious fanaticism, human sacrifice via the Inquisition, abuse of women, creation of ignorant masses, system of privileges and plutocracy, etc.). This explains a psychological principle today that asserts "you are what you see...if you see evil in everything, it is because you are obsessed with evil". There is no doubt that the myopic vision of the Spanish contributed to their obsession with evil.

[51] Hernando Alvarado Tezozomoc, *Crónica Mexicana*. One can readily see that there is a Roman Catholic education on this native writer. Still, other writings show a negative and distorted interpretation of mythology and events, e.g., *Codex Ramírez*, writings of Friar Duran, *Crónica Mexicayotl*.

[52] Probable foe may have been the *Kulhua*, *Tepankas* and *Xaltokans*.

[53] See *Anales de Tlatelolko*, p. 41.

[54] The *Temaskalli* is not simply a bath as many have thought but a place where one cleanses mind, body and soul through steam and heat.

[55] See Dr. Juan Luna Cárdenas, "*México: estudio de su significación*" originally presented to *The Mexican Society of Geography and Statistics*, Mexico, D.F. 1966. Cited are numerous interpretations:
(1)Cortés--Mexico is the as place of Colhuas,
(2)Códice Ramírez--Place of Mexicans
(3)Torquemada--Fountain or Spring
(4)Name of Ruler Named (Plane of the) Rabbit of the Maguey
(5)López de Gómara--Springs
(6)Motolonía--Place inhabited by the *Mexitin*
(7)Cristobal de Castillo--Place of those who eat quelites or Place of the sons of the Moon
(8)Orozco y Berra--Place of the God *Mexitl* or Founded by the *Mexitl*
(9)Codice Vaticano A--*Lugar de los que visten de piel de conejo*
(10)José María Cabrera--Place of Magueyal
(11)Mendieta--Place of those who eat Mexixquelite
(12)Galicia Chimalpopoca--Place of the Nobles
(13)*Tezozomok*--Place of the Springs
(14)Enrique Juan Palacios--Between Magueyes
(15)Angel García Conde--Place of Magueyes conquered by *Xiucactli*

[56] See Ixlilxóchit*l*, *Relaciones históricas*, tomo II, p. 478.

[57] One cannot blame the Native American for their distrust of foreigners' in view of the history of exploitation by the outsider. Regarding the Native question, I do not refer to the masses of Natives that have suffered centuries of inculcation by the Catholic Church and society. I refer to these few that have intelligentsia lineage that have cautiously preserved an autocthonous oral tradition. Such is the case of *Yakanini Metzli*

Kuautemok of the *Metzli* clan who traces his lineage to *Tultekah* rulers. As an elder, he has been cautious about the more sacred areas of his culture. He has seen that the knowledge will be passed on to people that possess the higher levels of thought, i.e., that can understand reality from the five mental spheres (dimensions); *Teonemilizzotl, Teomaniliztli, Teoizauhtli, Teomatilli, Teoyotl.* Only then can you understand the supreme science of *Ilhuikayotl*. It is the wisdom of the ancients shared by the great prophets of other cultures, the "ascended" masters, e.g., Jewish prophets, Krishna, Joshua, the Christic-One, etc.

[58] Juan Luna Cárdenas, *Historia patria* (México, D.F.: Editorial U. Tl. I. Aztekatl) p. 123. Luna Cárdenas states that the *Metzitin* used as warriors for *Akolhua* to fight *Tenankakaltzin*, a usurper ruler of *Tenayokan* and brother of *Tlotzin*, the latter, being defeated, left for *Tanpiko*, where his grandfather *Xolotl* resided. It is at this point that he is the seventh ruler of the *Cicimekah* dynasty. He, thus, becomes the Great *Tenayukan*, the post that his son *Tezozomok* will inherit upon his death.

[59] Carlos Muñoz Angulo, *Historia de México*. (México, D.F.: Editorial U.Tl.I. Aztekatl), p. 147.

[60] The death of *Ixtlixóchitl* is said to have been witnessed by his very young son who had hidden behind a cluster of *kapulli* trees; he cried over his father's cadaver in the darkness of night and in the silence of the woods, swore vengeance for his father.

[61] Luna Cárdenas, *Historia Patria*, pp.109-113. Dr. Luna Cárdenas further adds the etymology of the word *Çiçimekatl* as "People of Order, of Government". *Xolotl* was the founder of the *Çiçimekatl* dynasty; they had previously governed in Tampico and *Tomiyauh*. They were also the founders of the dynasty of the governing heads of *Tlaxkallan* who later ally with Cortés to attack *Metziko-Tenochtítlan* and complete the conquest.

[62] Don Fernando de Alba *Ixtlilxochitl, Obras Históricas*, pp. 62-63. The female here represents democracy and women's rights at its highest level. The "President Advisor" referred to (correctly spelled) was *Matlalziuatzin*.

[63] Luna Cárdenas, *Historia*, pp. 137-138.

[64] Carlos Muñoz Angulo, *Historia de México*, p. 150.

[65] Carlos Muñoz Angulo, p. 152.

[66] Ibid, p. 157.

[67] It is suspected that his death was due to a microbiotic type of infection inflicted in the jungles during the military campaigns. *Ahuizotl* was an exemplary ruler; legislator, lover of fine arts, historian, architect and exemplary military leader.

[68] In the *Kalmekak,* potential leaders of society were taught discipline and were required to balance mental and spiritual work with manual labor. This brought about discipline, dignity and integrity.

[69] Jorge Gurría Lacroix, *La caída de Tenochtitlan* (México, D.F.: Ediciones Conmemorativas , 1974).

[70] Gurría Lacroix, *La caída...,* p. 96.

[71] María del Carmen Nieva López, *Mexicayotl* (México D.F.: Editorial Orion, 1969), pp. 165-169.

[72] In measuring a time period of 1,040 years, the Julian calendar would have been off by eight days, one hour, five minutes and two seconds; the Gregorian calendar would be off by slightly less than eight hours but the Aztec calendar would have accumulated only one hour, five minutes and two seconds in 1,040 years.

[73] The *Tlatokans* at the local, regional and national levels included a council of women. At the federal level it was called *Weyi Çihuakoatl.*

[74] According to Dr. Juan Luna Cárdenas, the parents had the responsibility to educate their own children (father-son; mother-daughter) through the first four years. Between four and six years, they shared the educational process with the *Peukalli,* a type of kindergarten of which the *Kuikalli* was part, teaching dance, music, sculpture and art. The *Kalmekak* (House of Formation) taught boys and girls mathematics, biology, sculpture, discipline, music/dance and writing. At age twelve the sexes were separated; *Telpochkalli* (boy), *Ichpochkalli* (girls). The highest level of education was the Teyokalli (ages 16-20), which contained the study of professions (medicine, mathematics, arts and literature, astronomy, agronomy, metaphysics.

[75] The *Tonalámatl* was the sacred 260-day calendar in which a numerological/psychological personality profile system was developed to better track its citizens into the appropriate professions. See Hannerl Gossler, *La ciencia celeste de los Aztecas* (México, D.F.: Editorial Posada, S.A., 1974).

[76] Contrary to popular opinion, the pre-Columbian *Aztekahs* believed in the One Supreme Force (*Zentéotl*), which brought about *Teyokoyalitzli* (the Force of Creation), which in turn created *Mixkóatl,* the nebulous serpent or galaxies or the galactic universe; from here the stars of day, *Zitlaltonak* and of night, *Zitlalkuey.* Next is the Solar Force *Tonaktekuhtli,* which brings about the duality in nature represented by Tonaltuhy and *Tonaziuatli,* giving *Omeyokan* or the Place of Duality. Finally, there are the manifestations of the Supreme Force (*Zentéotl*), i.e, *Tezkalipoka, Ketzalkóatl, Xipe, Uitzilopochitli, Ikkozouhki, Tlalok,* etc., notwithstanding the 13 causes of the Creative Force on Humanity.

[77] The *Fuego Nuevo* was celebrated cyclically every 52 years as a symbol for renewal. Fiestas were also celebrated every year, every four years and every 52 years. See Juan Luna Cárdenas, *La ceremonial del Fuego Nuevo* (México, D.F.: Editorial Aztekatl, 1990).

[78] I refer here to the *Soles* or planetary cyclical ages: *Nahui Ocellotl, Nahui Echékatl, Nahui Quiyáhuitl, Naui Atl* and *Nahui Ollin.*

[79] The botanical gardens in *Metziko Tenochtitlan* were medicinal and were categorized according to its medical use. The early Europeans studying the pre-Columbian pharmaceutical knowledge (Carulus Clusius [1574, 1580], Dr. Monardes, Dr. Francisco Hernández [*Rerum Medicarum Novae Hispaniae Thesaurus*, 1628] were amazed at the great variety of cures, therapies and surgical procedures that existed, e.g., they had over thirty four homeostatic remedies to stop internal bleeding (this antedates European homeostatic remedies by three centuries), dentistry, plastic surgery, cranial plates, removal of cataracts, and obstetrics that were not only sound, but advanced for their times. See Gustavo A. Pérez Trejo, *La Medicina Prehispánica* (México: Editorial Aztékatl).

[80] Soustelle, *Daily Life...*, pp. 216-244.

[81] Miguel León Portilla, *Los Antiguos Mexicanos* (México: Fondo de Cultura Económica, 1973), pp. 173-186.

Inquisitional Torture used against Jews and Natives in Europe and Spanish-Speaking Americas

CHAPTER II

THE CULTURAL DOMINANCE OF SPANISH

COLONIALISM

NATIVE CULTURAL COUNTER-HEGEMONY

THE EUROPEAN MEDIEVAL CULTURE: CHURCH AND STATE
The historical, cultural and political origins of racism can be traced to the Teutonic tribes in the Sixth Century in Spain. It is these tribes that establish a cultural and social foundation of racism that will continue, through the centuries, not only in Spain, but throughout Europe. These tribes bring into the Latin territory the concept of Aryanism, a warrior spirit and a barbarous culture; a culture that is primitive in comparison to Greek, Roman and Moslem cultures. They establish a military aristocracy within the nobility and introduce into New Spain the concept of the indivisible kingdom which will provide for Spain the final justification for the re-conquest and the expulsion of the Jews and Moors about the same time that Columbus reaches the Antilles. It is important to note that the justifications for the expulsions were motivated not only by political and religious reasons, but also by racial considerations, since within the Castillian mentality there existed reflections of racial purity and Aryan superiority. This Teutonic heritage survives throughout the centuries and will form the basis for racial discrimination in the Americas. As a consequence, the Hispano-Romans and Visigoths formed an Hispano-Gothic aristocracy,

viewing themselves as one race; the *gens gothorum* or *hispani*. Moreover, the Church and State become one united governing structure in view that since 559 A.D., with the Third Council of Toledo, there exists religious, cultural and racial persecution against Jews which continue successively until their expulsion in 1492. The power of the Roman Catholic Church in Spain is felt in 561 A.D. from the Councils of Braga and from Toledo (633 A.D.) in which the primacy of the Pope of Rome is recognized. The monarchy develops during this epoch with the Christian Church as a collaborator, and will, notwithstanding, survive the Moslem conquest with very little change. During the Moslem occupation, there will be eighteen bishops in *Al Andalus* and Visigothic law, moreover, will be imposed. On very few occasions was a caliph consulted for the naming of a bishop. In the end, the re-conquest and the expulsion of the Moslem state creates a rebirth of the neo-Gothic state and with Mozarabic assistance with absolute racial and religious prejudice promotes the idea of an imperial state. And with the onslaught of the Crusades and the occupation of the Middle East in 1096 begins the ascent of the temporal and religious power of the Roman Catholic Church largely through Holy Wars, religious orders and the Inquisition.

During the European Medieval period, man and woman live essentially in a primitive state; power is provided by mules; everything is made by hand; peasants are almost all servants in a feudal society. There are no systems of drainage or running water; writing is limited to a few urban clergy since most of the provincial clergy were illiterate; children go about unclothed until the age of seven. In the cities, the urban middle class is disorganized and is dominated by a nobility who retain the right to make war and impose taxes. This is the only class with liberty, a governing class with indisputable power which has maintained the military aristocracy of Teutonic origin and whose sons are professional soldiers. The Church is all-powerful; it retains armies to protect its own interests; they recruit members of the nobility as well as the masses for their protection; they control education; they are the scribes, counselors, secretaries, accountants, lawyers and jurists. The concept "might makes right" is fundamental for feudal lords who are the oppressors of the poor in view that they have the right to beat their servants to death without legal opposition and are judged only by their peers. Women have few rights; they are the only ones who are required to be faithful, and failing this, they are subject to the penalty of death. Men notwithstanding, are allowed to have concubines and retain the right to divorce through no more than a declaration of consanguinity. It was common for the nobility or the clergy to offer a daughter or a mother in order to establish an alliance. The average life span during the Middle Ages was thirty two years with infant mortality at seventy-five percent. Medicine was primitive; there existed, for example, the primitive practice of bleeding and the abuse of purgatives. Antiseptics were still unknown and, consequently, hot oil was applied to open wounds which only caused additional infections. Death from hunger was common and the majority of the afflictions were recorded as poisonings.[3]

With regard to the rise of the Medieval Roman Catholic Church as a religious and political power, one notes that the Medieval Church, with its participation in the Crusades for several centuries, becomes a powerful economic and political institution, controlling all levels of society with the Inquisition, an institution characterized by violence, fraud, religious intolerance and absolutism. The Popes decreed absolute power with their dogma of *plentitudo potestatis* over all Christianity including Byzantium. These temporal princes performed more like emperors in search of power than as shepherds of souls. It was through the Council of Trent, that the Roman Catholic Church sought to eliminate Christian reform, maintaining the *status quo* and the general structure of the Medieval period. Holy War was promoted and justified by the concept of *bellum justum* established by Saint Augustine. More precisely these were wars of conversion that were, moreover, aggressive religious wars of territorial expansion designed to advance the Papal idea of a Universal Church.[4] With the Crusades and the Spanish re-conquest, European religious colonialism and imperialism developed; underlying these were the motivating forces of materialism which created avarice and cupidity. The Medieval nobility's concept of "might makes right" fomented despotic and imperialist tendencies. During the Thirteenth and Fourteenth Centuries the centralization of power continued in Rome. After the re-conquest, enormous properties were conferred to the nobility and the army, the majority of which was still controlled by the Church. Moreover, members of the military class, from the King to the most common knight, were bound to the Order of Knights and as such, were exempt from taxes and had exclusive right to the tribunals for their class through their participation in the King's court. These privileges were extended as well to the clergy, who were, in many cases, illiterate. Such was the abuse that the Spanish courts complained that the clergy lost considerable time in gambling, fighting and drinking, and consequently, contributing to the problem of celibacy. Celibacy became a problem for the Church, not so much for spiritual as for economic reasons in view that ecclesiastical property was lost to the children of the clergy. In 1391 the hatred of Jews (and other races) reached its peak. Incited by the sermons of archdeacon Fernando Martínez, the masses assaulted and sacked the Jewish community of Seville. Moreover, in 1449, the *conversos* were robbed of their property and as an act of persecution were called *marranos*.

It is during the last century of the Medieval period that there is social upheaval in the greater part of Europe: peasant rebellions, dynastic struggles and ecclesiastical rebellions. While Europe is fragmented by religious schism, the structure of the Roman Catholic Church in Spain is modified only slightly due to (1) the Spanish censure of all information originating in Europe and (2) the counter-reformist movement initiated in the Council of Trent. Spain, consequently, by not being part of the reform movement, decided to continue in the Medieval tradition that, from a civilized point of view, is at the height of decadence. The morality of the clergy is manifested in the general abandonment of spiritual responsibilities by bishops and priests. Even monastic discipline appears to have degenerated to a relaxed state. The religious and military orders of knights, likewise, are ignored or abandoned, as well as responsibilities for prayer, fasting and chastity; instead, they are enmeshed in political labyrinths in search of power.

Soon after Columbus' voyage to the Americas, the unification of Spain is established through the marriage of Isabela and her cousin Fernando, thus unifying Castille and Aragón. It should be noted that the good intentions of Isabela have been greatly exaggerated. The truth is that she is responsible for having submitted

Spain to one of the most insidious institutions in the history of mankind: the Inquisition, and this by secret injunction in 1478 There are other political maneuvers at her disposition that bring about political control: (1)annexation of the military orders to the Crown in 1494, known as the *Consejo de las Ordenes* (Councils of the Orders), (2)control over all naming of bishops, by order of Pope Innocent VIII in 1494, (3)the creation of a language based on her native Castillian; naming Antonio de Nebrija to establish a grammar, that establishes the rest of the peninsula under her control. While Isabela is an obstinate person, there is no doubt that she was a competent administrator but, perhaps, even more important were her political and religious propensities. She was a religious fanatic who imparted her racial prejudices of the old nobility against the Jews, the *conversos* (converted Jews) and the *mudéjares* (Moorish Christians). Previous to this time, these groups had already been persecuted since the Council of Tortosa in 1119 when the King declared the right to persecute all heretics. The Tribunal of Seville in 1481 had already sacrificed 800 persons and sentenced 5,000 Jews to life sentences. The Inquisitor Torquemada, under his rule, had sacrificed 8,000 to their death. The "reformist" Cisneros had 2,500 sacrificed alive, 1,378 tortured and burned facially and sentenced some 7,073 others for other infractions. He is, moreover, responsible as a "reformist" for the expulsion of Jews in 1492 as well as the expulsion of 50,000 Moors Incredibly, upon the death of Isabela in 1504, the Inquisitor Francisco González Jiménez de Cisneros was called to direct the politics of Spain; it is this Inquisitor who will dominate political and religious politics not only with respect to Spain but Africa and the American colonies, for thirteen years, i.e., until 1517, the year of his death at age eighty two.

SPANISH NEO-FEUDALISM: NEW SPAIN

In the Americas, the most severe impact of the Inquisition was felt in New Spain. The greater part of the expeditions that arrived in New Spain brought clergy from the Dominican Order, the first order responsible for the administration of the Inquisition. It is not surprising, then, that the first Bishop of Mexico, Juan de Zumárraga, is, moreover, the first Bishop with Inquisitorial powers. He is, historically, one of the most infamous personalities in the history of Mexico, for having burned in his own patio, most of the valuable historical, scientific and cultural documents of the Aztecs. This is especially important, because by destroying Aztec history, he had destroyed the autocthonous perspective, thus providing an open pathway for the clergy to create their own historical, religious and cultural revisionism with the European Medieval/Western perspective as a basis for interpretation.

For this reason, the invasion of the Americas is an extension of the Crusades and the *reconquista,* characterized by unscrupulous sacking, sexual assault, massacres and a vicious disregard for propriety, customs, culture and the religion of the Amerigenous population. Specifically, the most notable factors of Medieval origin transferred to the Americas were: (1)imperialism and expansionism; the acquisition of new lands through forced warfare, (2)avarice and materialism as motivating forces of the Spaniard (his first question asked is about gold), (3)religious intolerance and fanaticism. They forced their religion on the Amerigenous population through wars of conquest and wars of conversion, (4)the idea of the Roman Catholic Church as the Universal Church with the Pope as the governing head of the spiritual world.

There are other characteristics of European/Spanish society which are transported to the Americas: (1)there is the continuation of slave trafficking; in "the Indies", the Amerigenous peoples are made slaves, working under inhuman conditions, often to their death in gold mines. According to Bartolomé de las Casas, after 40 years of Spanish invasion, 24 million natives were eliminated in the Indies, Guatemala and New Spain, (2)the prejudices and lack of respect for other cultures. Incredibly, the majority of the Spanish believed that the natives had no soul and, consequently, they could be treated as beasts. In this sense, there was a preoccupation on the part of the ecclesiastical authorities for the creation of a Christian community among the natives, (3)the importation of European illnesses, that in part, contribute to a decrease in the Amerigenous population, (4)the false idea of protection for the Amerigenous people established by the New Laws of Isabela in 1599. Instead, this was a document that permitted them to abuse the natives through administrative clauses ("Free, unless they are cannibals or captives"). The ridiculous *Requerimiento* that was read from a hill, announced to the unsuspecting Amerigenous population, that by Spanish law, they were now subjects of the Spanish Crown, and upon attacking them, they became captives and therein the loophole and weakness of the New Laws,[13] (5)the importation of African slaves after the decrease of the Amerigenous population to work in silver and gold mines, (6)the continuation of a neo-feudal order by means of legalized labor, forced through the institution known as *La Casa de Contratación* in 1503. It is through this economic institution where the Lord was owner of a number of natives who would become victims, along with their children, of forced labor for the rest of their lives. Its consequence was the vicious cycle of inheriting debts from one generation to another, creating a labyrinth of slavery. This is the precursor of the *latifundios*, the *haciendas* and   the terrible *caciquismo* that reached its height in the Nineteenth Century in Spanish America.

What were the implications of the Spanish invasion with regard to the autocthonous populations? There is no doubt among historians that the invasive and destructive impact for the Amerigenous peoples of the Americas at the hand of the British, French and Spanish had major social, cultural and economic consequences. The cultural and religious intolerance on the part of the Europeans brought about not only the loss of lands to the natives, but also the denial of their customs, their religion and their human dignity. It was a negation of their existence, of their history, compounded by the deleterious effects of Christianity that, in Spanish America, was represented by the *Santo Oficio* or the Inquisition. It is in New Spain that the first Bishop and unofficial inquisitor, Juan de Zumárraga, will burn in his patio, hundreds of Aztec codices, erasing scientific and historic knowledge of the Aztecs. This is significant, because it opened the door for the Roman Church to interpret and relate the history of the natives from a Medieval European point of view. Every document written during the Colonial Period was subject to the censorship of the Inquisition and consequently, every document written after the Conquest cannot be considered authentic in view of the alteration and the interjection of a Medieval European perspective. Even the *"viejos"* (elders) used by Padre Sahagún represent individuals who had been educated under the supervision of the clergy and whose testimonies, moreover, had passed through the[14] censorship of ecclesiastical concepts prior to their publication. Unfortunately,

Page of Inquisitorial Treatise against Heretics circulated in Mexico.

these are the documents utilized by today's anthropologists and historians; representing a revisionism of the history and consequently a false interpretation of the religion, culture and politics of the Amerigenous populations of the Americas. North American investigators have also fallen into this trap, in view that they also carry a Western European perspective which is utilized to interpret an autocthonous society devoid of European values. According to Eugenio Chang Rodríguez:

> The counter-reformist zeal is to a great extent responsible for official thought control, as well as the means of expression in Spain and her dominions. In theory, punishment was by means of death and confiscation of goods for the possessors of books included in the *Index Librorum Prohitiorum* and for those who tried to print or were printing other unapproved books. The best instrument of censorship and thought control in America was the *Santo Oficio* or the Inquisition. It was established first in Lima (1571), then in Mexico (1579) and later throughout the Ibero-American continent, with the exception of Brazil.[15]

Thus, the Colonialism established throughout Spanish America was a transplanted neo-feudalism whose goal was to maintain the *status quo* and the continuation of the Medieval European structure promoting, simultaneously, a counter-reformist movement. This system was based in the Medieval vertical concept of life where God, the Pope and the Kings with their nobility represented the higher levels and, conversely, the masses comprised of non-Spanish "serfs", comprised the lower levels on the social scale. Because of inherited prejudices and ignorance, the Spanish saw the native as inferior and as such, assigned him within the Medieval stratum of servant. This now implied the imposition of forced labor; it implied the imposition of a new religion, language and culture; it implied the implantation of prejudice based on race, on color and on gender; it implied subordination of the woman to an inferior level in view that sexual abuse was established during the first moments of the European/Spanish invasion; it implied an imperialist imposition making the invasion legitimate through the Medieval concept of "might makes right" which provided the excuse to impose later what[16] North Americans unjustly established as "manifest destiny"; it implied the destruction of a democratic/communal system replaced by an exploitive feudal system based on capital; it implied the destruction of ancient autochthonous knowledge and its reinterpretation from a European/Western perspective. The result was the creation of a privileged class (the religious and civil plutocracy) and the maintenance of an enormous illiterate mass for more than 300 years. Following Independence from Spain and France, the Colonial structure and attitude continued to be present, appearing within the models of contemporary government. The same occurs in North America, where racism based on color and prejudice against women, cultural genocide, etc., are but perennial aspects of contemporary Colonialism in the United States. Finally, it is these harmful social, political, economic and cultural factors from the Medieval epoch which are responsible for the inequities in today's Mestizo-America, i.e., avarice and the abuse of power in a capitalist/exploitive system, where there is discrimination against women, discrimination based on social class (earlier, a semi-caste system); religious myopia, intolerant and dogmatic; prejudice based on color and against native cultures and the arrogant and righteous attitude of governing classes. These are but a few of the characteristics inherited from the Colonial period that directly or indirectly affect and impact the problem of identity and *mestizaje* throughout Mestizo-America.

A century after the arrival of Admiral Columbus in the Antilles and after four generations of colonialism, there appeared, according to Professor Arrom, the first generation of *criollos* (1564-1594).[17] Between 1571 and 1574 the geographer Juan López de Velasco, on a scientific voyage to America, observed: "Those born of these, are called *criollos*, and in all respects are cared for and had by the Spanish, they are known to come out differentiated in color and size..."[18] In the same way, a Sevillan doctor living in Mexico in 1591 states: "There is no man, however ignorant he may be, who cannot see who is *cachipín* and who was born in the Indies." From[19] this point on, they began to use the word *criollo*. These were the children of the Spanish nobles born in America, even though there was little legitimate nobility not only in the Americas but also in Spain during the final phase of the Medieval period: "There was a pro-aristocratic mentality in Castille, a disdain for work, a desire to share the esteem enjoyed by the nobles, especially to be exempt from taxes as were the clergy...all of this inspired too many men to aspire to the privileged state of nobility to such a point that the courts declared in 1432 their complete discontent to the supreme authorities."[20] In reality, the majority of the first Spaniards that reached the "New World" were people of the lower classes, without titles, property or fame. Even Columbus had to negotiate for his title of Admiral. By the fourth generation, the impact of the Amerigenous populations as much as the impact of the environment, forges the new character of the *criollos*. Hundreds of native words and foods are introduced, helping form a new personality. A distinction should be made, however, between the *criollo* and the Spaniard; it was not based on biological, racial or cultural differences. The *criollos* began to see and feel American things as their own. This vision "of the Americas" rightfully has its roots in the autochthonous population, seen most clearly in the Mestizo and in the native tribes, in spite of the fact that a vertical concept of life had been implanted into these new lands, notwithstanding, a Medieval prototype with all its social and racial discrimination, within the aristocracy and plutocracy. As a consequence, the Mestizo and the Amerigenous peoples, consequently, lost their social rank and rights, but maintained, concurrently, a sense of both worlds. Similarly, this approach was imposed on the *mulatos* and on Africans, now the lowest on the social and economic scale of the Colonies. And with regard to the *"cachupin"* (now, *gachupín*), there were many who neither founded nor wrote nor worked; but simply were vagabonds. Thus, Fray Jerónimo de Mendieta notes:

> Beyond the ocean in this region, the lowest scoundrel of Spain is considered as the best gentleman, and since all bring so much decoration that they must be served by the Indians for their gracious gestures, there is no man among them, villain that he may be, that lends a hand to lift a hoe or a plow, because they realize that whenever they enter among Indians, they will not be left without (much to their dislike), the meal of a guest, and thus they remain idle, going about as vagabonds like the flower of the water cress.
>
> January 1, 1562[21]

Consequently, the Spaniard creates his own "nobility" designating everyone with "Indian" blood as inferior, a concept that continues to be expressed in contemporary Mexico. European feudalism is transplanted and Medieval scholasticism and counter-reformation are demanded; religion is forced on the Amerigenous population, including Jews residing in the capitol. Moreover, one must not forget the atrocious acts of human sacrifice at the hand of the Inquisition during the Colonial period, the "plagues" affecting the Amerigenous population and the censorship of all "pagan" or "profane" documents as declared by the Inquisition.[22]

Inquisitional and fanatical reality was a serious reality in New Spain:

> One of the most celebrated processions that occurred in Mexico, in the Sixteenth Century, was for doña Francesca de Carvajal, a noisy and important procession for having rounded up don Luis de Carvajal, the Saxon governor of the new reign of León, in New Spain, and all of his family, many of them burned at the stake. Again, confirming that the prestige of the Inquisition was above the nobility and the governing classes, these being rejected, victims of the fanaticism inculcated among the people for their own ends. Doña Francesca de Carvajal was a noble matron of Mexico City, whose only crime consisted of privately practicing, Judaic Law, for which she was denounced by the *Santo Oficio*, and discharged against her all the rigor of their arbitrary repression...whose sentence of torment was given by the said Inquisitional Lords...Arias de Valdés, Alcalde y Pedro de Fonseca, Portero...and with this was carried to the torture chamber...was again admonished to..tell the truth, if you do not want to see this punishment and danger...and with this admonishment, she was ordered to undress, and with some *zargüelles* and her shirt down, naked from the waist up, was again admonished to tell the truth...after binding her arms...seeing that she did not want to confess the Christian law, they began wrapping a cord around her arms at least five times...and she continued protesting that she had merely practiced law taught to her as a child...for which she was...executed along with her daughter doña Mariana de Carvajal, a maiden of 29 years. She was, moreover, condemned and taken through the public streets mounted on packhorse and forced to proclaim with a voice her crime and that she be

clubbed until dying naturally, and that she be burned in fiery flames until converted into ashes and out of that there remain not a memory of her...[23]

The religious intolerance on the part of the authorities of New Spain carried within itself the stamp of religious fanaticism and imperialism. Everyone outside the Catholic religion was considered a heretic, belonging to the domain of hell and, consequently, condemned. The natives, whose religious perception was to be in harmony with the universal laws of nature, were considered *a priori*, to be outside the law of Christianity and were accused inquisitionally of hundreds of falsehoods to justify the existence and dominion of Roman Catholic Christianity of the Fifteenth Century. For this reason, the Amerigenous individual, was established, from the beginning, as an inferior and all natives of mixed blood (*mestizos*) in the same manner. It is not strange, therefore, that they were seen as people without souls or as beasts. Fray Bartolomé de las Casas states:

> All who are true Christians know and even those who are not, such action is heard all over; that to maintain and feed said dogs, many Indians are brought through the roads and chained such that, they are led as if they were herds of pigs, and they further kill them and conduct a public butchery of human flesh, and they say to one another: "Loan me a quarter of this scoundrel to give to my dogs to eat until I kill another[24] as if they were loaning a quarter of a pig or of a sheep.

The aforementioned recalls images of Medieval human sacrifice, of fanatical religious intolerance and the racial prejudices, avarice and greed of imperialist commercialism. They hold roots of contemporary bloody ethnic and religious wars, avarice and greed of imperial colonialism by powerful nations both worldwide and in particular, Latin America. And the woman, as the first victim in the Americas, continues to be abused in every way: socially, physically and mentally. She was in the beginning an object of Spanish commercialism. Bartolomé de las Casas further states: "This lost man, in laudable fashion, approached a venerable clergyman, saying that he had worked as much as possible to impregnate many Indian women, so that by selling them pregnant and as slaves, he would get more money for them."

There is no doubt that beneath this historically and socially absolutist and inquisitorial scenario, there had been a significant historical, philosophical and social alteration of documents by the dominant Spanish groups. Napoleon said it well when he affirmed that history is always written (invented) by the conquerors and not by the conquered. And as such, the modern myths invented by all invaders. One notes that in the United States, for example, it was believed for some time that the Amerigenous people had established the custom of scalping North American soldiers as a type of trophy; the opposite was the case. The North American army had instead offered a reward for each Amerigenous individual killed and to prove it demanded that the soldiers return with the scalp of the native person; this is but another example of the invention of history by the invaders in order to justify their atrocities. Religious ministers, in the early formation of the North American colonies, also hanged (like the Spanish Inquisition), natives who refused to become Christians; there is evidence of campaigns and massacres directed by religious ministers against the native tribes of the region. But the North American histories praised only the actions of the recently arrived Europeans, justifying and creating for them heroic deeds. It was not until the seventies, when civil rights movements broke out among all minority groups suffering from racial and cultural discrimination in the United States, that interest arose in Native-American Studies, African-American Studies, Chicano Studies, Women's Studies, etc. Unfortunately, this type of Ethnic/Amerigenous Study has not arisen in Mexico, directed toward and taught to all public school students of the Republic, a study that eliminates all European falsehoods with regard to the history of the autocthonous groups. In the United States, this has been accomplished to a great degree by the Amerigenous peoples; they are the only ones who can know their own reality. Why is the word of the native peoples disdained in Mexico when one seeks to write about autocthonous concepts?[25] Self-criticism, as Samuel Ramos suggests, does not exist. The Mexican is closed off within himself. This recalcitrant individualism, inherited from the European/Spaniard, is harmful and counterproductive. Until it is eliminated, there will not be a true vision of the historical and cultural past of Mexico. When this is accomplished, the Mexican will see all of the inherited foreign and European prejudices as well as the legitimate and original cultural and philosophical grandeur of their autocthonous ancestors.

AZTEC COLONIAL MYTHS: HISTORICAL RELIGIOUS BIAS AND MISINTERPRETATION

In pre-Columbian America, the cosmogony of the various high cultures (Olmekah, Teotihuakan, Maya, Toltekah, Meztzikah-Aztekah, Inca) is seen through science, i.e., astronomy and mathematics. Thus, they did not have a religion as we know religion today, i.e., with dogmatic theology. The pre-Columbian view of reality is non-Western.[26] It is more similar to ancient Eastern cultures (China and Tibet). Native Americans including Lakota, Pima, Hopi and Algonquian tribes understood astronomy. They guided their whole existence via planetary cycles. That is why the autocthonous holy men known by the Spanish as pagan priests were, in fact, astronomers and sages, who were able to read the esoteric and abstract symbolism of the writings of codices and sculptured images. According to *Yakanini Metzli Kuautemok* (Juan Luna-Cárdenas), their supreme science was known as *Ilhuikáyotl*, which was a type of *kosmosofia* or cosmogony.[27] It is this inheritance of thought, taught through oral transmission within select families, that comprises of five spheres or dimensions of mental thought. In order to understand the symbolism of the Aztékatl nations, in codices, they must be read via five mental levels.[28] The first level relates to our analysis of the pre-Columbian cosmogony. It affirms the idea of *One* Supreme Force that cannot be interpreted because it is invisible. Its generic name is *Teotl*. In order to express its greatness, they used epithets of an expressive nature to give its greatness and power, e.g., *Ipalnemoani*, which means "the force for whom one lives" or *Tloke Nauake*, which means, "the force that has everything within it". This supreme essence was assisted by natural representations or manifestations of the Supreme Essence. These provided life to the planet; without them this would be nothing but a cold, dead planet (the sun, moon, rain, etc.).

They understood, like the Chinese, the role of energy and its connections. It began with the One Supreme Force (*Zentéotl*) that connected in particular to all people via an energy flux to the immortal spirit called generically *Tonalli*. There were two types of spirit/energy, one for humans (*Tetona*) and one for the animal and plant kingdoms (T*latonal*). There were special dimensions in which the immortal spirit departed, all of them positive, for the pre-Columbian people did not believe in demons or hells; this was the invention of the Europeans (*Hölle*). One was expected to live in harmony with the laws of nature; when an elder lived such a harmonious life, it was celebrated because he had progressed the spirit of his people to a higher-evolved level. The spiritual dimension reached depended upon the evolvement of one's spirit, but *never* did any spirit suffer damnations or hells brought on by Satan or demons as exemplified in Western Judeo-Christian thought. And like many ancient civilizations (Egyptian, Chinese, Tibetan, early Greek), reincarnation was understood as a means of spirit evolvement. The *Tlamatinimi*, the scientist/priests, were responsible for providing knowledge of astronomy, botany, mathematics, hieroglyphics, ecology, agronomy, medicine, the arts and metaphysics. Students under their tutelage in the *Kalmekak* and *Teyokalli* learned to read the abstract codices, to practice cleansing via abstinence, prayer and discipline. They learned techniques propitious for elevating the spirit to higher dimensions of truth and thought. The sage scientist/priests knew when and how to access higher forms of thought. They had the most advanced mathematics and calendars in the world. They even had a psychological/philosophical framework or system (*Tonalámatl*) for determining ones vocation or profession that used mathematics as a base for its development.

Thus, the high civilizations of pre-Columbian America did not use dogma created by an imperialistic church as did the Spanish; their metaphysics ("religion") was based upon thousands of years of scientific observation and the hard sciences. They were intent on discovering higher truths as opposed to fallible interpretations of dogma by theologians of the medieval Roman Catholic Church. They understood the planetary cycles, the interrelationship between animals, plants and humans ecologically balanced in a cyclical pattern nurtured by the energy of the One Supreme Force of *Zentéotl*. Thus, to refer to multiple gods is to project a medieval Western

Christian perception of reality as seen through the worship of hundreds of saints, virgins and trinities. It is no wonder that the Moslem and Judaic religious groups accused the medieval Catholic Church of polytheism. *Miktlan,* as a religious concept, was interpreted as Hell by the early clerics as well as Sahagún, an error that has subsequently been repeated by scholars to date.[29]

THE MYTH OF MIKTLAN AS HELL

It was the missionaries who first interpreted the myth of *Miktlan* as Hell, projecting their own medieval world of demons, damnation and punishment. Since, most serious scholars have seen it largely as a place of the dead. Chavero does not concede *Miktlantekutli* a personality but rather thinks it refers to *Tonatiuh* or the sun. Moreover, he affirms that the soul was not judged and, like Sahagún, professed that they were materialists.[30] Chavero is correct only in that the soul was not judged and sent to *Miktlan* as in the Christian tradition with Hell. He is incorrect in thinking *Miktlantekutli* refers to the sun and that the pre-Columbian people were materialists. The interpreter of the Codex Magliabecchiano scorns the clerical version, stating, "...this is a great falsity, that they had [hell] as a name, and thus when the friars preached to the natives that when they were not good keepers of the [Christian] faith of God, that they would go to *Miktlan*; nothing was given to them and then they were to go to the house of the devil".[31] León-Portilla cites 13 celestial levels in addition to nine underground levels in which the dead were to undergo obstacles en route to *Miktlan*.[32] This level was not the dark void inhabited by ancestors that had few worldly possessions as Fagan attests;[33] rather, the place where humans go that have died a natural death on earth, without considering social rank or status.[34] *Miktlan* should not be considered an underworld as is the case with Western Christian thought; neither should it be a final resting place. It is merely one of many space/time dimensions within the infinite cosmos that have to do with the energy source at the spirit level. To the pre-Columbian peoples, the spirit was immortal; death was not a finality. The evolvement of spirit was the key; the higher-evolved and purer a spirit, the higher plane it was assigned. *Miktlan,* on the energy scale, was merely on the lower levels. The spirit of the persons here were far from illuminating; that is why the color of darkness is used to describe this level. Anyone, regardless of position, who did live by the laws of nature (as observed for centuries by the sages) would go to the corresponding spirit/energy levels. It was a temporary place where the spirit was to regain its light to continue its path in its evolvement. Thus, the introduction by the clerics of devils, hells, punishments and other grotesque descriptions, were designed to (1)discredit the original positive metaphysical concepts of the Aztecs and other native peoples and (2)use the old medieval tool of fear inculcation by the Inquisitional Catholic Church, in this case, to the natives as a means of cultural and religious control.

THE COLONIAL MYTH OF FATALISM

Fatalism is a common charge that follows a pattern within Western culture vis-a-vis native and/or Mestizo peoples. The literature is replete with stereotypes of *Mexicans* (and *Mexican*/Americans) in the late nineteenth-century and early twentieth-century dime novels. Paredes cites the hatred of Anglo Westerners against *Mexicans* originating from Native-American peoples.[35] The origin of this bias by the Spanish appears to be in their lack of comprehension of the *Tonalámatl*, a ritual and sacred 260-day calendar read only by designated sages. There is no question that both the 365- and 260-day calendars were ultimately tied to all activity since astronomy, mathematics and metaphysics were the basis for understanding the cycles of all living things on earth. The misinterpretations begin with the insertion of magicians, sorcerers and general superstitions about bad luck by various ecclesiastical sources. Padre Mendieta creates a detailed description of the formation of the ritual calendar in which he inserts special days for each *devil* that was celebrated, speaks of idolatrous gods and creates a fable as Orozco y Berra notes in his study.[36]

Padre Sahagún speaks of the use of the *Tonalpouhqui*, the person who "knows the fortune of those who are born" and his use of the ritual calendar in determining his sign. He gives examples of the "good" sign and a "bad" sign. A bad sign may mean he will be a thief, carnal and full of vices; he will never gain fortune and will become lazy, a drunkard..."[37] Alfonso Caso refers to the *Tonalpouhqui* as astrologers who predicted good and bad luck corresponding to each person born.[38] Soustelle describes man as "inserted automatically into this order and in the grasp of the omnipotent machine" and this sign will "govern him until the day of his death his$_{39}$ whole fate is subjected to the strictest predestination..."[39] Fagan asserts that the "magico-religious pattern of the day count determined ones destiny." He does, however, point out that these readings were not absolute, that a person's deeds on earth could alter his fate...[40] Nigel Davies reiterates the ideas of the post-Conquest Florentine Codex where the example of Nine Crocodile is represented exclusively to "being perverse and full of vice...one of the lesser faults would be a propensity towards slander and rumour-mongering; so incapable would he be of taking care of himself that he would be destined to appear dressed only in rags and tatters..."[41] Eric Wolf sees the association of numbers with cosmic and magical concepts..."such magical numerology may have been the root of a lunar count...it measures both recurrent social time and recurrent individual fate."[42] Finally, León-Portilla regards the *Tonalpohualli* (calendaric count) or *Tzolkin* of the Mayas as one of many astrological systems found in other cultures; it permits one to discover within the rhythm of change, bad and good influences that determine and give meaning to life vis-a-vis the universe and the multiple relations with the divinity...[43]

It is clear through the vocabulary used by Padre Mendieta that he is duplicating the medieval world he is familiar with, i.e., devils, idolatry and general inquisitional accusatory tone that attempts to portray a superstitious and evil native society. Padre Sahagún cites examples of the practice of consulting the *Tonalámatl* when a child is born but he clearly underscores in detail the vices of a bad sign citing theft, drunkenness, laziness, carnal propensities and poverty as outcomes. Ironically, these, with the exception of poverty, are common characteristics of the Spanish world in colonial Spanish America. It should be pointed out that in pre-Columbian America, drinking (source--*Metl*) was prohibited. Only the very elderly were permitted to sip a drink from time to time; drunkenness was considered counterproductive for a nation that was intent on creating a total person. Theft was not natural in view that possession of material things were just not part of this non-materialist society. Bartolomé de las Casas cites numerous examples of how the Spanish would invade the homes of natives from the very beginning at Española, noting that the doors had no locks and moreover were always left open. It is not until after many abuses of theft[44] by the Spanish that the natives begin to protect themselves. Inca Garcilaso de la Vega, similarly, cites that among the Incas, locks on doors just did not exist since taking and possessing material things were not part of the morés of the native populations[45] In terms of laziness, such an act was considered negative and unproductive for the Aztecs. If there is one salient characteristic of the Aztecs, it is the discipline and will to be productive. Padre Garibay, in his translations of Aztec codices, cites the example of the noble governing head and his exhortation to his sons; here, he advises his sons "to never be idle nor go about without[46] something useful to do...Don't pass the day or night in vain....". Moreover, he asks that they refrain from sexual desires, that they not stoop to the level of an animal. In the *Kalmekak* (equivalent to college prep) the young student learned discipline and the sciences. He also received austere surroundings, coupled with the nocturnal baths that provided means to deal with sexual urges. It was clear that the time would come when as a responsible and mature adult, he would[47] enter into the very serious and sacred ceremony of matrimony. In terms of poverty and riches, these are not part of a person's objectives in the non-materialistic pre-Columbian world. Everyone had all of the basic necessities in a system when even in extreme economic conditions caused by drought or other catastrophic events, there were always reserves of food held for just such occasions in both the Aztec and Inca societies. Money was non-existent as we know it today. The *trueque* or exchange barter system provided all of the needs of a society. Thus, these negative characteristics of fatallism are not part of the pre-Columbian world and refer more specifically to the world the Spanish knew in the European Middle Ages.

Caso's assertion of good and bad luck predicted by "astrologers" is carried further by Soustelle completing Caso's implication that a person's whole fate is subjected to the strictest predestination. Similarly, Fagan asserts the day count as a determining factor in ones destiny. To begin with, the science known to *Tonalpouhqui* was based on numbers, ergo, it was numerology and not astrology. It is interesting to note that the Spanish still have astrology as part of their curriculum as late as the Seventeenth Century. Fagan does correctly identify it as numerology and, moreover, qualifies his statement on destiny by declaring that the reading was not absolute, i.e., one could, through good deeds, alter the course designated. In the case of Nigel Davies, there is, unfortunately, no critical commentary. Rather, he reiterates a questionable and biased post-Conquest document in which Nine Crocodile is represented as perverse; such a person destined to a kind of Spencerian biological determinism. According to the *Tonalámatl* or sacred 260-day calendar, *Cipactli*, or Crocodile, is not a negative symbol. A "crocodile person" is industrious and an achiever, generally cautious and conservative, optimistic, sociable and generous. The number nine is a negative number but it represents only one of three forces at play.[48] Thus, with the cosmic sign of *Ketzalkóatl* (scientist, philosopher, poet, researcher) and the favorable psychological personality profile of "crocodile", this person in a system of discipline and productivity, as is the case with the Aztecs, would have no problem being a productive member of society. It is clear from the exhortations of the noble governing head to his children that there is no such thing as bad luck or destiny and that one can change one's patterns through one's will.[49]

THE COLONIAL MYTH OF POLYTHEISM

The idea related to the belief that the Spanish were thought of as gods can be traced, not to pre-Columbian sources, but to European projections of egocentricity. It is in the *Diario* of Columbus that we see the reactions of a Spaniard who is unable to communicate to the natives and is overcome by his admiration via the native's generosity, spirituality and civil behavior.[50] To the natives, communal sharing is a way of life; to the Europeans it is unknown, for booty is the spoils of war and conquest. He cannot believe that the doors in all houses are left open and are without locks and that these people are "*harto mansos*" (extremely docile and kind) and concludes that they are indeed good candidates for conversion to Catholicism. It is at this point that he concludes that these people see him as a god, an assertion that is based on his own perception and not on the native's point of view. While it can be argued that Columbus was treated as "royalty" or as a special dignitary, this does not mean he is above mortality in the view of the native peoples of the Caribbean. Indeed, it was customary to receive visiting heads of state from other nations, and as in the case of the Confederation of

Anauak, they were allowed to rule side by side existing rulers for a period of six months. What is important here is that it did not come from the mouth of the native because it is clear that there was no communication between Columbus and the natives as late as 1493, when he writes a letter in poor Castillian, the contents of which are subsequently transcribed in Latin by a friar.[51] It is here that he proclaims (after the customary salutations and formalities) that he has just crossed the river *Ganges*! Had he been able to communicate to the natives, he might have known where he was and might have learned about the real perceptions of native peoples.

One notes that after the Spanish began behaving in an uncivilized manner, i.e., entering the native houses and taking in their possession material articles to their liking, the natives began to distrust these intruders, who were accustomed to plunder, rape and booty since the days of *Reconquista* and the Crusades. The subsequent enslaving of natives and inhumane treatment via starvation and work in the mines notwithstanding separation of the men from their families, is the type of knowledge that became known and was widespread regarding these invaders; thus, they became known later to the Aztecs as *Popolokas* (barbarians). Information of the attacks by the Spanish in the mainland was received by courier (runners of the Confederation) on a daily basis to Moctecuzoma Xokoyótzin. They were aware that many had died, including knowledge of their horses.[52] The idea of being gods was fruitful and strategic in the general plan of conquest by the Spanish, particularly in the creation of the myth regarding *Ketzalkóatl*. What begins as an historical figure by the name of *Nakxitl Topíltzin*, a military ruler who, because of internal political factions, must leave the Toltec nation, is strategically changed to a priest with Christ-like characteristics, who, like Christ, is run out of the city, has a following and leaves with the idea of returning (from the East). What follows is the creation of the myth in which the Spaniards are the representation of the return of *Ketzalkóatl*.

THE MYTH OF KETZALKÓATL AS A GOD

According to the Aztec scholar and native Yakanini Metzli Kuautemok, the historical Toltec figure is being intentionally confused with the celestial force that *Ketzalkóatl* represents, i.e., as brother of the light representing harmony of thought along with

Tezkalipoka, Xipe, Uitzilopoçitl and *Ixkozauhki.*[53] Cecilio Robelo quotes Padre Mendieta, that with reference to *Quetzalcoatl* (*Ketzalkóatl*), there are so many fables and fictions that natives invented regarding the deities, so diverse for different nations that there is not one person that can declare its verity. There is reference to *Quetzalcoatl* as son of the Supreme Force, as son of *Chimalma*, as a representation of the morning star (Venus) and even as a priest from Iceland and as a Jewish Apostle from the East who came to the Americas to preach the Gospel. As a man, he is said to have had his kingship in *Tollan* or *Chollolan*. However, it is pointed out by Robelo that history and mythology are not in accord with the role of destruction of the *Tula* (*Tollan*) and *Ketzalkóatl*. According to *Ixtlilxóchitl* the most authoritative historian of the Toltecs, the kingdom of the Toltecs was founded in the Seventh Century by the heads of Xalisco in a three-year war. The last Toltec ruler was *Topilzin* and during this lapse of time, there appears no memory (before and after the war) of any emigration or abandonment of the city; thus, the exodus of the mythical *Ketzalkóatl* with the masses of Tollan is pure fable.[54] It is the friar, Padre Durán who confuses *Topíltzin*, the last Toltec king without the deific force of *Ketzalkóatl*, perhaps also because of the existence of a Toltec priest by the name of *Huemak.*[55] *Topilzin* is not only a king but a warrior and as a participant does not even fit the characteristics given to the mythical "messiah priest", i.e., peace-loving, Christ-like. In fact, some historians have said that this mythical priest was to have hated war, and some have added that when he heard of it, he would cover his ears. According to Luna-Cárdenas, when the 52 years of rule by *Tekpankalzin* had ended, *Nakxitl Topíltzin* was designated ruler along with *Kuauhtli* (from *Koliman*) and *Maxtlatzin* (from *Tlapallantonko*) third head and chair of the Supreme Council of the Confederation. The barbaric heads of the northern invaders were not pleased and subsequently declared war. It was a time that experienced atmospheric disturbances which brought about hunger and misery such that, for ten years, crops were lost. The battle known as the Battle of *Tultitilan*, was a major war with two lines of battle drawn; (a)from the coasts of *Miçhuakan, Tollan*, the *Tlahuika* to the gulf, and (b)from the coasts of the *Panoko* to *Xalixko* and the pacific. The Confederation was subsequently destroyed by the barbaric invaders from the north and it marked the end of the Toltec Confederation.[56] In the end, *Ketzalkóatl* as a deific force is confused with historical figures, i.e., *Topíltzin* and/or *Huemak* and a myth is created by Spanish chroniclers to project the banished "messiah figure" as returning one day from the East to provide redemption to the *Metzikans*. Thus, the Spanish are placed as gods and as redeemers conveniently fitting the interpretations of Padre Durán.

THE COLONIAL MYTH OF AZTEC IMPERIALISM

The idea of imperialism is well-documented as an historical legacy of Western civilization. The examples are numerous, e.g., Roman, Nordic, Visigothic, Normans, Franks, Angles and Saxons and, more recently, the centuries of crusading warfare and the imperialism of the French, Spanish, English and Americans in the East, Africa and the Americas. War and conquest are concepts that are understood within the context of European and Spanish noble families. It is the Teutonic legacy that survived within the nobility in Europe. After years of battle during *Reconquista*, the Spanish continue the pattern of war and conquest in the Americas. What is interesting to note is the myopic view of society that the Europeans possess with regard to the acquisition of territory. It is this idea of imperialism that is firmly embedded in the minds of Spanish chroniclers that will prevail as the principle mode of explanation of the acquisition of territory. What is paramount in understanding pre-Columbian/Native American thought regarding land and territory is the concept of non-ownership, so characteristic of all Native Americans. Land cannot be purchased. Thus, it cannot be owned. It is there for the communal use of the all. The idea of possession is foreign to the native peoples in the Americas, save a few personal items revolving around the immediate household. What is often obviated in the accounts of history of native peoples is the idea of Confederations. The history of pre-Columbian Mexico written by Europeans repeatedly alludes to emperors, using European linguistic and cultural markers. To use this terminology is to think in terms of European hierarchy and governance. This is a vertical conceptual structure, totally and diametrically opposite from the pre-Columbian mode of governance. For native peoples of the Americas, the communal structure varied in its development but the ends were the same; all shared the goods of production and election of governing heads was by democratic process via councils. Men and women had responsibility in the elective process as seen by the councils of women from Mohawk/Algonquin tribes to Aztec/Inca/Maya state cultures. With respect to Aztec nations and cultures, there was a great degree of sophistication at all levels of society. We note that the Toltecs had inherited great and advanced ideas within the arts and sciences from the *Teotihuakan* state culture. In its governing evolution the Toltecs formed Confederations as exemplified in the last reign of the democratic triumvirate of *Tollan*, *Koliman* and *Tlapallantonko*. In addition to alliances, the extension of territory was accomplished through marriages between the families of principal governing heads of different tribal nations. A case in point is the case of governing head *Tekpanekatl* who was of the Chichimec lineage.

Fleeing from the northern invaders, these *Akolhuas* from the provinces of *Miçhuakan* asked *Xolotl* for lands in which their nation could be established. An agreement was reached and the head of the *Akolhuas* was subsequently married to the daughter *Xolotl*, living in prosperity, constructing large edifices in the newly-formed territory of Atzkapotzalko, establishing their new name of *Tekpanekah* (builders of large temples/palaces). Later, with the Confederation of *Anauak*, there is the triple alliance of *Texkoko*, *Tlakopan* and *Tenochtitilan*. A subsequent rebellion by *Maxtla* from *Koyohuakan* is quelled by *Moktekuzoma Ilhuikamina*, who is named as governor of *Koyohuakan*. This forms the quadruple alliance of the Confederation. In later years, Iztapalapan was added to the Confederation, giving it the character of a quintuple alliance. Commerce was ultimately important to the Confederation of Anauak as it had trade routes to distant places beyond its boundaries. Other non-Aztec tribes, fearing the industrial and commercial power of the Confederation, would attack and kill merchants with the motive of cutting off the economic current. Thus, many wars were begun; these were not wars of conquest but civil wars that had a direct bearing on national unification and confederation. It should also be noted that there were many non-Aztec tribal nations that were not in accord and harmony with the Aztec Confederation, i.e., the *Purépecha* (Tarascans), the *Tlaskallan* (the betrayers, allied with Cortés), the *Mixtekah*, the *Zapotekah*, the Maya. Once a territory came into the bounds of the Aztec rule, they were allowed, unlike Western tradition, to live in peace and harmony. This was accomplished by the principle of self-determination. They were allowed to keep their tradition, religious practices and elect their own governing heads. Such was the case in *Yukatlan* (now Yucatán) where, after peace was established by the armies of the Aztecs (between the *Totol-Xiuh* and the *Kokom*), the Mayas were given the right to elect their own heads after the signing of the peace accord in Mayapan.[57]

THE COLONIAL MYTH OF AZTEC SLAVERY

The question of slavery merits little consideration in view that this was decidedly a Western practice. The slave trade was indeed lucrative to both the Spanish and the Portuguese. It was the Spanish that first instituted slavery in the Americas, first by enslaving the Native Americans of Hispaniola to work in the mines and secondly, by importing black slaves from Africa into the Caribbean. The concept of slavery in terms of its justification, is credited to Plato. Thus, Plato was the consummate philosopher, par excellence, of the Middle Ages. The idea that a ruling class could subject a lower class gives medieval Europe its justification for slavery. The idea of possession and/or ownership consequently was an idea that was in the European psyche and was one that was imported to the Americas. The friars and Spanish chroniclers customarily used the term *vasallo* (serf) to refer to natives, who were considered heathen and of the lowest estate. The latter is explained by their biased contention during the first century of colonialism that the natives had no souls.[58] The concept of slavery, therefore, was introduced by the Spanish chroniclers, notably Díaz del Castillo, Sahagún and Durán. This unfortunate misnaming referred largely to the social/commercial group that provided a variety of services and/or the penal group that was sentenced to work off their transgression to the strict societal mores of the Aztec Confederation. Bernal Díaz del Castillo, like many of his contemporaries, cannot understand the human dignity involved in working off a debt to the person who has been inflicted, nor can he and his contemporaries understand the joy of communal responsibility to neighbors as well as to the nation.[59]

In view of the hate and low esteem relegated to the native by the Spanish, it is convenient and natural to regard them as slaves. Fagan, believing Díaz del Castillo's misinterpretations, asserts incredibly that one had the option of becoming a slave! Later he declares they could have considerable authority$_{60}$ own land and the right to marry with children as free citizens It is clear that Spanish chroniclers but also contemporary writers, have tried excessively to fit a non-Western socioeconomic pattern into an established Western institution. Sahagún notes$_{61}$ that this group lived in poverty in his house surrounded by rubbish . What Fagan does not understand is that Sahagún is observing a post-Conquest society that has been destroyed and has been subjected to serfdom by the Spanish circa 1566. Father Motolinía, reiterating the term of slave, observed, nonetheless, a different practice: "The manner in which slaves are made by these natives of New Spain is very different from the practices of European nations it seems to me that those who are called slaves do not fulfill many of the conditions of a slave properly so called.$_{62}$

Soustelle, like Eric Wolf, reiterates the concept of slavery as a$_{63}$ justification for a servile group within a growing complex society Nigel Davies, moreover, attempts to create a social strata citing nobility, warriors and priests at the top, officials and merchants at the center and serfs and slaves at the bottom of the social scale. It is clear that the latter are inherently part of the hierarchy of the European Middle Ages and, upon checking his sources, it is traced back to medieval-minded Spanish friars$_{64}$ via Soustelle and Katz that serve as the foundation for his assertion.

THE COLONIAL MYTH OF CANNIBALISM AND HUMAN SACRIFICE

Among the myths created by the Spanish chroniclers that caused the most damage to the high Aztec culture and civilization is that of cannibalism and human sacrifice. After researching the medieval Christian church and its nefarious ties to the state and the Inquisition, it is clear to this writer that as sanguine invaders of a civilized people, the "New World Crusaders" created fictitious accounts of cannibalism, in part to justify their own acts of butchery throughout the Americas. Anthropologist William Arens shares this view and further adds that as Christians, the Spanish felt they had a divine mission to wipe out paganism and that chroniclers like Sahagún "highlighted cannibalism$_{65}$ and other idolatries partly out of their own fear of the inquisition". Arens suggests, moreover, that these accusations were political and argues that no conquistador actually saw any evidence of cannibalism. There are several other factors that are important which shed light on the motivations for the creation of a fictitious Aztec "black legend". Aside from the military invasion, plunder and search for gold for the Spanish Crown, the mixture of religious fanaticism and state, the intolerance of all religions, making all who are outside of the "medieval" Christian church heretical, there is the problem of control between what is enacted as law by the Crown and what is practiced in the Antilles and New Spain (Mexico). I refer here to the *leyes de las Indias*, proclaimed by Queen Isabela in 1500, i.e., that hereafter, all natives will be free with the exception...and the exception became rule...that they be cannibals or captives of war.[66] It is this law that gave the Spanish colonists the legal impetus to defame the Aztec culture by accusing them of cannibalism, thus ensuring their lack of freedom and the irresponsible action of attacking village after village with the ridiculous *Requerimiento* (pronouncement of conquest), thus assuring them captives of war.[67] In terms of the friars' fears for the Inquisition, there may be a grain of truth but I suspect that it was the religious and fanatical "divine mission" of conversion that blinded the chroniclers, not to mention the prejudice and hatred established through their racial/color bias imported from the European noble family structures. What may not have been invented in the first draft of a document was altered by the censors of the *Index Librorum Prohibitorum* of the Inquisitional ecclesiastical councils which lasted 300 years in Spanish America.

What is most ironic, as Dr. Juan Luna-Cárdenas asserts, is the track record of the Europeans in human sacrifice. This custom has taken many forms, be it Roman or the *Santo Oficio* or the Inquisition. It is estimated that over one million innocent women were tortured and sacrificed alive to the fire in Europe; incredibly, they represented the last of the knowledge keepers of medicinal herbs and botany during the Dark Ages. This European religious practice of human sacrifice is transported with the Inquisition to the Americas and it is Christopher Columbus' brother Bartolomé that initiates this practice very early on as he orders the burning alive of six natives "for acts against the Faith and the Religion".[68] Shortly before returning to Spain, Chistopher Columbus constructs a fort that he calls "Fort Nativity". It is here that we see the first act of cannibalism by the *Colonos* (colonials) left behind. They began to kill natives, whom they ate roasted or raw and, upon seeing such savagery, the natives fled, leaving the colonials alone. Soon they fought each other, consuming each other until the last of the Spanish cannibals died of hunger not realizing the bounty available in the jungles of the Antilles.

Let us not forget that, had it not been for the Native Americans' teachings of survival in the wilds to the first settlers on the Eastern Seaboard of the United States, they certainly would not have survived one winter. Ironically, there are a number of other accounts of Spanish cannibalism, e.g., Galveston, Texas, Venezuela, etc,[69] as reported by soldiers and friars disillusioned by their misfortune. It is not difficult to understand that chroniclers Father Sahagún, Father Diego Durán, Bernal Díaz del Castillo and other colonials were biased. What is difficult to understand in our age of rationalism is (a) the irresponsible and naive belief by current researchers of what are essentially censored documents (post-Conquest codices) by the ecclesiastical councils of the Inquisition, and (b) the contemporary rationalizations of biased assumptions. One can understand (without justifying) the modern *Mexican's* dilemma as he views a contradictory culture that he has inherited. What is inexcusable are ludicrous rationalizations of a myth as exemplified by Harner who incredibly asserts that it was a matter of providing meat protein for a[70] population in an environment where meat was in short supply! If there is one thing that is ultimately clear in the research of Aztec society, it is their great abundance of meats, vegetables, fowl, medicines, fruits, etc,[71] Cortés was amazed by this abundance in his *Cartas de Relación.* To date, there has not been archeological evidence, i.e., broken bones, roasted bones, in Mexico's pre-Columbian sites.[72]

The friars and chroniclers that are responsible for creating an Aztec black legend of cannibalism are the same who go a step further and recreate abominable acts of human sacrifice. It is Diego Durán himself who speaks of the Holy Church that orders him to receive the "True Body and Blood of our Lord Jesus Christ."[73] This physical manifestation of the divine is an inherent characteristic of the religious medieval mind. the butchering of natives by the military is so overwhelming that it causes Fray Bartolomé de las

Official Inquisition Building in Mexico City during Colonialism.

Casas to revolt against the barbaric acts of the Spanish committed in the name of conquest and avarice. It is Fray Montesinos, much earlier in the Antilles, who provides the first spark of rebellion against the un-Christian acts of the Spanish.[74] The so-called sacrificial stone referred to as the *techcatl* has now been declared a falsity by historian and head librarian of the Museum of Anthropology in Mexico City, Antonio Pompa y Pompa. According to Pompa y Pompa, it is not a sacrificial stone but rather a monolith that is commemorative of *Tizoc*. The error of calling it Stone of Sacrifices appears to have begun in the Nineteenth Century by the uneducated masses and this error prolonged into the Twentieth Century by many without real knowledge or credentials. Pompa y Pompa has known this for over 30 years[75] and cites the engraved commemorative deeds of Tizoc as proof. Most important is the fact that there are no *pre-Columbian or pre-Conquest codices* that show that such a practice ever existed. Finally, Dr. Luna-Cárdenas points to a medical problem among the Spaniards that may explain the psychosis and illusions among the military and clergy. He refers to *ecomanía*, a mental disturbance in which anguish creates fantasy and delusion. I would add, moreover, that the soldiers and many of the clergy were involved in unmitigated sexual activity, violating native women daily. Moreover, infection with syphilis and gonorrhea and other diseases was widespread and uncontrolled. It is known that Bartolomé Colón (the admiral's brother) and Cortés were pathologically sickly cases and were both involved in extreme butchery and inhuman acts. It is also well-documented that priests did not observe celibacy in the Americas even as late as the Nineteenth Century in New Mexico. Thus, in cases of advanced venereal diseases, the mind was insecure and twisted. This may account, in part, for the extreme violence and deviant behavior among the Spanish. It must be remembered that these two cultures were diametrically opposite in thought and deed. Sacrifice in the pre-Columbian sense, was accomplished largely through offerings of prayer, incense, flower, clay and corn; it was a symbolic representation of the cyclical sustenance provided by nature and the divine forces now being returned through its own growth.

After wars, captives were granted permission to become part of the Confederation and, in so doing, permitted to retain their customs and culture. This is clear in the writings of Inca Garcilaso de la Vega,[76] as with the conscription of people for war by the *Aztekah-Tlaxkaltekas* (alliance with Cortés) after attacking their villages. Finally, the taking of life (other than by defense of home and nation) violated a most important religious principle of the Aztecs, i.e., reincarnation. Each person had the duty to live by the laws of nature to the fullest so that their greatness in this life could be manifested even more so in the next, providing greatness to the race in their pursuit of happiness on this earth.

THE COLONIAL MYTH OF DIPSOMANIA

The question of drunkenness as a social problem can only be considered within an historical framework. Much of this is due to the European sociocultural impact on the Native Americans. It is only after the Spanish destroy the sociocultural/religious base that[77] drinking becomes the rule rather than the exception. Most researchers admit that drinking was strictly prohibited in pre-Conquest times. For a high priest to drink or steal was considered an outrageous offense against the principles of *Tloke-Nahuake*. The penalty was death for a priest/sage who had to possess the ultimate and highest selection of ideals. Drunkeness violated the sacred principles of the total spiritual/intellectual development of humankind.

Davies contends that "under the stress of change and faced with the dissolution of their society, the native population...literally...took to drink, so severely controlled in pre-Hispanic times and largely limited to religious ceremonies."[78] Friars intent on massive conversion projected a condemning view of sacred plants used by the Aztecs in spiritual ceremonies. Sahagún referred to *péyotl* (peyote) and *teonanakatl* (a sacred fungus) within the demonic context of drunkenness. The Lakota Nation, as well as many other Native Americans in the United States, still use *péyotl* as a sacred plant in their religious ceremonies; here, they achieve harmony with the universe and through visions are able to obtain a high level of precognitive vision. Sahagún, however, does admit that "nobody drank wine (*octli*) excepting those who were already aged, and they drank a little in secret, without becoming drunk".[79] Since social drinking was severely prohibited and recognized as a deterrent to the total development of a person, why were deities of drink and drunkenness created by the friars during the post-Conquest colonial period? In every case concerning religious practices of pre-Columbian peoples, there is immediate condemnation of their rituals and religious symbolism. Fagan cites maguey as being represented by a four-hundred-breasted goddess, *Mayahuel*. She and her children, the Four Hundred Rabbits, inhabited the world of drink and drunkenness.[80] What is obvious is the intent to portray a negative and discrediting image of the religious practices of native peoples. Ironically, this is an exact picture of ancient Western gods and paganism reminiscent of Greek/Roman decadence. Fagan, in discussing the 260-day *Tonalpohualli*, incorporates into the *Tochtli* (rabbit sign days) *Mayahuel* as the deity of pulque and intoxication "because the drunkard weaved and strutted about in the same erratic and unpredictable way as a rabbit".[81] Moreover, he cites *Ometochtli* as associated with maguey and pulque, whose assistants were known collectively as *Centzon Totochtin*.[82] There appears to be confusion among the chroniclers of post-Hispanic codices. It is also possible that the original sources were altered by Inquisitional tribunals of the Roman Catholic Church who were totally intolerant of any religious ideas beyond the established theology of their dogma.

THE PROBLEM OF USING POST-CONQUEST SOURCES

The significance of *Tochtli*, *Mayahuel* and/or *Ometochtli* have little to do with drink but rather with manifestations of the planting/growth phenomenon. Soustelle comes close as he refers to *Centzon Totochtin* as the lunar and terrestrial gods of plenty and harvest.[83] With the introduction of Catholicism comes the anthropomorphic interpretation of the divine forces. *Ometochtli* (2 Rabbit) is a calendaric sign/symbol that, when used with the 260-day sacred calendar and *Tonalámatl*, has special significance with respect to one's personality and propensities as humans on earth. The Spanish brought medieval superstition, ideas of evil, and bad luck, and quickly introduced these distortions into the interpretation of pre-Columbian sources. Sahagún spreads ideas of drunkenness and debauchery for all those born under this sign and adds that *Centzontotochtli* (*Centzontotochtin*) means "four hundred rabbits" because there are many diverse manners of drunkenness.[84]

The Tonalámatl was a sacred calendar read only by the scientist/priests; it has been referred to as the "cuenta de los destinos" or the count of the destinies, probably because of its predictive capabilities, i.e., its ability to categorize twenty personality types and thus accommodate to the appropriate vocations and professions. Analyzing *Tochtli* within the context of this mathematical/psychological system, there is no reference to drink or drunkenness. A *Tochtli* personality type is one that is passive, always in the background, concerned with the welfare of others before his own. He is not dull-minded but rather possesses an alert mind. He is humble and prefers an ambiance of tranquillity, abhors power, is kind with wise counsel as an educator and guide. As can be concluded, this personality type is contrary to the models created by the colonial friars. Others confused *Ometochtli* with *Tezkatzónkatl*; some relegated *Ometochtli*[85] as high priest of *Tezkatzónkatl*, the ultimate deity of drink. Other names were attributed to *Tezkatzónkatl*, e.g., *Tequechmecaniani, Teatlahuiani*. The problem with the latter is that it contradicts any sanctity or positive nature of a divine force since they signify "he that chokes" and "he that denies", respectively. Thus, this is a confusion on the part of the colonials or a post-Hispanic deterioration of values and symbols. *Tezkatzónkatl*, through its etymology, refers not to drunkenness or debauchery but rather to an enlightened and luminous state.[86]

According to Robelo, it refers to *tézkatl* (mirror) *tzóntli* (hair, 400) and *katl* (that which is) or he who has its crown (of hair) like a mirror, i.e., illuminating. This is a spiritual state that one aspired in sacred religious rituals, e.g., "baptism" ritual in the naming of a child or young man in various stages of maturation.

Mayahuel, likewise, has been anthropomorphized as a goddess of wine or pulque with considerable and varied interpretations. They range in origin from Olmekah to Maya to Aztekah/Metzikah. Generally, they point[87] to a woman who discovered the drink and was later made divine. There does not appear to be any connection with the plant maguey *(metl)* and *Mayahuel*; neither is there any historical proof of the existence of a person by that name. The invention of the varied properties of the maguey plant are known. By the time of the arrival of the Spanish, the maguey plant already yielded medicinal preparations, fibers for cape manufacture, needles for sewing[88] and rituals; the leaf pulp and salt were also used to dress wounds. *Yakanini Metzli Kuautemok*, in his historical recreation of

Aztekah/Toltekah society, cites a intelligent young female chemist called *Xóchitl* because of her natural beauty, as the inventor of a[89] variety of properties derived from the maguey plant. This occurs during the reign of *Tollan* (*Tula*) during the epoch of *Tekpánkaltzin*. *Xóchitl* is the daughter of *Papántzin*, a scientist and sage in the court of the governing head *Tekpankáltzin*. Together they dedicate their research to a science called *Keyíyotl* (similar to biology and chemistry). Among their inventions were liquid detergent from the plant *kuahmetl*, dyes from the maguey (*metl*) and paper from its fiber, but most important are discoveries from the juice of the maguey (*nekhuatl*).

It began with observations of the maguey plant. She noticed that small animals nourished themselves without harmful effects from the juice of the maguey. Through a process of filtration, *Xóchitl* was able to produce an almost transparent liquid with *Xoxoktik* (acid) taste and thus it was called *Xoxoatl* (acetic/acidic water). After much thought it was decided to experiment with its other properties, i.e., the sweet extractions. This led them to extract a sepia/blackish-colored honey called *nekuth* because it was the sweet substance of *nekhuatl*. Another experiment included a powder called *tekulli*, a porous rock called *texalli* in a filtering process that produced thick white liquid drops that, after a few hours, formed into small white granules called *çiankakatl*, which were pleasingly sweet to the palate without the odor of the plant. The *Aztekah/Çiçekatl* historian of *Tetzikuko*, *Ixlilxóchitl*, refers to the aforementioned as authentically historical and the invention of refined sugar from the dark honey of the maguey juice occurred in the year 13 *Kalli* or 900 A.D. of the Christian era, which antedates the German discovery of sugar by seven centuries. *Xóchitl* subsequently became the wife of *Tekpankaltzin* and bore a son called *Nakxitl Topíltzin*.

Historically, the real name of *Xóchitl* is not known. *Xóchitl*, meaning flower or rose, was a name given to her by the sovereign head of *Tullan*. What is interesting is *Xóchitl* as the inventor of wine, medicinal uses, paper and dyes, as well as sugar and *agua miel* from *metl* or the maguey plant. Moreover, of special significance is the introduction of a significant amount of calcium and other minerals and vitamins C and B.[90] Wolf refers to scrapers used with the maguey plant to increase the flow of juice from the heart of the century plant found in the Teotihuakan Valley. This, however, does not prove that it was filtered or fermented by the highly advanced theocratic Teotihuakan culture.

Dr. Juan Luna-Cárdenas contends that in pre-Columbian times, it was the unfermented *agua miel* (literally honey water) that was used by the populace. The sages knew of the deleterious effects of the fermented acidic juice and thus, like sweet unfermented cider, it provided a nutritional base for society at large. Thus, the image of the drunken native is a stereotype that was created during post-Conquest colonial times when severe exploitation, disillusion and hunger were the effects of the cultural invasion of the intolerant Europeans.

THE COLONIAL MYTH OF AZTEC MACHISMO AND THE DEBASED WOMAN

Native-American women generally have been portrayed in Aztec society as secondary citizens in a patriarchal structure. Sahagún is largely responsible for this negative view of women, asserting, notwithstanding, the existence of prostitutes and harlots.[91] The female in Aztec society was highly respected in all stages of maturation. She was the ideal of the race. She was meticulously dressed, bathed often and allowed to achieve the highest characteristics of her feminine nature. According to Yakanini Metzli Kuautemok, she could never wander alone or date freely and never could she deal with more than one man. If married, she was totally in charge of the household and all decisions were hers without interference of the husband.[92] She enjoyed the independence of retaining her own property and she could do business, entrusting her goods to itinerant traders or exercise a profession suited to her abilities be it that of a priestess, a midwife, a healer or a governing head.[93] Sahagún's own projection was largely that of a woman whose main duty was childbirth, whose pregnancy was filled with superstitious directives and whose baby would face a place of hard work and suffering. He speaks of soothsayers predicting the fate of a child, their honor or dishonor, their richness or poverty.[94]

What Sahagún is describing is essentially a European medieval model for women, i.e., women as objects, as secondary citizens with little future in a world of superstition. There is no question that the first victim of the Spanish invasion in the Americas is the Native American woman. She was raped, beaten and prostituted by the

Spanish. She was subsequently enslaved as a concubine, much like the European medieval model. The honor and respect that she enjoyed in pre-Columbian times was destroyed forever by the brutal and violent Spanish. After the conquest, women became objects of exploitation by the Spanish. It is estimated that each Spaniard had an average of 20-30 concubines in his *encomienda* for his folly and pleasure. Thus, the woman fell into disrepute and was encouraged to paint her face and become a courtesan. It is the post-conquest female that Sahagún is observing and not the pre-Columbian model. In the post-conquest model, the woman had no right in colonial society. In the pre-Columbian model she could participate in major governing decisions in the Council of Women at the various levels of government; she held supreme power in Tula[95] and it appears that a women (*Ilancueitl*) was at the origin of power in Metziko-Tenochtítlan.[96]

Old women, like old men, were highly respected and esteemed and had a place in society until their death, which was celebrated with great joy for having contributed to the greatness of the nation. Adultery, like drunkenness, was severely prohibited under the punishment of death. Neither practice was part of the social mores. As a wife, she could divorce the husband on grounds of lack of support, abandoning the children or other equally-damaging factors to the household. The conjugal property was equally divided between the two former spouses. The divorced woman was free to marry again whenever she chose.[97]   Finally, when a woman died during childbirth, she was relegated the highest place in the sacred dimensional world. Like the esteemed warrior who died in battle, their spirit forms would go to *Tonálkatl*, a region where the regent of the glorious energy of the Sun resided. In the transition to the spirit world, there were *danzas*, music and general celebration throughout until dawn. It was thought that after four years of glorious existence in this place, the spirits could then animate the clouds or sacred birds with beautiful plumage.[98]   Finally, the female in Aztec society could belong within any of the many options available to her according to her talents and propensities. Her personality type usually was a signal for the direction she would take. A personality type of *Akatl* projected women with great leadership qualities, innovations, individual rights and generally governing heads. Due to her focus in the world of law, business or governance, she was often not interested in wifehood. In the end, each person was seen as equal because he or she was seen within a spiritual/metaphysical framework. It was the inner spiritual qualities that brought about greatness and, once recognized, these people became the select heads of society. In the final analysis, it was not power of materialism that mattered but the highest spiritual ideals. Thus, nobility must not be viewed in the same light as medieval Europe but rather in the definition of sublime dignity and moral/ethical character.[99]

SUMMATION

In summation, the history and interpretation of native peoples and in particular the Aztec, has been subjected since the beginning of the invasion of the Western world, to alterations and distortions by medieval minded writers and censors attached to ecclesiastical councils of the *Santo Oficio* or the Inquisition. The negative picture portrayed in chronicles and post-Conquest codices of native peoples has often been a direct reflection of medieval European reality with all of its barbarism, superstition and violence. Moreover, the backwardness of the Spanish, particularly in the sciences, did not permit them to objectively understand the scientific vision of the universe as viewed by pre-Columbian high cultures; rather, it was seen as heretical and therefore, was condemned with the characteristic listing of medieval witchcraft accusations. It is precisely because the Aztecs and other high pre-Columbian cultures were urbane, humane and civilized that they were overtaken by the cannon and the sword. The high principles of these high cultures regarding humanity, brotherhood, true harmony and understanding of the principles of nature, their profound knowledge in high mathematics, astronomy, biology, engineering, architecture, agronomy and their creative genius as exemplified by their profound abstract art and poetry does not fit with the barbarous model invented by the Spanish. The contradiction has puzzled many researchers who have tried to rationalize or justify its existence. It does not fit simply because it is a myth invented like many in the history of invading nations. As one looks at today's world, it is evident that the Western model of institutional politics of the moment are symptoms of a very long pattern of conflict and denial. The moment is now upon us to seek as the Aztecs and other Native

Americans sought, the *Neltililiztli* or the "root and foundations of all things" so that we can attain a more profound understanding of the truth of things; so that our reality can be transformed into the center where light and understanding of humanity and the cosmos are experienced in a non-linear, multi-dimensional and interlinking unified reality.

ENDNOTES

[1] Religious/racial persecution by the Visigoths is seen in the following councils: (1)613 A.D. (King Sisebut) orders that Jews accept baptism, otherwise penalty of exile; (2)633 A.D. (Fourth Council) Jews have the obligation to accept baptism and accept Christian precepts. Their children shall be taken from them and raised as Christians; (3)681 A.D. (Twelfth Council) Baptism by Jews within one year or penalty of expulsion and confiscation of properties; circumcision prohibited, as well as Judaic celebrations or insulting Christianity. Punishment by the clergy; (4)694 A.D. (Seventeenth Council) Jews not accepting Christianity will be reduced to slaves and property will be confiscated; (5)1119 A.D. (Council of Tortosa) Kings have authority to persecute all heretics; (6)1197 A.D. Pedro II king of Aragón and Count of Barcelona, establishes the penalty of death by fire for all heretics.

[2] Under Gregory VII, the model army was converted into the *Militia Sancti Pictri* or the Knights of St. Peter; these were armed soldiers of the church with pontifical blessings form military campaigns. See Hans Eberhrd Meyer, *The Crusades*. Trans. John Gilligham, Oxford University, 1972, p. 21. "For having been in armed campaigns, some princes saw the Pope as a feudal lord and when it was necessary, the ecclesiastic reformists used force of arms mobilizing the feudal lords to war for their own interests. This change had positive consequences for the Church upon being approved totally by the feudal aristocracy. The Catholic Church had success in combining the expansionist ambitions of the aristocracy with Christian ideology." Cited in the unpublished manuscript of the author, *Tres civilizaciones del mundo medieval: Crítica, análises y crónicas de las primeras cruzadas*.(In Press with The Edwin Mellen Press, 1997)

[3] Recommended critical works on the Middle Ages include:
Jonathan Riley Smith, *The First Crusade and the Idea of Crusading*, trans., Marshall Baldwin y Walter Goffart.,   Fulberto de Chartres, *Historia Hierosolymitana*, ed. de Hagenmeyer, (Heidelberg, 1913), Oderic Vitalis, *Historia Aecclesiastica*, E. M. Chibnall (1969-79), 6. vols.,   A. Potthast, *Bibliotheca Historica Medii Aevi* (375-1500 D.C.), 2 vols., (Berlin, 1896). L. Bréhier, *L'Eglise et l'orient au moyen âge: Les croisades*, ed.(Paris, J. Gabalda et. fils., 1928).

[4] Arnoldo Carlos Vento, *Tres civilizaciones...*, p. 2.

[5] Santiago Valenti Camp, "La Inquisición," in *Las sectas de las sociedades secretas a través de la historia de México*, (México: Ed. Valle de México, 1975), p. 741. The word "marranos" is a corruption of a Hebrew word, "maranatha" that means "stigma upon you".

[6] The Council of Trent took place in Northern Italy on three occasions, 1545-47, 1551-52, 1562-63. The Nineteenth Council of the Roman Catholic Church was the principle instrument for reform, clarifying issues of doctrine, developing instruments for reform, clarifying issues of doctrine, developing definitions on all aspects of religious life. It also condemned the Protestant Reformation and began the counter-reform which gave way to the Inquisition within the Church.

[7] Valenti Camp, p. 742, states: "In 1477, the Dominican Fray Alonso de Ojeda with his preachings in Seville, was able to receive an inspecting ecclesiastical commission and not having much success petitioned to Sixto VI in 1478 who then dictated a Pontifical Bull authorizing two or three bishops or archbishops or other capable men to become Inquisitors in every part of the kingdom using, with regard to heretics, all of the power, jurisdiction and authority..."

[8] Valenti Camp, pp. 744, 751. See also, J. G. Rodrigo, *Historia verdadera de la Inquisición*, (Madrid, 1877); Antonio de Llorente, *La historia crítica de la Inquisición en España*.

[9] It is Alexander VI, who through Papal Bull, declares all lands of the New World under the sovereignty of Spain, a point of international right contested by Padre Vittoria from his seminary in Barcelona.

[10] Not only did they work without eating in the mines but the Spanish also separated the boys from their families, "and in this manner the generations ceased to exist...and in this way countless multitudes of people were killed on that island...", Bartolomé de las Casas, *Brevísima relación...*, p. 26.

[11] Bartolomé de las Casas, *Brevísima relación...*, p. 22.

[12] It is ironic that doubts remain even today after Columbus' observations in his *Diary* in which he remarks that, "There are no people more domestic...all of them with the most singular treatment, lovingly and with kind voice...and industrious...and I believe they can quickly become Christians."

[13] See Lewis Hanke, "Fundamental Laws: The Requirement. 1513, a most remarkable document," in *History of Latin American Civilization*, vol. I (Boston: Little, Brown & Co., 1967), pp. 93-95. "Originally designed to legalize the possession of lands by the Spanish. It was used first in 1514 by Pedrarias Dávila near Santa Marta; later it was used in different and unusual circumstances: it was read from trees, from empty huts, to aborigines while they slept or while they fled...the captains of ships

would read this document several leagues away from the island, and then at night, they would go in and attack.
[14] It was Ixlilxóchitl who gave testimony as to the alterations that the Spanish were committing: "I have read many histories written by the Spanish of things of this nation and all of them are very different from the original history instead of saying one thing, they say another, some speaking about passion, others speaking about industry and others relating fabricated fables in the language of the moment of these and others...the Spanish do not understand well our language or what the elders are saying..." See Fernando de Ixlilxóchitl, *Obras históricas*, 2 vols., Mexico (1891-1892).
[15] Eugenio Chang Rodríguez, *Latino-América: Su civilización y su cultura,*(Rowley, Mass: Newbery House Publishers, 1983), pp. 106-107.
[16] See Rudolfo Acuña, "Legacy of Hate: The Conquest of the Southwest" in *Occupied America: A History of Chicanos.* (New York: Harper and Row, 1981), pp. 1-23.
[17] Juan José Arrom. *Esquema generacional de las letras hispanoamericanas,* (Bogotá: Instituto Caro y Cuervo, 1963), p. 33.
[18] Ibid.
[19] Juan José Arrom, "Criollo, definición y matices de un concepto," *Certidumbre de América,* (Havana , 1959), pp. 9-26.
[20] Translated by the author. See, Joseph F. O'Callaghan, *A History of Medieval Spain,* (London: Cornell University Press, 1975), p. 612.
[21] Norma F. Martin, *Los vagabundos de la Nueva España,* (México: Siglo XVI, 1957), p. 38.
[22] From the work, *México a través de los siglos,* (Barcelona, N.D.), vol. II, p. 415, where one can see the atrocities committed by the Inquisition in New Spain proved through documentation.
[23] Ibid., p. 415.
[24] Bartolomé de las Casas, *Brevísima relación de la destrucción de las Indias,* (México: Colección Metropolitana, 1974), pp. 110, 163.
[25] An eminent Mexican Mayan anthropologist when presented with ideas of *Mexikáyotl* and its cosmogony as received by persons through centuries of generations via the oral tradition, rejected it all, declaring, "These people do not belong to any legitimate academy". The problem, then, is following the Colonial mentality. One has to unmask oneself and meet truth squarely, no matter how terrible it may be. The ones that truly understand the autocthonous metaphysics have not been recognized. These native teachers have had to function from their homes without any financial help from educational institutions. Such has been the case with the native teachers of autocthonous thought, e.g., Yakanini Meztli Kuautemok (Juan Luna Cárdenas) and Domingo Martínez Parédez.

[26] The early Christians, following the "revolutionary" philosophy of the Master (known as the Christed One) represent a non-Western view of reality; it followed the metaphysics of the Essenes, a monastic Judaic group whose existence was mysteriously left out of the histories.

[27] *Yakanini Metzli Kuautemok* (Dr. Juan Luna-Cárdenas) "Conoce ud. la ciencia suprema?" Lecture/address to the *Central Kosmosofica de Anahuak*, (Mex.: Editorial Aztékatl, N.D.).

[28] According to *Yakanini Metzli Kuautemok, Ilhuikáyotl kosmosofia* (Mex.: Central Kosmosófica de Anauak), the five mental spheres are:

(1)*Teonomilizzotl*
(2)*Teomaniliztli*
(3)*Teomazauhtli*
(4)*Teomatlilli*
(5)*Teoyotl*

[29] Sahagún, Fray Bernardino de, *Historia general de las cosas de Nueva España*, (Mexico: Editorial Pedro Robredo, 1938) vol. II, pp. 258-262. Sahagún states: "...hell, where Satan lived and called himself *Mictlantecutli* and also *Tzontemoc* and a goddess who was called *Mictecacihuatl*". Modern scholars reiterating this myth include Walter Krickeberg, *Mitos y leyendas de los Aztecas, Incas, Mayas y Musicas* (Mex., D.F.: Fondo de Cultura Económica, 1971) pp. 34-35. (From the German, *Märchen der Aztecen und Incaperuaner, Maya und Muisca)*; Jacques Soustelle, *Daily Life of the Aztecs: On the Eve of the Spanish Conquest*, trans. Patrick O'Brian (New York: The MacMillan Company, 1968) p. 108 (from the French, *La vie quotidian des Azteques a la veille de la conquête espagnole)*; Alfonso Caso, *El pueblo del sol* (Mex. D.F.: Fondo de Cultura Económica, 1953) pp. 81-82.

[30] Alfredo Chavero, *Mexico a través de los siglos, Historia antigua y de la conquista*, (Mex.: Ballesca, Espasa y Cia.) N.D.

[31] The Codex Megliabecchi is a post-Conquest manuscript stylized with native design but on European paper (92 pp.) written in the mid-Sixteenth Century. Its content is the calendaric *Tonalámatl* with interpretations written in Spanish. According to Luis Azcué y Mancera (*Codices indígenas*, p. 164), it does not clarify but detracts from the original concepts, e.g., characters referred to with pulque are interpreted as deities (housed in Florence, Italy).

[32] Miguel León-Portilla, *Toltecayotl: Aspectos de la cultura Náhuatl* (Mex.: Fondo de Cultura Económica, 1980) p. 186.

[33] Brian M. Fagan, *The Aztecs* (New York: Freeman and Company, 1984) p. 161.

[34] Noemí Quezada, *Amor y magia amorosa entre los Aztecas* (Mex.: UNAM, 1975) p. 25.

[35] Raymond Paredes, "The Origins of Anti-*Mexican* Sentiment in the United States", *New Directions in Chicano Scholarship*, ed. Romo & Paredes (La Jolla: U.C. San Diego Chicano Monograph Series, 1978).

[36] Fray Geronimo de Mendieta, *Historia Eclesiástica Indiana*, (Mexico, 1870), (reprinted by Chávez Hayhoe, Mex., 1945). See also, Manuel Orozco y Berra, *Historia antigua de la Conquista de México*, 4 vols. (Mex.: Atlas, 1880).

[37] Padre Sahagún, *Historia general...*

[38] Caso, *El pueblo del sol*, p. 88.

[39] Soustelle, *The Daily Life of the Aztecs*, pp. 112-113.

[40] Fagan, *The Aztecs*, p. 222.

[41] Nigel Davies, *The Aztecs; A History* (New York: Putnam and Sons, 1974) p. 25.

[42] Eric Wolf, *Sons of the Shaking Earth* (Chicago: University of Chicago Press, 1959) p. 88.

[43] León-Portilla, *Toltecayotl...*, p. 188.

[44] Bartolomé de las Casas, *Brevísima relación de la destrucción de las Indias*, (Mex.: Metro, 1974) pp. 24-25.

[45] Inca Garcilaso de la Vega, *Comentarios reales de los Incas.* See the translation of Clements R. Markham, *First Part of the Royal Commentaries* (by Inca Garcilaso de la Vega). (London: The Hakiuyt Society, 1st Series, nos. 41, 45, 1869-1871), no. 45, pp. 3-29, passim.

[46] Angel M. Garibay K., *La Literatura de los Aztecas*, (Mexico: Joaquín Mortiz, 1964) p. 116.

[47] Garibay, *La Literatura...*, p. 123.

[48] Hannerl Gossler, *La Ciencia celeste de los Aztecas* (Mex.: Posada, 1974) p. 126.

[49] Garibay, *La Literatura...*, pp. 101-131.

[50] Cristóbal Colón, *Diario de viaje*, transcribed originally by Padre Bartolomé de las Casas in his *Historia de las Indias.* See dated entries of Oct. 12-15; Oct. 28; Dec. 24.

[51] During the Nineteenth Century, Maggs Bros. 34 and 35, Conduit Street, London W. Advertised the sale of "the first edition of the Latin Letter Announcing the Discovery of America" for 1,250 lbs. in which he announces his recent discovery of the Ganges dated the third day of the calends. of May, 1493 (From the Rare Books Collection, Benson Library, University of Texas--Austin).

[52] The vision of *Xokoyótzin* is reproduced by the informants of Sahagún (vol. XII of the *Codice Florentino*); there is also a brief section in *Historia de Tlaxcala* by Diego Muñóz Camargo which reflects the dubious opinion of the *Tlaxcaltekas*, the allies of Cortés. See also Miguel León-Portilla,

Visión de los vencidos; Relaciones indígenas de la Conquista (Mex.: UNAM, 1972) pp. 1-11.

[53] Juan Luna-Cárdenas, *Ilhuikáyotl:kosmosofía* (Mex.: Central Kosmosófica de Anauak). In the scientific metaphysics of the Aztecs, *Tezkatlipoka* represents the force of dominance bringing about truth and justice; *Xipe* represents wisdom, *Uitzilopoçitl* fine, correct thought, artistic and spiritual and *Ixkozauki* the flourishing of mental activities.

[54] See *Ixlilxóchitl*, Fernando del Alba, *Relaciones históricas*, cited by Cecilio Robelo, *Diccionario de la mitología Náhuatl*, p. 233.

[55] Cecilio Robelo: *Diccionario de la mitología Náhuatl* (Mex.: Ediciones Fuente Cultural, 1951) p. 234.

[56] Juan Luna Cárdenas, *Historia Patria* (Mex.: Editorial Aztékatl, 1956) pp. 79-71.

[57] Juan Luna Cárdenas, *Historia Patria*, pp. 155-156.

[58] José Juan Arrom, *Esquema generacional de las letras hispanoamericanas* (Bogotá: Caro y Cuervo, 1963) p. 28.

[59] Bernal Díaz del Castillo, *Historia verdadera de la Conquista de la Nueva España* (Mex.: Ed. Robredo, 1933) p. 232.

[60] Fagan, *The Aztecs...*, p. 178.

[61] Sahagún, *Historia general...*, p. 31.

[62] Motolinía, *Memoriales* (Paris, 1903), p. 349.

[63] Soustelles, *The Daily Life...*, pp. 73-76; Wolf, *Sons of the Shaking Earth...*, pp. 142-143.

[64] Davies, *The Aztecs*, p. 81. Also cites on pp. 42-43, Katz, Friedrich, *Situación social y económica de los Aztecas durante los Siglos XV y XVI*, (Mex.: UNAM, 1966).

[65] Fagan, *The Aztecs*, p. 234, citing William Aren, *The Man-Eating Myth* (Oxford: Clarendon Press, 1969).

[66] José Juan Arrom, *Esquema generacional...*, p. 23.

[67] The *Requerimiento* was a legal document that had a multitude of legalistic purposes, one of which was the proclamation of land for the Crown; it was ridiculous because often it was pronounced from a ship or a hill before invading a village with innocent women and children. All would be killed with the exception of the young who were pleasing to the eye for rape and/or labor. See Lewis Hanke, *The Spanish Struggle for Justice in the Conquest of America* (Boston: little, Brown and Co., 1965) p. 34.

[68] Juan Luna-Cárdenas, *Sí hubo sacrificios humanos y actos de antropofagia en América*, (Mex.: Editorial Aztékatl, 1993) p. 13.

[69] Juan Luna-Cárdenas, "Sí hubo...", pp. 16-32.

[70] Michael Harner, "The Ecological Basis for Aztec Sacrifice" in *American Ethnologist*, 4, I (1977) pp. 17-135.

[71] Hernan Cortés, *Cartas de relación*, written circa 1520 from his second letter (*Carta de relación*) in *Historiadores primitivos de las Indias* (Madrid: *Biblioteca de Autores Españoles*, Tomo 22, 1946).

[72] See Bernard R. Ortiz de Montellano, "Aztec Cannibalism: an Ecological Necessity?", *Science*, 1978, 200. pp. 611-617 in which he questions the problem of cannibalism.

[73] Diego Durán, *Book of the Gods and Rites*, trans. Heyden and Horcasitas, (Norman: University of Oklahoma Press, 1971) p. 95. The idea of eating God's own blood is of Western medieval Catholicism; the idea is so embedded that Soustelle even reiterates the idea of "eating of God's own flesh that the faithful ate in their bloody communion" as a form of explanation. Soustelle, *Daily life of the Aztecs*, p. 98. In the end, researchers cannot reconcile the obvious contradictions, or what appears on the surface to Fagan as philosophical ambivalence between violence and benevolence, humility and mercy. There is a reason for it; the malicious intercalations and inventions of the Inquisitional censors are out of sync with the philosophy and metaphysics of the Universe as understood by the pre-Columbian peoples.

[74] The sermons of Friar Antonio de Montesinos (1511) were transcribed or reproduced by Padre Bartolomé de las Casas in his *Historia de las Indias*. See also, Lewis Hanke's, *History of Latin American Civilization* (Boston: Little, Brown and Co., 1973) pp. 91-93 for the English version.

[75] Originally appears as an article in a local Mexico City newspaper or journal; cited by Dr. Juan Luna-Cárdenas, "*Sí hubo...*", p. 57

[76] Inca Garcilaso de la Vega, *Comentarios reales...*

[77] Soustelle, *The Daily Life...*, p. 157. See also, Andrés de Alcobiz, *Estas son las leyes que tenían los indios de la Nueva España* (1543).

[78] Davies, *The Aztecs*, p. 297.

[79] Sahagún, *Historia general...*, vol. 1, p. 357.

[80.] Fagan, *The Aztecs*, p. 81.

[81] Fagan, *The Aztecs*, p. 217.

[82] Fagan, *The Aztecs*, p. 245.

[83] Soustelle, *The Daily Life...*, p. 156, cites Sahagún.

[84] Cecilio Robelo, *Diccionario...*, p. 198-199.

[85] Cecilio Robelo, *Diccionario...*, p. 200.

[86] Cecilio Robelo, *Diccionario...*, p. 167.

[87] Fagan, *The Aztecs*, p. 81.

[88] Juan Luna-Cárdenas (*Yakanini Metzli Kuautemok*), *La casa de jade* (Mex.: Editorial Aztekatl, 1950), pp. 19-20.

[89] Luna-Cárdenas, *La casa de jade*, pp. 27, 41. See also, *Ixlilxóchitl's Historia Chichimeka/Toltekah* (*Quinta Relación*).

[90] Wolf, *Sons of the Shaking Earth*, p. 66.

[91] Soustelle, *The Daily Life...*, p. 131.

[92] Juan Luna-Cárdenas, Video interviews at the University of Texas--Austin. Summers, 1991, 1992.

[93] Soustelle, *The Daily Life...*, p. 184.

[94] Fagan referring to Sahagún, *The Aztecs*, p. 150.

[95] Magnus Morner, "The Conquest of Women" in *History of Latin American Civilization*, ed., Lewis Hanke, p. 140. Originally from *"Race Mixture"* in the *History of Latin America* (Boston: Little, Brown and Col, 1967) pp. 21-27.

[96] See *Ixtlilxochitl*, Fernando de Alba, *Historia Chichimeca*, p. 29.

[97] *Historia de los Mexicanos por sus pinturas*, vol. III, p. 249.

[98] Ixlilxóchitl, *Relaciones*, p. 239.

[99] Hannerl Gossler, *La Ciencia celeste de los azteca*, (Mexico: Editorial Posada, 1974), pp.121-22.

CHAPTER III

MEXICAN COUNTER-HEGEMONY

AUTOCRITICISM, THE SEARCH FOR IDENTITY

AND THE CHICANO

THE ATENEO DE LA JUVENTUD AND *MEXICANIDAD*

The concept of *Mexicanidad* or the quality or essence of being Mexican reaches its culmination when Mexico is launched into the Twentieth Century with the *Ateneo de la Juventud* in 1909. Among the group of writers, philosophers and intellectuals were Antonio Caso, Alfonso Reyes, José Vasconcelos, Julio Torri, Jesús Acevedo, González Martínez and the Dominican Pedro Henríquez Ureña. The latter, in 1913 in a famous paper, proposed the theme of *Mexicanidad* and the research into its antecedents, namely through the work of Juan Ruiz de Alarcón. Although there were some who disagreed with his reasoning, there is no doubt that a Mexican way of viewing life did indeed exist.[1] Henríquez-Ureña pointed out the following Mexican stylistic and cultural characteristics: discretion, polite sobriety, keen observation concisely expressed, proverbial courtesy, as well as morality of purpose and a thoughtful temperament.[2] It is not so much in what Alarcón sees as much as what is, in his perspective, his independent criteria in observing the customs of Madrid through his dramatic works. There is no doubt that his view of society had already been formed in Mexico by the time he had reached twenty years of age; years of being raised and educated in Mexico as a *criollo*. In addition, aspects of *Mexicanidad* were also represented much later in novelistic form with *El Periquillo Sarniento* by José Joaquín Fernández de Lizardi, notwithstanding, the folklore and customs of the historic and romantic novels of the Nineteenth Century.[3] While a new mode of discussing and viewing reality is already visible, serious philosophical and cultural analysis is not accomplished until December 24, 1923, when Antonio Caso proposes a series of problems and conflicts within Mexican ideology, a problematic platform that serves as a basis for Samuel Ramos in his analysis of the Mexican.[4] Consequently, as an essayist, Antonio Caso is the precursor of Mexican ideological and philosophical analysis.

MESTIZAJE

Prior to an analysis of *Mexicanidad* and as an integral part of that analysis, is the concept of *Mestizaje*, indispensable for the understanding of its historical, political and cultural implications. Although the *criollo*, through his social and economic rank, is the most representative figure in literature and politics, it is the *Mestizo* who is the most representative of the essence of being Mexican as a bi-cultural product from the first generations of New Spain. Through the *Mestizo* the attitudes of the new culture toward race, color, women and religion can be profiled. There is no doubt that the new ideas New Spain were the same employed during the European Medieval period. With respect to the mixture of races, the Spaniard viewed the Amerigenous peoples racially and religiously as inferior in comparison to his own blood which was viewed with racial purity. Consequently, any person with Amerigenous or *Mestizo* blood, carried within themselves, a stigma of inferiority. Even Garcilaso de la Vega of noble lineage will suffer discrimination in Spain for having Inca blood. During the early years of Colonialism, the problem of the Amerigenous population is debated; it is doubted that he has a soul and consequently, is not fit to be a Christian. Fortunately, the Amerigenous people will be defended very early and eloquently by Padre Montesinos, succeeded, moreover, by Padre Bartolomé de las Casas and Padre Pérez de Oliva y Vitoria. But, unfortunately, the prejudices of the "Old World" will have been planted in the colonial society of New Spain. Even today it is affirmed in Mexico, that "better white than dark" or "better than a barefooted Indian" (vestiges of the European Medieval colonial mentality). The irony is that the Spaniard was not pure-blooded but rather already a *Mestizo* with Moorish, Roman, Phoenician, Iberian,

Jewish and Visigothic blood, a *Mestizo* even more varied than the autochthonous races of the Americas.

After five centuries of *Mestizaje* in Mexico, it appears that among the Mexican intellectuals and philosophers, there is a unanimous consensus: *Mestizaje* is a process, and as such, is still developing; consequently, what results is an inconclusive product in the making. Nevertheless, one can see cultural characteristics (some contradictory) that profile the personality of the Mexican in all his/her complexity. According to José Iturriaga the bloods of the two respective cultures are in perpetual conflict; historical symbols are seen in conflict: Cortés/Cuauhtémoc, Cortés/Las Casas. Iturriaga affirms: "It would seem that our two bloods will not be able to rest until the two and one-half million bilingual and monolingual indigenous peoples are completely established at the median cultural level and at the median economic level of the country; and perhaps then, we will be able to view Cortés with objectivity and without animosity and we will recognize him as one of our grandfathers, as he is, in effect [5]

Mestizaje, in its broadest sense, that is to say as a mixture of many races (probably a representation most suitable for the Mexican) is used by José Vasconcelos as a positive or inevitable development of human consciousness beyond today's science and logic. The basis of this future development lies in integration and synthesis: integration and synthesis of the human personality at the individual level and at the social level: integration and synthesis of ethnic groups at the political and social level that will form an ultimate race, the cosmic race. His vision is one in which the world rejects the military/political and primitive states (in the evolution of civilization) where man and woman live in a regressive political and economic state; Vasconcelos desires a state beyond the antiquated rationalism and the adulterated intellectual state, one that he calls the aesthetic/spiritual state. Here woman and man now no longer suffer the prejudices of economics, the false logic and politics nor the decadent systems of religion and of social conduct. According to Vasconcelos, the new nations will do away with national interests and move into universal matters. Man and woman now leave behind the individual materialism centralized in the ego and now advance toward a universal unity, a higher of consciousness and perception, toward a more profound understanding beyond the material and the necessities of the senses. It is a liberation of things intellectual and of the illusions of the mind that are in league with the violent and aggressive systems of today, characterized by avarice, the abuse of power, Darwinist survivalism and materialism. It is a passage toward a higher dimension where there is unity and no conflict, where there is happiness and love as proper and essential manifestations. It is a departure from the archaic materialism of today toward a superior metaphysical plane.

JOSÉ VASCONCELOS: *MESTIZAJE* AS A DEVELOPING
HUMAN CONSCIOUSNESS

The ideas of Vasconcelos are laudable and noble. The problem with his vision and idealism resides in his hope that Mexico will make a sudden change; from Medieval neo-colonialism to a philosophical metaphysical system of a future age. After suffering from the "fraud" of Mexican elections when he ran for the presidency of the Republic, he suffers a depression and a disenchantment with Mexican politics. Many years later after various exiles, he confesses that the social evolution of mixed groups follows a slow process and possibly takes centuries before reaching the universal cosmic plane. I agree with the latter although it would appear on the surface difficult to see the society outside of today's exploitive systems. However, it is only necessary to see the disintegration of the Soviet Union and of communism. Who would have believed this ten years ago? Its old economic cycle has been terminated; now it begins a new political/economic/social cycle. All that is lacking now is the purification of North American capitalism, and the social/economic revolution of this country whose social structure is in dire disintegration. The great autocthonous cultures (Maya, Toltekah-Aztekah, Inca) knew that, in this world, everything spirals cyclically, including societies and nations. For this reason, the vision of Vasconcelos, although not immediately practical, is valuable, as a philosophical goal, as a direction and path toward a future of peace and harmony.

In speaking of *Mexicanidad*, one refers to that which is particular or unique to the Mexican in contrast to the other nations of Spanish speakers. At the beginning of the Twentieth Century there were two attempts to define the Mexican and his cultural characteristics prior to 1920. Both were participants in the young group known as the *Ateneo de la Juventud*; the first was Pedro Henríquez Ureña and the second is Alfonso Reyes. The first noted the unique Mexican characteristics in the work of Alarcón while the second came out of his classic work and investigation of Aztec culture in his *Visión de Anáhuac*. Unfortunately, the work of Reyes did not represent an autocthonous vision but a reiteration of the Western and European clerical perspective. According to Octavio Paz, it is Samuel Ramos who is the first Mexican writer that presents a systematic and comprehensive system of the Mexican in his key work, *El perfil del hombre y la cultura* and, which represents a point of departure for key future research for Leopoldo Zea, Emilio Uranga, José Iturriaga, César Garizurieta and Octavio Paz. There is no doubt that this work published for the first time in 1934 is a systematic and comprehensive study but is not the first to analyze the contemporary Mexican in his/her cultural aspects.

ANTONIO CASO: *EL PROBLEMA DE MÉXICO Y LA IDEOLOGÍA NATIONAL*

It was Antonio Caso's book, *El problema de México y la ideología national* (1924) that antedated the work of Samuel Ramos by a decade. Antonio Caso saw national problems not following a uniform, dialectic and gradual process but one that had developed cumulatively. He saw the Conquest as an immense wrong vis-a-vis the Amerigenous population of Anahuak, which implied "a pain, a sacrifice, and above all, an extremely difficult problem to resolve in Mexican history: the adaptation of two human groups at very diverse cultural levels. How, in the end, to integrate into one congruent whole the same incongruencies of the Conquest?".[8]

According to Caso, affirmations by both Democrats and Republicans were premature, particularly in view that the unification of the cultures had not been resolved prior to Independence. He States: "While our anthropological, racial and spiritual problem remains unresolved, while there remains great human differences between individual and social groups, Mexican democracy[9] will remain imperfect, one of the most imperfect in history." He continues, stating that political and social theories implemented "were not rooted in this nation but rather were taken from European[10] consciousness and have remained here with us". According to Caso, there is not a constructive ideology; even Catholicism was

almost converted to paganism by syncretism. The problem is not
with a new idea but within the spirit:

> Within the intimate, the cordial, a feeling, an attitude, of a faith,
> old or new like humanity...There needs to be an act of
> sacrifice...not Christ King, but Christ Nation: here, the
> maximum and the act that can save us. Most urgently within our
> teachings is to preach forgiveness for our offenses and love to
> one's brother...Avarice among the dispossessed was engendered
> by the avarice of the powerful. The social problem in Mexico, as
> in other parts, is a moral one...[11]

Caso further states that for being an imitating nation, Mexico
has not been an inventive nation. Its originality lies in its
autocthonous culture "one of the few original elaborations of all
times...rated at par with the great oriental civilizations: Chinese,
Hindu, Persian, Egyptian and Chaldaic-Assirian".[12] For Caso,
Mexico should not continue to assimilate the attributes of others:
"Our contemporary misery, our inverted revolutions, our tragic
bitterness are but bitter fruits of non-reflexive imitation".[13] He wants
idealists to see Mexico from the ground, their customs, their hopes
and desires to see oneself as one is in reality. Idealists should not try
to explain society extrinsically but rather intrinsically through the
spiritual; to do otherwise is to negate society "within an absurd
materialism which hides the originality within the historic
creations".[14]

In terms of Mexican collective consciousness, Caso points to
the problem with exalted individualism which isolates oneself from
other brethren, our brothers. He asks: "How can we love others when
we cannot love ourselves.?" The recalcitrant individualism does not
result from spiritual superiority but rather,

> It originates from our terrible, psychological limitations, from
> our irreconcilable emotions. What few genial men has Mexico
> given to humanity: a Morelos, a Sor Juana Inés de la Cruz...The
> majority of the inhabitants of this country do not distinguish
> themselves via exceptional and powerful psychic individuality
> but through absurd outpouring of deep emotions, surging forth
> devoid of reason. That is why we want to be in first place and
> we curse those who occupy it. That is why we struggle endlessly

Colonial Construction using forced Native Labor

in private and public deb\u0105s. That is why we injure and tear
ourselves without a truce...

We have here the voice of an honest and sincere Mexican
intellectual who reveals himself without a mask. Antonio Caso is a
patriot who loves his country but as a philosopher and intellectual,
he feels he must speak truths without fear. These are words that most
Mexicans do not want to hear; words that open wounds from the
legacy of conquest/invasion. Although written in the early part of the
twenties, much can still be applied to the contemporary corrupt
politics and *compadrazgo* of Mexico. It is in the end, as Caso states,
a philosophical problem, a moral problem.

SAMUEL RAMOS: *EL PERFIL DEL HOMBRE Y LA CULTURA*

Samuel Ramos' work, *El perfil del hombre y la cultura*, is
basically a psychological study connected to historic analysis with
the intent to reveal the perspective and personality of Mexico.[16] In
this work, Ramos alludes to a feeling of inferiority, not stating the
Mexican is inferior but rather that his feelings are the result of
frustration, which suggests the need for confidence and security. He
believes the problem is from being neither European nor American
and therein, the conflict; as a consequence, the Mexican is
predisposed to imitate. His lack of balance is the result of trying to
do much more than he is able to do. Thus, he feels frustrated and
depressed. The origin is in the Conquest and in Colonialism. It is the
latter that oppressed his spirit obviating initiative. This irritation is
felt from his initial beginning as a *Mestizo*. According to Ramos, the
Mestizo needs to stop imitating and readjust his values. The *Mestizo*
personality here is the result of an historic accident; nonetheless, he
can change his borrowed character.

In order to understand the mind of the Mexican, Ramos
examines the "*pelado*" as a social type representative of the most
elemental design of the Mexican character. This type belongs to the
lowest social levels, the most unwanted personality in town. Life has
been hostile to him all around, ergo his resentful attitude towards
life. By nature, he is an explosive verbal type who is generally
accustomed to affirm himself via aggressive and coarse language.
His irritability, his sense of hostility, is not directed toward humanity
but rather it is a means of elevating his depressed ego. His sexual
allusions (*tener muchos huevos*) as well as patriarchal references (*yo*

soy tu padre) suggest symbolically the idea of power and from this, *Macho* values of aggressiveness, a passionate spirit. But from behind that offensive veil, there is a fictitious valor, a continual fear of being uncovered and consequently, a distrust of all those who surround him. The *pelado*, in the end, has two personalities: one real, the other fictitious.

In terms of the characteristics related to nationality, Ramos associates the concept of manliness with nationality by noting his susceptibility to patriotic feelings and his exaggerated expression through words and shouts, all pointing to Mexican's national insecurity. Proof of this can be seen also in intelligent, cultured Mexicans who belong to the bourgeoisie. Another social Mexican type is the city dweller who also displays distrust. Ramos states:

> It is about an irrational distrust that emanates from the intimacy of his being...his distrust is not circumscribed to humanity; it is extended to all that exists, all that happens...he does not profess a religion, a social or political creed. He is the least idealist possible. He negates all without reason because he is the personified negation himself.[18]

Another characteristic of the urban Mexican is his non-reflexive action, i.e., without any real plan. Each person is only concerned with the immediate end and as such suppresses the future. The Mexican distrusts each gesture, each movement, each word. He interprets all as an offense which is why he constantly fights to protect his "I" within himself and thus, simulate power and courage.

The third social type is the Mexican bourgeoisie representative. This type does not suffer from economic, intellectual or social inferiority; rather, he expresses himself with an exaggerated courtesy. As a member of the upper classes, he is different by his total and hidden feelings of lesser value, like the inferiority feelings. Ramos asserts:

> The Mexican ignores living a lie because of the unconscious forces that have been driven to him and perhaps if he were aware of deceit, he would stop living like this...he has an extraordinary susceptibility to criticism and he is defensive, ready to duel his neighbor. And for the same reason, self-

criticism is non-existent. He needs to realize that the others are inferior to him. He will not admit, consequently, any superiority and does not know veneration, respect or discipline...Each individual lives enclosed within himself with an attitude of distrust towards others, displaying malice so that others can stay far from him. He is indifferent to collective concerns and his activity is always individualistic.[19]

Although it may not be possible to acquire a Mexican culture for Mexicans, one can see society with Mexican eyes. Ramos elucidates: "We have a European sense of life but we are in America and the latter signifies a vital sense within a distinct ambiance, therefore, it must be achieved in a distinct manner".[20] Inherited *criollo* culture since Independence has brought about a soul for Mexico but one without a body. For Ramos, very few have been able to express themselves beyond the parochial, the provincial, and as examples, he cites Vasconcelos (*La Raza Cósmica*) and Rodó (*Ariel*) as the highest thought in *criollo* culture.

For Ramos humanism and a spiritual sense or feeling are fundamental in the creation of high culture. It is necessary to have an autocthonous sense to appreciate universal values but, concurrently, one needs criticism of extreme nationalism. He sees the masses as the greatest obstacle due to the ignorance and illiteracy and, as such, education is the key for change.[21] In addition to having followed the problems found in Colonialism, Mexico has launched itself into the modern world which conversely abandons culture and invades humanism. The obsession with mechanization and technology produces within humanity a dehumanized product, i.e., a lack of sincerity, lack of eliminating prejudices, *caciquismo* (political tyrants). There is, moreover, the danger of imitating the North American Yankee, thus falling into dehumanization and utilitarianism.

THE METAPHYSICS OF VASCONCELOS: *LA RAZA CÓSMICA, INDOLOGÍA*

It is in 1908 that Mexico will enter the Twentieth Century when Justo Sierra dispenses with Positivism and asks the nation in 1910 to "Mexicanize knowledge". These are the years of transition when the *Ateneo de la Juventud* searches for a unique personality and culture. Later Luis Urbina will speak to the essence of the Mexican and Vasconcelos will proclaim "The spirit will speak through my people". Before Ramos' publication of *El perfil del hombre y la cultura en Mexico* (1934), Mexico will discover the human and metaphysical philosophy of José Vasconcelos in *La Raza Cósmica* (1925) and *Indología* (1926). While it is not a specific analysis of the Mexican, it is representative of profound thought into the *Mestizo*-American. He shares with Rodó and Ramos the idea of the danger in following contemporary materialist ways.

Vasconcelos saw Mexico in the Twentieth Century following the goals of Positivism with its slogan of order and progress, notwithstanding the aspirations of the governing classes. He was the only one who saw the Mexican Revolution as a failure and treason since none of the goals of the Revolution were realized. Instead it represented the creation of a materialist state imitative of the United States, motivated by the profit of the dollar and personal convenience. Vasconcelos' idea was to create a total man/woman (and not partial as exemplified today); to go beyond the socio-economic level and biological aspects. He was not interested in the confining and narrow parameters of science; his base was creative and intuitive. What is interesting in this analysis is that Vasconcelos not only recognized the danger of imitating materialist systems (cited already by Caso) but also was formulating very early a futuristic platform and vision justifying the mixture of races, functioning on a universal plane within synthesis. This synthesis would take this future model to a higher consciousness that would bring about an international world ethic. *Mestizaje* in itself is not fruitious; it must go through its social evolution and replace antiquated systems where military, political, economic and technical systems dominate. The difference between Ramos and Vasconcelos resides in that for Ramos there is a psychological analysis of the Mexican whereas in Vasconcelos there is within his cosmovision, the analysis of the various stages of civilization in the world. Vasconcelos, moreover, develops a futuristic universal philosophy based on integration and synthesis. In each case, the problem resides in not developing a concrete plan to achieve a new cultural product.

OCTAVIO PAZ: *EL LABERINTO DE LA SOLEDAD*

For Nobel laureate Octavio Paz, the contemporary problem for the Mexican man/woman is in the lack of identity, isolationism, the loss of creativity, loneliness and desperation produced by modern technology, political and totalitarian systems and wars. Man/woman needs to make the change and restructure himself/herself in their beliefs. They should reject the false concepts of contemporary society, particularly, materialism as an index for happiness, as well as the erroneous notion that time is linear progression and that history is progress.[22] Man/woman needs to rediscover their instinctive values of creativity. There is a need to return to the original and integral state, as an entity in harmony with the universe. For Paz, it is not possible to define nor to analyze *Mexicanidad*; it will reveal itself when one least expects it. In accord with the majority of Mexican intellectuals, he sees *Mestizaje* as an incomplete phenomenon. For him *Mexicanidad* is a problem between solitude (loneliness, isolation, nationalism, the parroquial, provincial) and communion (the others, universality). In agreement with Ramos and Zea, he sees the need for *Mexicanidad* to participate and integrate into universality. Nonetheless, in *El laberinto de la soledad*, he does cite predominant cultural characteristics of the Mexican that keeps him on a parochial plane, i.e., his mask (he encloses and preserves himself), his manliness/*Machismo* (not allowing himself to give in, to open up), distrust, stoicism, love of form, modesty, homophobia, simulated behavior, love as conquest, sense of inferiority for being different, zeal for self-destruction, sadness, sarcasm, passiveness of women, the negation of others, and *Malinchismo* (traitor colonial aspect). In the end, he describes the Mexican or *Mexicanidad* as "the rupture and negation...as a search, as a will to transcend that state of exile.[23]

For Octavio Paz, humanity is in need of a rebirth of an authentic person that can reconcile himself/herself with the universe. This is the major problem of contemporary society. The solution is in the validation of reality. This seems to me very important, particularly in the analysis of contemporary societies; however, it is also important to recognize the distorted history written by clerics and Spaniards under the guise of the Inquisition and censorship. How can one understand the autocthonous ancestors of the past great civilizations when the history has not been written by them? Even Paz relies on this prejudicial and fallacious history left by colonial clerics, erroneous ideas that justify the atrocities of the Spanish: the abandonment of the "Gods", the mythical insecure Moctecuzoma, the

Catholic religion as a model for the domination of the Aztekah-Metzikah, the idea that the pre-Columbian nations were freed by the Conquest, the fascination of the natives with death, the notion of sin, etc.[24] Unfortunately, this only implants into the Mexican psyche, not only a false interpretation, but a negative view of his/her autocthonous ancestors.

Paz, like Caso and Ramos, has fallen into the trap of false and altered pre-Columbian history. Nonetheless, his perspicacious observations on *Western* societies are truly accurate. Using the ideas of Zea's ideas of marginality and the disjointed center, Paz establishes that Mexicans have always lived in the periphery of the Western world; but at the same time, one notes that the Twentieth Century has given testimony to a disintegration of ideas. Like Ramos and Zea, Paz argues that history has returned to its original point...to the meditation of man. For Paz, all men are lost in labyrinths and each hides behind their masks. His "dialectics of solitude" is a final commentary on solitude and communion, reason and myth, present and future times, the trauma of birth, love and poetry. It is a summation of his philosophy, of his poetics in opposition to modernity, a summation of the current crisis that Mexicans and other nationalities find themselves in today. For Paz, rational modern myths represent the political utopias where human dignity and liberty are lost. Finally, he states that perhaps the most horrifying labyrinth may represent a ritual of discovery of oneself as well as one's penance.[25]

JOSE ITURRIAGA: "*EL CARACTER DEL MEXICANO*"

José Iturriaga in his article entitled, "*El carácter del mexicano*", continues the twentieth-century Mexican tradition of self-analysis and *Mexicanidad*. He points to the complexity of the historic Mexican past, the diversity of autocthonous groups before the arrival of the Spanish. Like Octavio Paz, he asserts that the Spanish were not truly Europeans but rather *mestizos* of Celtic/Iberian and Arabic origin (among other groups). He also underscores the fact that Spain had not eliminated the Medieval lifestyle when it conquered the Americas, particularly in view that it promoted a vigorous counterreformist movement. Moreover, he shows the contrast between Mexico and its neighbor to the north, noting the roots there as reformist, free examination while Mexico, geographically, is fragmented into a plurality of isolated areas. And as has been concluded by his predecessors, *Mestizaje* is incomplete and as a result, there are two bloods in constant conflict. Like Garizurieta, he concludes that the unique spiritual profile of the Mexican (the collective national subconscious) is found in the poor and rural classes. Iturriaga feels that the Mexican suffers from a deep sense of inadequacy, of his feelings of technical inferiority amidst the conqueror and for having been the result of the subsequent *Mestizaje*. Not through love but through violence. It is from here that one sees all of its virtues and all of its defects. In his article, Iturriaga cites twenty-five character traits of the Mexican, some of which appear to be contradictory: (1)timidity, (2)reserved, feigns actions, (3)jealous, (4)distrustful, (5)a sharp sense of the ridiculous, (6)individualistic, (7)deep ties to friendship, (8)prefers to practice politics in anonymity, (9)*Machismo*, (10)erotic preoccupation, (11)emotional and exalted patriotism, (12)severe governance, (13)little reflexive or analytical, (14)richness of imagination, (15)sober in his habits but can be baroque, (16)impulsive, (17)suffers from indecision, (18)spendthrift, (19)great power of adaptation, a powerful facility to imitate, (20)improvisation, (21)fatalistic and superstitious, (22)predisposition for the minute, (23)violent but also sensitive, (24)moderate in gestures, (25)sentimental, speaks little in low tone and uses many diminutives. These characteristics correspond largely to the poor or popular classes that reside in the center of the Mexican Republic. But there are also contrasts in other regions. In the Veracruz coastal areas, the Mexican is neither timid nor introverted; rather, he speaks in a loud voice, (Tabasco region as well). In the Northern regions, the Mexican is frank, and energetic, with weak religiosity. Iturriaga finally concludes that these character descriptions can disappear quickly as economic, political and social conditions are modified; still, there is one great quality hidden in the Mexican that can rescue his national personality and that is his great spiritual quality or force.[26]

Nonetheless, one needs to pose the question: What do these characteristics have to with the woman? Upon examination, it is clear that he is thinking of man and not woman, e.g., what does number 9, i.e *Machismo* have in common with the passive woman; Likewise, the erotic preoccupation (number 10), the security in governance (number 12), spendthrift (number 18), violent (number 23) and practicing politics in anonymity (number 8)? What are the characteristics of the woman? It is proper to follow an outline which divides Mexican society into (1)the impoverished masses, (2)the middle class, and (3)the upper (monied) classes. Unfortunately, in social and interpersonal matters, the woman has been relegated to the same role that was imposed during the Colonial period, i.e., the man can have another woman (from Medieval and Colonial concubinage) or a lover while the woman must remain faithful. Generally, it is the man that regulates and maintains power over the family with the woman playing a passive and secondary role. The female of the impoverished class does not have time for imitation; she only has time to persevere economically due to her severe or extreme economic existence. This directly affects any opportunity for education or development. On the other side of the social class pendulum, the woman within the bourgeoisie and upper classes does have a propensity to imitate the European and the North American; she prefers not to be called Esperanza but rather Betty. She speaks using Anglicisms and is prejudicial toward those women not on her social level. The few independent women that have been able to climb out of the Colonial pyramid are the ones who have been able to pursue important professional careers in their society.

ROSARIO CATELLANOS, LEOPOLDO ZEA AND EMILIO URANGA

According to Rosario Castellanos, the Mexican Mestizo shows hostility toward the female when she becomes a professional. One needs, Castellanos suggests, to eliminate (1) The severe handed father and the stereotypical sweet and timid female, (2) the formal boyfriend who values himself to an extreme and sells himself highly, and (3) the white dress with a crown of orange blossoms as symbols of virginity. She adds, further, that maternity is not the road to sanctification and husbands are not the miracle of Saint Anthony.[27]

Leopoldo Zea cites the problem as one of adapting Mestizo-American circumstances to a European concept of the world instead of adapting the latter to the former. The Mestizo American has, as a consequence, imitated and not realized his own personality and has not recognized that they are different. It is necessary to the Mexican Mestizo to tell the world its truth with sincerity and without pretensions. He/she needs to create culture and resolve problems from the Mestizo-American point of view.[28]   Emilio Uranga, moreover, observes the dualism within the Mexican, the mixture of humanism and nationalism. The Mexican has great compassion when he refers to plants and animals and has a tendency to call everyone *"pobre"*, but conversely, he can be indifferent, brutal, inconsiderate and cold. According to Uranga, he has an unlimited capacity for humanism but he always falls back on nationalism. Nationalism is described here as a refuge where the Mexican is protective of his riches. This, he says, is an official and popular business concept. It is a solution that is anti-moral and not an ethical conduct of human beings.[29]   He criticizes Paz' labyrinth of solitude concept; rather it should be a labyrinth of community, and should be directed toward the underdeveloped community. He states, further, that one has to go back to origin and move away from *privatisimo* where the self and the singular aspect is paramount, where man/woman separate from the rest. This, according to the author, has filtered into the political movements of Mexico. In the end there is only extreme skepticism, even cynicism and false and decadent intellectuals. There is need for a doctrine that communicates to the people.

CONTEMPORARY ANALYSES: ROGER BATRA AND SARA SEFCHOVICH

Contemporaneously, Roger Batra and Sara Sefchovich view the problem from the social and economic arenas.   Sefchovich foregrounds the problem of the Mexican living myths: (1) the burden of weight of the paternal and maternal figures, (2) the weight of the atavistic servitude (3) the weight of the Catholic Church originally imposed by blood , (4) the weight of what is considered "sacred" in Mexico and (5) the weight of the North-American life style. The Mexican's reality lies between the modern world and the third world. In Mexico a true concept of culture does not exist. The only existing concept is the business and authoritarian concept that flows from the top to the bottom. Sefchovich suggests: (1) taxation to the rich as opposed to the poor, (2) care of Mexico's natural resources, (3) a new mode of thinking, away from business, toward modesty, a change of values and (4) an true effort in recuperating all of Mexico's cultures in all of its plurality and differences.[30]

Roger Batra in his penetrating study of the Mexican looks at the history, politics, economics and the social state of the Mexican.

He notes the elusive characteristics of the *Pelado* which , ironically, best describes the bureaucrats of government that create a labyrinth of contradictions. He identifies, moreover, new social types that affect the Mexican character: (1) *el importamadrismo*, (2) *el desmadre*. (3) *el apretado*. The first social phenomenon literally means "the I don't give a damn attitude" and is directly attributed to the ruling classes that imposed a Hegemonic process on the native masses. The second relates to dishonoring the mother, literally "to take away the mother", the lost mother left alone "*a la chingada*" but is used contemporaneously to refer to the chaotic, nonsensical and often violent result. The third concept refers to the personification of the dominant class. Here, the idea is give the impression of seriousness, a serious and elegant appearance of power, of propriety, high functions and money. Literally, it means "the tight one". Thus, when ordering at a restaurant, one must have this demeanor in order to be recognized.[31] Most interesting is his analysis of the Virgen and the *Malinche*. He concludes by saying "It is convenient to see the *Malinche* as a sinner so that she can then be exorcised by Mary."[32] Batra suggests to the reader the study of the political system, how it uses cultural connotations, how it manipulates myths of historic figures of the revolution and how it uses the hegemonic cultural values of the U. S. and Europe. Historical symbols , though static, are often used to glorify the national powers, numbing reason in the process. It creates nationalism as a legitimate source for the dominant system of exploitation. Identity has been lost in a world of disharmony and contradictions. The Mexican does not fit, he is not alike; he is another.[33]

CONCLUSIONS TO THE ANALYSIS OF THE MEXICAN CHARACTER

It seems just and proper to situate the conquest/invasion of the Spanish at the root of the problem relative to *Mestizaje* and *Mexicanidad*, much like Antonio Caso, Samuel Ramos, Octavio Paz and José Iturriaga have concluded. It is from this origin that we begin to see the incongruity as a result of a neo-Medieval mode of existence; the lack of respect and understanding of the high religious, scientific and cultural principles of the autocthonous cultures; a *Mestizaje* brought about through violence; cupidity and avarice established as a Colonial model engendered by the rich and powerful; the rupture of communal/fraternal structures with the

replacement of a capitalist model characterized by exploitation, alien
to universal principles; the creation within *Mestizaje* of a feeling of
frustration, of resentment, vengeance and rejection; the propagation
of a modern social and political system influenced by *a priori*
attitudes reflective of Colonialism, not so much in its form as from
its spirit in which the modern bourgeoisie and the plutocratic class
have merely changed clothing. They follow a modified form of the
vertical concept of society where a minute percentage of the society
(the power and money class) governs and controls an enormous
mass, of which nearly fifty percent are illiterate and ignorant of their
history and rights. At the core of the problem is the inability of
Mexico to eliminate or solve the sociocultural inequities left by
Colonialism. It is Antonio Caso who points to the lack of legitimate
Democrats or Republicans at the start of Independence. Samuel
Ramos further establishes that all that was given was "a body
without a spirit". José Vasconcelos goes further by categorically
stating that the Revolution was a failure in which a materialist state
(imitator of the Yankee) motivated by the dollar and personal
accommodation was created. In more subtle ways, *caciquismo* and a
recalcitrant individualism exist in the governing classes. As Silva-
Herzog has stated: "In Mexico, there have been rebels and
revolutionaries: of the first (ambitious and morally inferior) we have
had many; of the second (goodness, an apostle or hero), we have had
few.[34] What is needed is honesty, integrity and sincerity. The modern
world, as has been seen by Ramos, invades humanism and develops
a lack of sincerity, social and racial prejudices, political *caciquismo*
and the imitation of the Yankee. One needs, as Paz has pointed out,
a rebirth of values, of society and a reconciliation with the universe.
Mexico needs to make a *quantum* leap and purify itself of its past
Colonial models. The history of Mexico, as Pedro Henríquez Ureña
has noted, is divided into two classes: (1)honest rogues and (2)decent
thieves. The liberals belonged to the rogues, the imperialists to the
other class.[35] One major danger always present is with those who
mask themselves as progressives and as revolutionaries, when in
reality, they are conservatives, lacking in the spirit of change. The
latter want to maintain the status quo, the plutocracy and desire to
leave the oppressive structures intact. All great philosophers and
thinkers have recognized that the only inevitable certainty on this

earth is change; thus, one needs to recognize this universal reality. To think that Mexico, the United States or the Soviet satellites would have the same political or philosophical form in the future is to be closed, conservative and myopic. As Silva-Herzog has stated: "Living...is action in motion, happening and there cannot be an event nor an activity without change, because change is the essence of the activity or event".[36]

On a daily basis, Mexicans charge politicians with theft. These are the "very decent thieves" of the power positions and the honest rogues in the lower positions. Piracy during Colonialism was abusive; it was accepted as a privilege of the master. It is possible that this attitude of deserving booty as a privilege is part of the current political posts. I believe that Caso is correct when he cites the social problem as a moral problem; it is a problem of the spirit, of attitude, of a lack of sacrifice (by those at the top) and a lack of spiritual humanism (by the governing class). Ramos sees the key in education for future change. But who is going to educate the governing classes with a sense of ethics, spiritual humanism and social equality? It does little good to eliminate the feeling of inferiority to the masses, if the governing classes are to continue with the same social and political inequities of yesteryear. Antonio Caso, as is the case with Ramos, Vasconcelos and Paz, recognized the importance of not imitating that which is foreign, of not imitating the European. How is it possible to reject a society based on a European model? Caso sees the autocthonous cultures as the only tie to the Americas. But how can we appreciate the autocthonous cultures if the history was written with European eyes? There are, for example, many erroneous ideas introduced by Spanish clerics and chroniclers that interjected a European reality: (1)the idea of polytheism; this is of Greek origin. In fact, Medieval Christianity was often accused by Moslems and Jews of being polytheistic due to the multiple worship of saints. For the Aztekahs, *Zenteotl* represents the one cosmic divine principle that is responsible for all; (2)the idea of Hell. This is a Christian idea that conforms to the ideas of Christian penance and purgatory. *Miktlan*, for the Aztecs has no relationship to punishment or sacrifices; (3) regarding the idea of human sacrifice, there is not one single case that was witnessed by the Spanish nor are there any *pre-Columbian* codices that refer to such an act. The historical *post-Conquest* codices were written under the guise and censorship of the Spanish Inquisition, thus, these documents are invalid because of the alteration and intercalation of Spanish/European ideas. The ritual of human sacrifice was quite common in Europe in view that millions of innocent people were tortured and sacrificed alive at the stake with fire by the Inquisition in Spain, Italy and other parts of Europe; (4)the way of seeing reality in society by the Spanish was at the *physical and material level*: their religion and their god was seen anthropomorphically, governance was by an emperor or a king, surrounded by the privileged class with serfs or servants at their disposal. From this reality, the exploitation of the masses, slavery and exploitation through the profit motive; the woman as a passive figure without rights; the ideas of black magic; the idea of death as a finality, with the only path to heaven, purgatory or hell; power based on money, inherited posts, or brought about through the brute force of arms (might is right); the concubinage within the privileged class, the sexual abuses of the clergy...

One only needs to see the Spanish clerical versions to see the aforementioned Medieval/Colonial reality accommodated carefully into the *Aztekah-Metzikah* society. Without realizing it, many chroniclers and clerics were projecting their own vision of reality and since that is the only reality that they knew, it was natural for them to project it as such. What is incredible is that historians and anthropologists have accepted this distorted European version (with few modifications) as the autocthonous reality and they have done so because they are the descendants of the Europeans who know only the Western Greek/Roman European mode of seeing reality.

There have been a few, like Agustín Yáñez, who have come to delineate and understand some of the autocthonous concepts. Yáñez, for example, was able to recognize that the autocthonous reality was one that projected a dual perspective. In reality it goes beyond duality, it is multiple-dimensional, seen from five dimensional spherical planes of reality.[37] That is why it is incorrect to interpret from a Western or European point of view, within the physical/material one-dimensional plane. The few who have understood the autocthonous reality, its true metaphysics and concepts of the world, have been ignored by academics at the top (*gachupín* mentality); these academics cannot fathom how these other native types (without power or fame) can have such distinct ideas from theirs. They become offended easily and they launch themselves to the attack as Ramos states of the middle class and the bourgeoisie. Perhaps the first step towards developing a new high culture is to recognize that the recalcitrant individualism (European, left by the Hispanic/Mediterranean-Castillian/Moor) is not a propitious characteristic that is fruitful in developing a spiritual humanism, much less for realizing a true brotherhood among themselves. But the masses need a model and true leadership; there needs to be a national leader, a President with the vision of Vasconcelos to impose radical philosophical and educational change. There needs to be ethics and social equality at all levels of the national infrastructure. In agreement with Castellanos, the female must not be viewed in the traditional medieval role assigned to her since the colonial days but rather in a positive role at all levels of society. The Mexican must admit that he has been living under an illusion and an artificial and foreign legacy. He needs to underscore the importance of respect, human dignity and discipline in all activity. He needs to be a universal model so that others, as Uranga asserts, can leave their narrow parochialism and nationalism so that he can effect synthesis, integration and harmony with the universe. Octavio Paz, as universal man, understands the artificial nature of Western culture; the disintegration of Western ideas is becoming clear. That is why we need to question our mode of living, as Sefchovich outlines, our inherited philosophies that are in dire decadence. One needs to see, as Paz has asserted, the validity of reality. Have we not been functioning via the rationalism of the Seventeenth Century and the mechanistic Newtonian world of the past century? When will we, as society as a whole, begin to accept the multiple dimensions of reality of the new physics (realities known to pre-Columbian cultures)? When will we know and practice the autocthonous philosophical and cosmic idea of world brotherhood (*In Lakesh, Tloke Nauake* --we are tied to one another like the fingers of a hand)?[38] When shall we begin to see a true version of the past autocthonous ancestors? Samuel Ramos has underscored the importance for Mexicans to practice self-criticism, not only within the masses but also within the philosophers, writers, and educators. I believe that the example of Caso, Ramos, Vasoncelos, Zea, Paz, Iturriaga, Yáñez, Castellanos, Uranga, Sefchovich and Batra are noteworthy and representative of the step toward self-analysis, but unfortunately, the levels of power, institutions that control ideas, have not been penetrated as Batra clearly demonstrates: the "image" of the nation, the modern myths, that which is permissible, be they in religion, politics, culture or socio-economic matters. And as part of the national educational program, there should be established the new field within academic curriculum of "*Mestizaje* and *Mexicanidad*" as serious study for all students. This is important for it recognizes, without detours or excuses, the historic background (barbarous as it may be) the subtle, origins and development in all of its complexity or contradiction relative to the essence and character of the Mexican. Upon considering, for example, the twenty-five characteristics of the Mexican cited by Iturriaga, one needs to look at its origin so that one can know the causal agent of the problem: the characteristics of shyness, feeling of self-denigration, censorship, severity of governance, lack of civic participation, the great capacity for improvisation and simulation are examples of *Colonial manifestations* while individualism, distrust, the preoccupation with the erotic, for dogma and doctrine, fatalism, superstition, lack of analysis, are characteristics of the Spanish culture and European Catholic Colonialism. On the other hand, moderation, speaking in low voice with diminutives, the delicate expression, courtesy, rich artistic tendencies, love of Mother Earth, a deep universal/spiritual sense, a positive attitude towards death and the tendency towards the universal are useful aspects of *pre-Columbian* traits that exist within the Mexican soul. One can add, further, the pacifist inclination, peace, alliance and accords rather than war, universal intelligence (as noted by Reyes), not ivory tower, inclination towards synthesis, rooted in the earth, more internationalist, non-linear perception of time and space (the preponderance of Magical Realism in writers).

While there was an artistic German post-Expressionism movement which gave rise to the idea of Magical Realism in the Twenties, there was literature in Mexico prior to this movement, that was exemplary of this concept. The short story "*La Cena*" of Alfonso Reyes, written in 1911, has the imprint of Magical Realism. That is

XIX Century Mexico: A Mestizo Nation in Formation

why Magical Realism is authentic as a *Mestizo*-American phenomenon. All of the aforementioned pre-Columbian characteristics are not only notable but positive and important in the creation of an authentic Mexican soul or personality. In its march towards the elimination of the Colonial traits, the *Mestizo*-Mexicano needs to adapt himself/herself to a world that is Mexican where a spiritual humanism prevails, unity and respect for others, love and respect for ecological and universal principles of Mother Earth; he/she needs to express within art and literature a profound and universal spirit; he/she needs to maintain the unity of the family, eliminating *Machismo* and violence; it is necessary to follow the pre-Columbian spirit of communal collaboration, to see and understand time, the cycles and the universal dimensions. This revolution of conduct and philosophy requires, furthermore, a structural social and political revolution. In agreement with Paz, Vasconcelos, Uranga, Sefchovich and Batra, one needs to create a new system far away from the abuses of materialism (capitalism), a new system that offers equality in its socio-economic structure, where the worker and management are part-owners and share the product equally; a system where work is not a curse but a blessing; a collaboration and justice. Then, the Mexican will recuperate his dignity and will be able to think in universal terms and be part of the harmony of the universe. Nonetheless, what is certain today is that the Mexican has within his being, a great sense of spirituality and universality that places him/her on the path towards a humanistic, international cultural development for the future.

THE U.S. MEXICAN: THE CHICANO/TEJANO/MEXICAN AMERICAN

The Chicano/Tejano/Mexican American of the U.S. much like his counterpart, the Amerigenous *Campesino* of Mexico have one thing in common in their historical roots: both have suffered an economic, cultural and political invasion. The former suffers the Anglo-American land grab of the southwest and the imposition of a new language, culture and society; the latter, likewise, suffers through invasion of the Spanish/European conquest, losing ancestral lands, language and religion. There is little difference between the political and imperialistic objectives of the Spanish and the Anglo-Saxons that formed the first colonies of what is now the United States. The Anglo-American religion, albeit reformist and

Protestant, carries a religious platitude of intolerance. That is why amerigenous communities in the Eastern seaboard were invaded by zealous preachers and corresponding flocks which led to hanging or outright massacres of peaceful communities of native women, children and men. For the Native American of all the Americas, there existed no private ownership of land; neither could the land be exploited for the benefit of others. The practice of exploitation of land is decidedly Western and carries within, negative consequences in terms of the formation of society as well as the environment. The invasion and the land grab of Native peoples does not end until the Anglo-Saxons arrive in California; in the same manner, the Spanish continue the invasion of territory and cultures from the Antilles to South America. The result is the creation of a privileged European class on both sides that carries with it religious intolerance and racial prejudice against all Natives and people of color. Spanish law protected the special interests of the Spanish much like the U.S. Constitution protected the European Anglo-Saxon populace. Both European cultures profited from slavery, exploiting man/woman and cultures of color in their plantations and/or *Encomiendas*, respectively. Both showed a disregard for other manners of venerating the Deity so much that punishment for Natives often led to their death. Both European cultures rejected the mixture of native or African bloods with the European stock; the Spanish considered the Native-American as inferior to the degree that they were often referred to as "beasts" in their chronicles.[39]

It is interesting to note that the Mexican American/Chicano, as a Mexican *Mestizo* comprised largely of Native American and *Criollo*/Spanish blood has to suffer at least four cultural/political invasions i.e. the Spanish, French, the Porfiriato *caciquismo* and the Anglo-Saxon North American invasion of Mexican territories; in the latter stage, he is converted to a *persona non grata*, whose land titles and professions are not respected and whose language, traditions and religion are considered inferior. The socio-political segregation of the native peoples, heretofore, imposed by the Spanish, are now felt at the hands of the Anglo-American. The result is racial and cultural discrimination for all peoples of Mexican descent living in the U.S. While they pay taxes, they do not have the right to eat in restaurants frequented by Anglo-Americans; as in the case of the African-

American, Mexican-Americans must eat in the kitchen of a restaurant as late as 1950 in Texas[40]. They have educational rights but their schools are segregated conveniently by districts from the rest of the Anglo-American community. They are the recipients of pejorative labels such as *Meskin* or *Greasers* much like the Spanish did with respect to Jews and Amerigenous peoples i.e. *Marranos* and *Indio-pata rajada* while at the same time not allowed to mix socially. In the U.S. and as late as 1955, an Anglo-American girl was not permitted to date a Mexican American boy in South Texas. At the base of these two cultures was hatred towards other groups not European, of color or native to the Americas. This characteristic, along with religious myopia and the application of the inferior status to women are typical of Western medieval/European culture. After 1848, the Mexican American/Chicano like the amerigenous *Campesino* is assigned the lowest social and economic position in society; as his brothers of yesteryear in colonial Mexico, they are the new serfs of society.

More than a century has elapsed since the Southwestern land grab. Since 1848, the Mexican American/Chicano within the educational process has slowly developed bridging two languages and two cultures. As a bilingual/bicultural product, he has been able, in that span of time, to achieve high positions at the federal level as well as the university level. Nonetheless, in order to understand his/her essence, one must probe into the various socio-economic segments that he/she belongs to within U.S. society. Much like in Mexico, one must divide the economically deprived poor (from the Native American to the *peladito*) from the middle class urban class and the oligarchy comprised of the money rich class. Likewise, one must separate the various socio-economic classes for the Mexican American/Chicano into the following categories: (1) the economically deprived class, the common laborer, often times new arrivals or undocumented Mexican workers living in the poorest *Barrios* or *Colonias*, (2) the middle class which constitutes a large number, comprised largely of Americans of Mexican descent (Mexican Americans) residing in the suburbs (the teachers, counselors, merchants public officials) and (3) the professional and owners of substantial businesses (tenured professors, politicians, lawyers, Md.'s, engineers, the moneyed class).

It should be pointed out that the higher the person rises in the socio-economic ladder, generally, he/she is more likely to assimilate into the Anglo-American culture (the exception are activist educators and professionals). The Mexican American/Chicano legacy of bilingualism and biculturalism can be traced to 1848 after the signing of the Treaty of Guadalupe Hidalgo; this is a critical moment in history when the Mexican *Mestizo* decides not to abandon their ground, a link not only to the *Escandón* expedition but to his Native American heritage and lineage. While there are important Mexican American/Chicano researchers prior to the Chicano movement of the sixties and seventies (Aurelio Espinosa, Alonso Perales, Ernesto Galarza, George I. Sánchez, Américo Paredes), there is an explosion of investigative production after the "Chicano Renaissance." Besides the individual effects of the aforementioned Mexican American/Chicano writers, there exists scattered throughout the Southwest, a plethora of newspapers written in Spanish which include cultural and political essays as well as poetry and short stories. Still, the dominant Anglo-American culture controls the major presses and power positions in the decision making process and, the result, is the existence of censorship (like Mexico until Independence) of Mexican-American/Chicano materials which obviate the publication of novels, short story, or poetry. Thus, what the Independence was for Mexico, the Chicano movement was for the Mexican American/Chicano; it marked his independence and his rebirth. For the first time, as a result of rallies and a cry for equality, federal moneys became available, albeit short-lived, for Chicano presses and public service programs. There was a veritable explosion of creativity in all genres of literature by students, professors and housewives. Additionally, there was a proliferation of journals and newspapers throughout every *barrio* in the U.S. The word Chicano was adopted because it applied to the oppressed, the underdog; it linked, moreover, the Chicano/a with pride to his/her Pre-Columbian past, the Aztekah/Metzikah/Maya. It was understood, that the word Chicano was of autocthonous origin. The Chicano movement did not permit middle class attitudes; it was activist and radical. Whoever did not participate was considered a coconut i.e. brown on the outside but white on the inside. Of the many definitions given to a Chicano the following defines the Chicano within the context of the

Chicano movement: "A person of Mexican descent that resides in the U.S. who has suffered cultural and racial discrimination by the Anglo-American dominant culture who recognizes his culture both past and present in socio-political, economic-historical terms [41] As stated, the etymology of the word Chicano is Pre-Columbian and it has, further been verified as existing in both Maya-Quiché and Aztekah-Náhuatl by Mayan native and scholar Domingo Martínez Paredes and Aztec native scholar Yakanini Meztli Kuautemok (Dr. Juan Luna Cárdenas).[42] There is moreover, an archeological zone in southern Mexico called *Chicanna*.

Among the hundreds of articles written during the Chicano movement regarding the Chicano, Rendon's *Chicano Manifesto* stands out for attempting to define the Chicano and his culture. He cites the following characteristics as predominant: (1) individualism, (2) stoicism, (3) spiritual integrity, (4) a deeper understanding of human dignity, (5) dependence on familial structures and internal resources, (6) independence of social services, (7) tolerance for exaggerated speech and dress, (8) elder reaction against military, (9) love of fiestas and rituals, (10) love of tradition within the extended family (*quinceañeras*, weddings, dances, fajita cookouts), (11) mixture of two languages (code-switching), (12) active not passive.[43] Moreover, one could add to Rendon's list: (13) the Mexican American/Chicano's sense of *carnalismo* or brotherhood as a *Mestizo* of a long tradition, (14) the family as a base for all decisions with love, respect and unity, (15) a great respect for the land and Mother Earth, (16) he/she sees himself/herself as a new *Mestizo*, recognizing his/her Amerigenous and Spanish roots but adding a third culture making him/her not only bilingual but multicultural, (17) he/she is proud of his multiculturalism beginning with the *Mestizo/Mestiza* tradition but not excluding the Anglo-American culture, (18) he/she is a rebel when necessary as has been the case with past heroic rebels i.e. Gregorio Cortez, Juan N. Cortina, Reies López Tijerina, César Chávez, (19) according to his/her socio-economic class and region, he/she carries with him/her a linguistic variety that includes Mexicanisms (largely Aztecisms), archaic Spanish (includes Arabic derived words), caló (gypsy Romany) and hispanicized English expressions, (20) there is no one cultural/linguistic model for the Spanish-Speaking; they range from those that speak little English (new arrivals/undocumented) to those that speak little or no Spanish (upper class, assimilated types), (21) prevalence of *Machismo* at all levels; an unfortunate Western/Hispanic cultural inheritance, (22) some, particularly at the lower socio-economic levels see material things as a necessity, (23) many at the lower working levels see work as survival and not as a puritanical value predominant in the Anglo-American culture, (24) those closer to the Mexican Mother Culture see the poet, the teacher, the philosopher, the musician with more reverence than towards the businessman, (25) including the professional and middle class, he/she sees time/space more in the present than in the future, (26) those closer to the Mexican culture, show respect and courtesy to his fellow man, (27) the less assimilated groups are more conscious of their sense of touch, of feelings and smell as they deal with other people (28) the more assimilated (middle class and upper class) sees his Mexican undocumented worker "brother" or new arrivals with social reservation, often using the pejorative label of *mojado* (wetback), (29) generally, all Spanish-Speakers have a good sense of humor continuing the tradition of joke sessions in a number of social settings, (30) in the *Barrios* and *Colonias* where life is difficult, young Chicanos/as have a tendency to be territorial, particularly with the predominance of gangs among these areas (31) the Chicano/a is varied in their musical tastes form Caribbean Salsa, Columbian Cumbia to Chicano Polka, Country, Rock, Schottische, *Taquachito*, (32) the Chicano/a can dream or make love in English or Spanish according to the person and (33) he/she is hardworking, not lazy and knows how to manage his/her money.[44]

Since the Mexican American/Chicano functions under a Mexican cultural base, he has much in common with his brother/sister south of the border in terms of the socio-cultural qualities or deficiencies of that society. He/she is, different, however, in the sense that he/she can distance himself/herself from the Mexican culture and thus be in a more objective position to analyze it. As a bridge or link, the Mexican American/Chicano, as a *Mestizo-American* in the U.S., through education and evolution is creating a rich and varied culture and purifying negative cultural traits from the old culture as well as the dominant Anglo-American culture.

As in the case of the Mexican woman, it is proper to make certain clarifications on the Chicana/Latina. Although the woman has bettered her position on both sides of the border since the nineteenth century, there is no doubt, that the Chicana/Latina in the U.S. is at the forefront, principally because of her access to educational opportunities and a more open arena for discussion of women's issues. With the exception of the lower socio-economic group (*Barrios, Colonias*) the Chicana/Latina has greater opportunity to finish high school and receive grants and loans to colleges and universities. It is here where our Mestiza leaders have distinguished themselves in the various professions (law, education, literature, science). These, while in the minority, are a growing number. It is an assertive group who demand equality in the workplace as well as respect and dignity as a woman. From a cultural point of view, one of the growing problems with the middle class and professional group is the problem of total assimilation to the dominant Anglo-American culture. There are hundreds of cases of mixed marriages with Anglo-American men; too often the offspring becomes whitewashed culturally and linguistically. One of the complaints (and well-justified) of women is the unbridled *Machismo* with Chicano/Latinos. Unfortunately, *Mestizo*-American men throughout the Americas have inherited this Eastern/European and Mediterranean trait from the Spanish culture. This arrogant individualism injected by the visogothic and Arabic character caused the Spanish character to deform to the degree of barbarism as we see the uncivilized treatment of native women, the perpetuation of concubines/slaves and general disregard for the individual capacity and potential of the female. The modern Chicana/Latina is aware of this historical legacy and will not tolerate this European/Mediterranean *Machismo*. While the Anglo male still carries chauvinistic attitudes, particularly at the workplace, he is seen by some Chicanas/Latinas as less *Macho* or more flexible in terms of their rights and liberties, ergo the rise in mixed marriages. The latter is seen largely with middle and upper classes of the Chicana/Latina population. The danger here, however, is the curtailment of the Chicana/Latina culture and language with the offspring. As a professor in Academia for over thirty years, I have had numerous students lament that their parents never emphasized the value of their native culture and language; consequently, they express a loss, a lack of fulfillment and a lack of identity for their Chicano/a-Latino/a culture and language. There is a growing trend, however, among some married Chicana/Latina educators to maintain their Spanish surname and thus their identity.

Another problem among *Mestizo*-Americans in general is to fall prey to the materialistic philosophy of dominant Anglo-American culture. Mexican intellectuals from Antonio Caso to Octavio Paz, have clearly seen the problem as one of imitation of a foreign culture, not properly rooted in the spirit of the Native - American from where we gather our greatest spiritual insight and originality. Thus, Chicanos/as as well as the rest of the Spanish-Speaking must reject all negative cultural traits of both the Hispanic and Anglo models and create their own unique positive model that is rooted in universal and equitable principles.

Fortunately, a small number but important Chicano Studies programs have survived the conservative Republican (Reagan/Bush) years of minority cutbacks. It is here where important research related to *Mestizo* Americans of the U.S. is taking place. It is also a place where Spanish surnamed students can recover their pride and culture, completing their cultural identity. Even Mexican students from Mexico have praise for the knowledge they receive in these programs. I have had many well-prepared Mexican students from south of the border assert that the information on the Mexican identity and related problems in my classes too often are circumvented in the educational process in Mexico. It is paramount to educate not only our brothers south of the border, the Chicano/Chicana but also the Anglo-American. These future leaders will be in a position to make real and significant change in all levels of society. It can be argued that this is but a small percentage of the minority population. How then can significant change be brought about to that enormous mass of Spanish-Speakers that need a higher education? This, beyond the normal avenues for education, will have to be projected by the most effective means of communication, radio and particularly television. To date there have been some penetrating studies via documentaries in PBS regarding color, racial prejudice and consumer fraud. They have focused to a great extent on the problems facing the African-American and the Native American in the U.S.; documentaries of any great magnitude have been few and far between for Chicanos/as. The Chicana/Latina, as in the case of the woman in other societies, must win her struggle for rights, dignity and respect as a human entity. When this struggle is won, she will be able to use her greatest talents and contribute to the formation of a new society. While, it may sound ironic, given the cultural-political malaise of this nation, she will not only figure in the more important decision making positions in the future but will have the pivotal and key world vision for the twenty-first century. The prophets of the future society will no longer be dominated by men but by the sensitive, intuitive and talented woman.

CONCLUSIONS TO THE ANALYSIS OF THE CHICANO

The Mexican-American/Chicano as a *Mestizo*-American has much in common with his Mexican brother/sister south of the border. On the one hand, he has inherited all of the negative European characteristics and on the other hand, he carries within his/her culture the negative Anglo-American cultural characteristics as a result of being recipients of both the European and North-American cultural/political invasions. At first glance, it appears that there is, as a consequence, a dual risk in view of the danger pointed out by Octavio Paz (among others), i.e. the danger of the utilitarianism and materialism of the West. Nonetheless, the Mexican-American/Chicano continues to resist the Anglo-American Culture, particularly among those closer to the Mexican Mother Culture; moreover, those that have had the opportunity to study the Mexican identity question, have become aware, since the seventies, of cultural negatives of the inherited Mexican Culture. Thus, the Mexican-American/Chicano/a has acquired through education, a more advanced consciousness as he/she becomes the bridge of two cultures. This new prototype is in a better position to objectively view and analyze both cultures. As such, these are the keys for his/her integral formation (1) education, (2) a strong humanist base in the family structure, (3) a balanced and positive identity as a multicultural product eliminating colonial notions and attitudes from both the Mexican and Anglo-American Cultures, (4) tenacious idea of brotherhood/sisterhood, (5) unity and strength within the family structure, (6) love and respect for Mother Earth and ecological concepts, (7) the creation of a new *Mestizaje*, i.e. multicultural and universal.

It has been projected that by the middle of the next century, the Spanish-Speaking, as the fastest growing minority group, will become a major force as a majority group. This critical mass of the future carries with it important cultural, political and social implications. Since the seventies, there has been an explosion in literature i.e. the poetry, the critical essay, the theater and particularly the prose-fiction with the woman writer becoming more predominant each year.[45] The impact of Chicanos in U.S. cinematography increases each year with films manifesting Chicano/Chicana culture, i.e. *Zoot Suit* (1980), *La Bamba* (1987, Luis Valdez), *Born in East L.A.* (Cheech Marín), *Milagro Beanfield War* (1988), *Stand and Deliver* (1988), *American Me* (1992), and *And the Earth Did Not Swallow Him* (1995). Similarly, in the documentary area Jesús Salvador Treviño and Hector Galán represent a growing number of documentors of Chicano/Chicana culture as represented in *Songs of the Homeland* (1994, Galán), In 1994, Galán received a grant to film for PBS, *Chicanos: The History of the Mexican American Civil Rights Movement*, a film in eight segments focusing on the roots of the conflict, the worker's activism, the educational reform and the Chicano Power. It will, moreover, deal with the role of the student in the Chicano movement, their art and literature, the civic and political organizations of the twenties and thirties as precursors for the defense of Chicano/a Civil Rights.

In music, the Chicano of the sixties and the seventies brings in the traditional conjunto music and integrates it into the big band sound of the seventies exemplary of Little Joe y la Familia ("Nubes").[46] New instrumentation and styles create a unique Chicano/Tejano sound that began with female vocalists like Laura Canales that continue into the nineties with the international and varied Chicano/Tejano pop music of Selena. Currently, as the Chicano/Chicana "Renaissance" continues to proliferate in all areas, the Chicano/Latino Cinema appears to be the next and most promising field for *Mestizo*-Americans as we approach the end of the twentieth century.[47] At this juncture, it is difficult to say what impact English and the Anglo-American culture will have on *Mestizo*-American culture in the U.S.; since the seventies,

Chicano/Chicana (Latino/Latina) literature has shifted to English. Nonetheless, as long as there is a continued migration and contact with new Mexican arrivals, there will always be a strong cultural/linguistic base with the Mother Culture.

As the *Mestizo*-American expands its multicultural base, the Mexican-American/Chicano and *Tejano* like the brother/sister south of the border, will continue to maintain within his/her soul, a marked universal and spiritual capacity that foreshadows a culture which is more humanistic, and global for the future.

The Identity of Mestizo Americans: A Mural by José Antonio Burciaga

ENDNOTES

[1] Antonio Castro Leal, *Juan Ruíz de Alarcón, su vida, su obra.* (México: 1943), p 205-207.

[2] Ibid.

[3] With the rise of Romanticism comes the validation of values of the country, the language, customs etc. See *Jicontencal*, anónima; Manuel Payno, *Los bandidos del Río Frío* (1889); Luis G. Inclán, *Astucia* (1865), Ignacio Altamirano, *Clemencia* (1869); Emilio Rabasa, *La bola* (1888); Rafael Delgado, *La Calandria* (1890).

[4] Antonio Caso, *El problema de México y la ideología nacional,* (México: Libro México Editores S. de R.L., 1955). One notes the first edition to be by Editorial Cultura en 1924.

[5] José Iturriaga, "El carácter del mexicano", *La estructura social y cultural de México,* (Mexico: Fondo de Cultura Económica, 1951), Chapter VII, pp. 227-228.

[6] See Chapter entitled, "El mestizaje," de *La Raza Cósmica* (1925); *Indología* (1926).

[7] The Ateneo de la Juventud was founded in 1907 with the name of *Sociedad de Conferencias* in the Casino de Santa María. Among the many papers presented, *Nietzche* por Antonio Caso, *Gabriel y Galán,* Pedro Henríquez Ureña. In 1908 another cycle in the Teatro del Conservatorio: *D'Annunzio* by Genaro Fernández MacGregor, *Max Stirner,* by Antonio Caso. In 1910 already with the name of *Ateneo de la Juventud* one see anew the participation of Alfonso Reyes *(La obra de José Enrique Rodó)* and José Vasconcelos (*Don Gabino Barreda y las ideas contemporáneas*). Later it changes its name to *Ateneo de México* which will last until 1914.

[8] Antonio Caso, *El problema...,* p. 26.

[9] Antonio Caso, *El problema...,* p 29.

[10] Ibid.

[11] Antonio Caso, *El problema...,* p. 65.

[12] Antonio Caso, *El problema...,* p 71.

[13] Antonio Caso, *El problema...*, p. 72.

[14] Antonio Caso, *El problema...*, p 77.

[15] Antonio Caso, *El problema...*, p. 81.

[16] Samuel Ramos, *El perfil del hombre y la cultura*, (México: Espasa Calpe Mexicana, S.A., 1965).

[17] Samuel Ramos, *El perfil...*, pp. 52-57.

[18] Samuel Ramos, *El perfil...*, pp. 57-59.

[19] Samuel Ramos, *El perfil...*, pp. 64-65.

[20] Samuel Ramos, *El perfil...*, p. 67.

[21] Samuel Ramos, *El perfil...*, pp. 66-81.

[22] Rita Guibert, "The New Latin Wave: Octavio Paz" (interview), *Intellectual Digest*, (Dec. 1972), pp., 67-74.

[23] Octavio Paz, "Los hijos de la Malinche," *Laberinto de Soledad*, (México: Fondo de Cultura Económica, 1959), p.. 74.

[24] Octavio Paz, "La Conquista y la Colonia," *Laberinto...*, p. 78.

[25] See in *Laberinto...*, the relevant chapters: "Máscaras Mexicanas," "Los hijos de la Malinche," "La dialéctica de la soledad."

[26] José Iturriaga, "El carácter del mexicano," in *La estructura social y cultural de México*, (México: Fondo de Cultura Económica), Second Part chapter VII, pp. 225-44. Reprint: José Luis Martínez, *El ensayo mexicano moderno*, (México: Fondo de Cultura Económica, 1958 pp. 345-368.

[27] Rosario Castellanos, *Mujer que sabe latin*, (México: Secretaría de Educación Pública, 1973), pp. 7-29

[28] Leopoldo Zea, "En torno a una filosofía americana" in *Ensayos sobre filosofia*(Editorial Style, 1948), pp. 165-77.

[29] Emilio Uranga, *Análisis del ser mexicano*, (Porrúa y Obregón S.A., 1952), pp. 38-45, pp.164-193.

[30] Sara Sefchovich, *México: País de idea, país de novelas*, (México: Editorial Grijalbo, 1987), pp. 235-39, 255-72.

[31] Roger Batra, *La jaula de la melancolía: identidad y metamorfosis del mexicano*,(México: U.N.A.M., 1987), pp. 173-181, 191-198.

[32] ibid. pp.205-224.

[33] ibid. pp.225-42.

[34] Jesús Silva Herzog, "Meditaciones sobre México, ensayos y notas," in *El ensayo mexicano moderno*, tomo I, p. 337.

[35] Jesús Silva Herzog, "Meditaciones...", p. 341.

[36] Ibid.

[37] This information is not known to the public; It is part of a series of private seminars given in the Centro Cosmosófico de Anahuak. It is about an Aztec metaphysical science called *Ilhuikayotl*; from here

originate the five mental spheres (1)*Teonemilizotl,* (2)*Teomaniliztli,* (3)*Teoizauhtli,* (4)*Teomatlilli,* (5)*Teyotl.*

[38] See the work of Domingo Martínez Parédez: on the theory of Mayan preamerican cosmogony in *El Popol Vuh tiene razón,* (México: Editorial Orión, 1976); *Parapsicología Maya,* (México: Porrúa, 1977). For Aztec culture, see Juan Luna Cárdenas, (*Yakanini Meztli Kuautemok*) *La Casa de Jade, Prehistoria de América, Leyendas aztekahs, La diseñometría aztekah, La matemática de los aztekahs, Tratado de etimología de la lengua aztékatl,* Editorial U. T. I Aztékatl, Apdo. Postal H-8433, 06002, D. F. México.

[39] Bartolomé de las Casas in his *Brevísima historia de la destrucción de las Indias* tells of a Spaniard asking another for a leg of a Native to feed his dog.

[40] Alonzo S. Perales, *Are we Good Neighbors?* , (San Antonio: Artes Gráficas, 1948), p.122.

[41] Arnoldo Carlos Vento, "Estudio etimológico: Una perspectiva socio-lingüística e histórica del habla chicano", *Work, Family, Sex Roles, Language,* Mario Barrera, Alberto Camarillo, Francisco Hernández (eds.), (Berkeley: NACS, 1979), p.. 195-207.

[42] The word "chicano/chicana" has been verified in both Aztec Náhuatl and Maya-Quiché by Aztec and Mayan teachers and scholars, Yakanini Meztli Kuautemok(Dr. Juan Luna Cárdenas) and Domingo Martínez-Paredez, respectively. The word does not carry a pejorative connotation as has been assigned by the middle class and upper class groups. Rather, it means a person whose demeanor is one of strength both of will and spirit. Its etymology is from the *Aztekah Náhuatl* ÇIKANI.. In the southern most regions of Mexico, there are some arquelogical ruins with the name of CHICANNA.

[43] Armando Rendón, *The Chicano Manifesto,* (New York: Collier Books, 1971) pp. 1-41..

[44] The following is a list of major and representative works by Chicanos and Chicanas:

THE SEVENTIES:

NOVEL	POETRY	THEATER
(1)Tomás Rivera	Alurista	Luis Valdez
(*Y no se lo tragó la tierra*)	Ricardo Sánchez	(*Zoot Suit...*)
(2)Rudolfo Anaya	Abelardo Delgado	
(*Bless me Ultima*)	Raul Salinas	Carlos Morton
(3)Rolando Hinojosa-Smith	Tino Villanueva	(*JohnnyTenorio*)
(*Klail City y sus alrededores*)	Lorna Dee Cervantes	
4)Ron Arias	Evangelina Vigil	

(The Road to Tamazunchale)   José Montoya
(5)Aristeo Brito   José Burciaga
(El diablo en Tejas)   Angela de Hoyos
(6)Jim Sagel   Bernice Zamora
(Tu nomás, Honey)
(7)Miguel Méndez
    (Peregrinos de Aztlan)
(8)Estela Portillo Trambley
    (Rain of Scorpions)

THE EIGHTIES AND NINETIES :

NOVEL :	*POETRY :*	*THEATER*
(1)Rudolfo Anaya	Jim Sagel	Luis Valdez
(Heart of Aztlan)	Gary Soto	Carlos Morton
(2)Rolando Hinojosa-Smith)	Alurista	
(The Avengers)	Ricardo Sánchez	
(3)Miguel Méndez	Tino Villanueva	
(El sueño de Santa María	Lorna Dee Cervantes	
de las Piedras)	José Burciaga	
(4)Sandra Cisneros)	Pat Mora	
(Woman Hollering Creek)	Alma Villanueva	
(5)Arnoldo Carlos Vento	Rosemary Catalcos	
(La Cueva de Naltzátlan)		
(6)Floyd Salas		
(Buffalo Nickel)		
(7)Lucha Corpi		
(Eulogy for a Born Angel)		
(8)Alejandro Morales		
(Rag Doll Plagues)		
(9)Victor Villaseñor		
(Rain of Gold)		
(10)Roberta Fernández		
(Intaglio)		
(11)Irene Beltrán Hernández		
(Heartbeat/Drumbeat)		

[45] The eighties became representative of the explosion of women writers at all levels of the new Mexican-American/ Chicana . The new writers include Sandra Cisneros, Lucha Corpi, Pat Mora, Roberta Fernández and Irene Beltrán Hernández among others. Not included here are the many Latina writers not of Mexican descent. See also the Chapter VIII concerning the Chicana Movement and its Literature.

[46] This is not to say that the traditional Conjunto sounds do not remain ; both new styles and old styles continue concurrently. In fact, Conjunto has received acclaim and popularity in Germany and as far away as Japan where several Japanese Conjunto groups exist including *Los Gatos* who recently made their U.S. debut at the Tejano Conjunto Festival in San Antonio.
[47] See Chapter VIII for information on the Chicano Cinema.

CHAPTER IV

THE CLASH OF TWO CULTURES

MEXICAN/CHICANO CULTURAL
AND POLITICAL RESISTANCE

FROM ENGLISH/AMERICAN COLONIALISM
TO XIX CENTURY IMPERIALISM:
Culture as a technical term emerged in the writings of anthropologists in the mid-19th century. English anthropologist Sir Edward B. Tylor used to refer to the "complex whole" of ideas and things produced by men in their historical experience. By 1910, the term was used to refer to distinctive groups of traits characterizing particular tribal societies. By 1930, Ruth Benedict discussed culture as a pattern of thinking and doing that runs through the activities of people and distinguishes them from all other peoples. Later it became a term to describe the distinctive human mode of adapting to the environment--molding nature to conform to man's desires and goals. Other definitions have it as the sum total of ways of living built up by a group of human beings and transmitted from one generation to another or the quality in a person or society that arises from a concern for what is regarded as excellent in arts, letters, manners, scholarly pursuits, etc.[1] As a term it is much broader than a society referring to the behavioral contents of society which allows for culture to be seen as an "improvement or refinement of mind, morals or tastes; enlightenment or civilization."[2] Culture is heterogeneous and it is, in fact, this heterogeneity that calls for many definitions since it refers not to a single reality but to innumerable

items at different levels of generality: ideas, sentiments, values, object, actions, tendencies, and accumulations.

When one refers to Chicano culture, one refers to a whole set of historical socio-political and religious patterns that have undergone a Hegemonic experience becoming in the process a subpattern or subordinate underclass. At the core are what Gramci calls the superstructured levels i.e. civil society (private) and state society (political) where societas hominum and societas rerum (directed by organic intellectuals to expand their own interests) has been mechanistic and determinist. These levels correspond to the function of hegemony and the intellectuals are the "deputies" exercising the subaltern functions of social hegemony and political government. [3]

In order to understand the Hegemonic process as it relates to the Mexican/Chicano, one needs to look at the roots of culture of both the Spanish and the English, in particular to colonial European ideas and traditions from their mother country. It is, however, important to employ caution in the selection of sources. It is important to avoid romantic versions of the Spanish and their culture[4] as well as biased perceptions of pre-Columbian civilizations[5] notwithstanding heroic nationalistic versions of northamerican culture.[6] While cultural friction existed between the Spanish and the English, there are various social European characteristics that are homogeneous to both as representatives of descendants of Greco-Roman culture i.e. Western culture. While there is religious hatred between Anglo-Saxon and Spanish cultures, there remains religious fanaticism and intolerance of Native spiritual beliefs on both Protestant and Catholic sectors of society. From this myopic stance springs cultural and racial prejudice against Moors, Gypsies, Africans, and Native Americans. The Middle Ages further contributed to the concept of might is right which facilitates the idea of invasion/conquest leading to imperialism and expansionism. The Middle Ages gave rise to crusading, conquests and booty, an ideal of possession and materialism as the reward. The Aristotelian ideal of the elect dominating the underclasses, additionally gives rise to the ideal of enslavement and the separation of classes. Within this Judeo/Christian Western model the woman remains a domestic and secondary entity in a society of privileged classes which constitute a religious/civil plutocracy. It is precisely the arrogant and righteous attitude of the governing classes together with a recalcitrant individualism that is directly responsible for cultural genocide against people of color and different cultures.[7]

Religious fanaticism by the Spanish in the Middle Ages is well documented via the Sanctum Officium or Inquisition. This has been detailed in the previous chapter. Holy wars in the Middle East during the Crusades lasting 300 years were not represented by the Spanish; rather it was represented by the English, French, and Germans. This military aristocracy within the European nobility can be traced back to the Teutonic tribes who brought to the Latin territory the concept of Arianism, a warrior spirit, a barbarous culture, notwithstanding racism.[8] The campaigns to the "New World" by both the Spanish and the English are motivated by the idea of profit, materialism and expansionism. Columbus' voyages were business ventures as were early expeditions of English companies in Virginia. These companies were not at the service of the crown. They served only their own private stock corporations and their individual self interests. Those who were not "indentured slaves" were stockholders, so that every trip to the "New World" was a business venture, a practice in commerce.[9] These private companies chartered by the crown consisted of pirates, gold seekers, lawbreakers, stockholders-- for the most part, their aim was to gather wealth in the "New World" and then return to England. Like the early expeditions of the Spanish to Española, these early English settlers were comprised chiefly of men who had been "prisoners in English jails and ruffians of the streets." In 1699 England exported a shipload of "young women of ill repute" who were sold for their weight in tobacco, others were sold for the cost of their passage.[10] Not finding gold, later settlers were forced to turn to manufacture agriculture and the practice of manifest destiny i.e. expansionism and the extermination of Natives as chosen or destined by God. On July 30, 1619, two burgesses (citizens) from each plantation met with the governor (appointed by the London Company) and six councilors in a small church in Jamestown. This "legislature" was comprised of plantation slave owners and members of the London Syndicate. In the same year the first cargo of Negro slaves was brought to the English colony by Hawkins, the English pirate. As tobacco became king, plantation owners demanded cheap labor:convicts and criminals from overcrowded prisons in England, kidnapped children, political prisoners and unfortunates who had fallen into debt were sold to Virginia. Soon after their labor proved profitable both in cotton and tobacco, many Negro slaves were imported.

Like the Spanish elite, the English colonial elite enjoyed the spoils of exploitation and commerce. They were fond of amusements, such as hunting, jousts, race meets, fishing and horse racing. Similarly, in the area of religion, both were intolerant of other religions. The "New World" English settlers belonged to the Church of England. It was unlawful to settle in Virginia unless he/she acknowledged the English king as head of the Church. No Catholic could vote, hold office, carry firearms or be heard in a court of justice. According to Gramci, Anglo-Saxon immigrants besides being a (dominant) intellectual group, were a moral elite group...relics of past regimes...that give the initiative of equilibrium of mediocrity.[11] English prejudice against Catholicism, Spain and the Aboriginal Natives of the Americas is experienced shortly after 1500, crystallizing during the Reformation and intensifying as Protestantism thereafter. Resentment against Catholics transcended religious issues, particularly political and social. Englishmen began to regard the Church as a supra-national power which sought to overthrow their government. Most important was their perception of color and race. The color black had already required a number of negative connotations in the English mind; thus, human beauty equated blond perfection of the northern European, while the African and the Spaniard was placed at the bottom of the scale. The Spaniard, according to Raymond Paredes, was seen as manifestly impure, being the product of Moorish miscegenation. To the English, Moor and Negro were used almost interchangeably.[12]

The Puritans and the settlers were ardent nationalists who saw themselves as guardians against Spanish penetration--missionaries who would carry the Gospel unperverted to the American savages. Most damaging prejudices were in the colonial literature as evidenced in John Foxe's *Book of Martyrs* (Catholic persecution), the collections of Hakluyt and Samuel Purchas (champions of English imperialism), William Bendford (governor of Plymouth Colony) *Of Plymouth Plantation* (separatist hispanophobia). Perhaps the greatest denunciations came directly from the pulpit and in religious tracts as exemplified by John Cotton and Thomas Hooker. Even the New England Primer (a text of over 150 pages) contained prejudicial hispanophobic excerpts from the *The Book of Martyrs*.

When one speaks of the pilgrims of the Mayflower, there is reference to religious freedom and self government. What is often neglected is the religious fanaticism that accompanies this group of separatists who did not want to follow the official Church of England. In the beginning they fled to Holland where they were dissatisfied with the failure of the Dutch to conform to their ways only to return to England calling themselves Pilgrims. From England they sailed to the New World in the Mayflower like many undesirables. What should be noted after the signing of the Mayflower compact is that freedom was to be an exclusive right only for themselves. They were, in fact, tyrannical toward all believers in any creed except their own. Catholics were denied the right to vote. People straying from their belief were banished to the wilderness. Suspicions, accusation, torture, forced confessions and execution were practices that caused terror in the colony.[13] By 1628, another settlement was made in Boston by Puritans or roundheads settling under the Massachusetts Bay Company. Like the Pilgrims, they showed no desire to establish religious liberty in their new home. Baptists, Quakers and Catholics were particularly hated. It was a harsh Puritan aristocracy that enforced exile of countless of people from their territory. It was an aristocracy of righteousness which made honest expression of opinion impossible. Quakers were hanged in 1660 on Boston Common. In 1692, nineteen persons, largely women, were hanged in Salem Village for witchcraft. Later, the Puritans banished Episcopalians. These were harsh, narrow and unbending people that dispensed "justice" freely, who, as members, were the only ones that could participate in government.

Most significant are the attitudes toward Native Americans, who were looked upon as savages and whose land could be given away by these companies. In 1637, Puritans marched to the Pequot Indian Village and massacred the entire population; only five survived. When Native Americans retaliated to protect themselves and their land, it gave the settlers a pretext to wage a merciless war systematically exterminating settlements and populations for more than 200 years. The European crusades with all of its religious fanaticism and materialistic imperialism were once again manifested in the expansionism of Manifest Destiny. According to Paredes, the political and military conflicts combined with the mass of literary evidence reveals that prejudices against Catholics and Spaniards transported to the "New World" at the end of the Elizabethan era, persisted among Anglo-Americans for two centuries without modification.[14]

The image of Mexico and Mexicans by the English-Americans was equally negative. Virtually every writer spoke of their indolence, their drunkenness, polygamy and incest. The Mexicans were vilified for their hostility to the Spaniards and their refusal to conform to the moral and cultural beliefs of their invaders. What is interesting here is the convenient use by the English of distorted and biased documents written by Spanish clerics on the native population. Only Bartolomé de las Casas, as a defender of Native-Americans, gave a positive image of the Native-Americans, attesting that they were not savage but to the contrary, were kind, loving, intelligent and possessed souls ergo excellent candidates for conversion.[15] Accounts by Oviedo, Cortés, Bernal del Castillo, Gómara, Acosta and even Sahagún projected largely a distorted medieval view of pre-Colombian society. There are two problems with these *Post-Hispanic* sources: (1) religious fanaticism and the desire to make Catholicism through conversion the Universal Church and (2) censorship by the Sanctum Officium (Inquisition) whose ecclesiastical councils censored and distorted all printed material with the *Index Librorum Prohibitorum* after the imposition of the first Inquisitor Juan de Zumarraga in Mexico City (1528). Thus, the negative and distorted picture of a barbaric, sanguine Satanist society depicted by clerics who projected their own medieval world of witches, Satan and evil, was used propitiously by the English-Americans against the native Mestizo Mexican population.[16] Likewise, Hakluyt and Samuel Purchas' work emphasized a negative profile of the Mexican's bewildered contempt and barbaric Mexican images grounded in distortion, fantasy and simple confusion.[17] Interest in Mexico can be traced to the end of the 17th century when Samuel Sewell, a devout Puritan invents a scheme to overtake and Christianize Mexico. His intentions went beyond religion in view of his interest as a merchant with Mexico's wealth and trade possibilities. He apparently had the support of New Englanders including Cotton Mather.[18] These Americans, naively believed that upon the defeat of the Spanish, the indigenous regimes would be receptive to Protestantism and English-American traders.

Around the middle of the 18th century, several newspapers carried articles speculating on the origins of Mexicans. Some argued that Mexicans had descended from ancient Chinese or Japanese voyagers; others resurrected the Elizabethan legend of Madoc Ap Owen, a Welsh prince who allegedly began a settlement in Mexico circa the 12th century. Paredes contends that no matter how inaccurate or trivial these reports were, they suggest curiosity about Mexico, an interest in the economic exploitation of Mexico and finally the information printed suggests nothing to challenge traditional negative images of Mexico as established by Spanish and English writers in the Elizabethan and Jacobean ages.[19]

These traditional negative images of Mexico continue with the writings of Thomas Gages (*The English-American)*, Samuel Nevill *(New American Magazine)*. Soon after, *The History of the Conquest of Mexico* by Antonio de Solis reiterated the biased accounts of Spanish chroniclers Cortés and Gómara; similarly John Harris and Edmund Burke's *Account of the European Settlements in America* treated Mexicans with disparaging antipathy. Still, the greatest impact on the American populace in the 18th century was William Robertson's *History of America*. A Scottish Presbyterian and licensed minister, Robertson's depiction of Mexicans and the Aborigines was one that depicted them not only as defective morally and intellectually but physically. He saw them as villains, vengeful, always fighting, incapable of tempering their rage, as signs of "savagism". In short, he stated: "we cannot but suspect their degree of civilization to have been very imperfect."[20]

To Robertson, Mexicans were made of two extraordinary breeds of scoundrels. About 1840, racialist thought emerged focusing on the "inherent" characteristics as opposed to those acquired during colonial times. Paredes observes that Robertson's portrayal of pre-conquest Aborigines and contemporary Mestizos were strikingly similar suggesting that he was influenced to the negative and biased accounts of the Spanish chronicler, Gómara. Paredes concludes that "of all the racialist theories, the doctrine of miscegenation, which held that the progeny of racially different parents inherited the worst qualities of each, had the greatest impact on American views of Mexicans. Racialists regarded mixed breeds as impulsive, unstable, and prone to insanity."[21]

XIX CENTURY INVASION/CONQUEST OF THE SOUTHWEST: CULTURAL CONFLICT AND RESISTANCE

Acuña cites the roots of the conflict extended back to as early as 1767 when Benjamin Franklin marked Mexico and Cuba for future expansion. Expeditions into Texas by adventurers and insurrectionist Americans date back to 1790. The Louisiana Purchase in 1803 stimulated American ambitions into the Southwest. By 1818 American military expeditions in east Florida seized several unauthorized posts to which the Adams-Oris treaty then ceded Florida to the U.S. while the U.S. renounced its claim on Texas. Nonetheless, there were many who followed Jefferson's expansionist schemes, notably James Long who led an abortive invasion to establish the Republic of Texas. When Mexico opened Texas to settlers, Stephen Austin founded the community of San Felipe de Austin. Soon large numbers followed, refugees from the depression entrepreneurs, adventurers looking for quick profit and cheap land. By 1830 there were 20,000 settlers along with about 2,000 slaves.[22]

Settlers agreed to the conditions set by Mexico i.e. that all immigrants be Catholics and take an oath of allegiance to Mexico. However, Anglo-Americans became resentful when Mexico tried to enforce their agreement. It was soon apparent that Anglo immigrants had no intentions of obeying Mexican laws.

By 1836, there were not more than 5,000 Mexicans in Texas; about 2,000 in San Antonio; 1,400 at La Bahía; and about 500 at Nacogdoches. Along the border, the *rancheros* of Santander (circa 1748) had been encouraged to settle along the Río Bravo (Rio Grande) in an effort to build a line of defense against the native tribes. Most came from the established communities of Guerrero, Camargo and Mier. The towns on the northern side of the Rio Bravo were Dolores (1761); Rio Grande City (1757); and Roma (1767), respectively.[23]

Central to understanding the potential conflict and invasion are the following points: (1) Anglo-Americans assume themselves as a superior culture, and as such, show no respect for Mexicans and/or

Mexican culture, (2) the U.S. blinded by Manifest Destiny, greed and expansionism will continue to coerce the Mexican authorities to give up Texas to its settlers, (3) hatred and prejudice towards all things Spanish, in particular Catholics, continues to flourish since Elizabethan and Jacobean ages, intensifying hostilities in the Mexican territory, (4) incompatible likewise, is the Anglo-American's colonial ways, in particular slave holding, which was outlawed in the Mexican territories. In addition to Anglo raiding parties (the Edwards rebellion), the U.S. Presidency begins placing pressure on Mexico in the hope of persuading her to rectify the frontier. The U.S. not respecting the Oris-Adams Treaty, desires the Rio Grande although the Brazos, the Colorado or the Nueces were also considered.[24]

By 1829, the Anglo-American in Mexican Texas had created a privileged caste in part due to their attitude and economic advantage given to them by their slaves. It is during this year that Mexico abolishes slavery. Anglo Texans not willing to give up their slaves circumvented the law by signing them to lifelong contracts as indentured servants. Incredibly, Anglo settlers considered the freeing of slaves by Mexico, an invasion to their personal liberties. As restrictions on immigration were placed on new Anglo settlers, Anglo Texans became more defiant and began a series of revolts. At the political level, U.S. Minister to Mexico, Anthony Butler, tried to bribe Mexican officials, offering 200,000 to "play ball."[25] Col. Anthony Butler, Jackson's Minister was, according to Carlos Castañeda, "an unscrupulous passionate and scheming character."[26]

In the meantime, Anglo land companies in Mexican Texas after 1834 were indiscriminately advertising and selling "landscript" without legitimate titles to the land.[27] By Sept. 19, 1835, it led to a full revolt to which John Quincy Adams labeled as a disgraceful affair promoted by slave holders and land speculators. Lincoln called the war immoral. The real problem was that the newcomers did not want to be subjects of a people they thought were morally, intellectually and politically inferior.[28] The Battle of the Alamo as well as Texas history in general is a mixture of hyperbole and myth. Walter Lord rectifies much of the myth of the good Texans, or the Alamo heroes as freedom loving defenders of their homes. In reality, two thirds of them had recently arrived from the U.S., and only six had been in Texas for more than six years. Most were adventurers; William Barret Travis had fled to Texas after committing homicide, abandoning his wife and two children; James Bowie, a ruffian and brawler was a slave runner who came to Texas searching for lost mines and more money; the aging Davy Crockett fought for the sake of fighting.[29] Vigil adds a more stark picture of these Anglo-Texas settlers in Mexican territory:

> The settlers were largely border ruffians, pirates and other undesirable adventurers recruited by the Anglos. As the rapidly increasing number of thieves, slave holders and others reached an alarming proportion, the Spanish-Speaking Mexicans were forced to issue an edict forbidding all further immigration... The Anglos retaliated by setting up their so-called Provisional Government and calling for volunteers who were promised two square miles of Spanish and Indian land...with the promise of loot and plunder and promises of all additional land they wanted at twelve and a half cents an acre and no down payment, the volunteers set out to organize their own cattle kingdoms...[30]

Vigil adds that "Anglo appetites, whetted by territorial gains in the South and Southeast turned their attention to the vast land areas of the Southwest--murdering, raping, and pillaging the Spanish - Speaking and Native-Americans...The spirit of conquest and self aggrandizement had already become the predominant characteristic of the Anglo-American..."[31] With regard to the Anglo characters of the Alamo, Vigil underscores their dubious character: "they were hotheaded, ignorant, lazy, thoughtless mob, and a continual source of trouble and embarrassment to a few Anglos of good will; they were the brutish dregs imported from Anglo America to commit brutal outrages. These "volunteers" were criminals who craved crime of every description...Jim Bowie joined pirate-thieving expeditions and smuggled slaves into Texas and quickly gained a notorious reputation as a brawler, slave dealer, smuggler, forger of land grants and an extraordinary restlessness in the pursuit of money through forged land grants he soon amassed over a million acres of Mexican-Spanish-Indian-American land...William Barret Travis murdered a man in a fit of jealousy, leaving a Negro slave to take the blame; he deserted his wife (expecting a second child) and set out to seek land grants in Texas, rightfully believing that he could conceal his identity...Davy Crockett, an illiterate, a curious freak, knowingly feeding on people's amusement. He held political office in Tennessee, but later was defeated after making a fool of himself...he set out for Texas to be a land agent. It didn't matter who already owned this land. He deserted his wife and children to go "whole hog" in a new land...These men together with many others of less notoriety such as Jim Bonham, James Grant, James Fannin and hundreds conscripted by emptying Anglo jails in the North, actually started the war for their own personal selfish gain. All of them, including Sam Houston and Aaron Burr dream of a Southwestern Republic..."[32] It is a time when Mexico was weak after years of fighting for independence; there were many problems left over form a medieval/colonial structure that was a carrier for reconstruction. Thus, Mexico was not only weak but divided. With regard to the outposts of northern territories like Mexican Texas, they were far away from the center. One notes that Santa Anna's army was ill equipped, his army having suffered innumerable casualties traversing thousands of miles of mountains, attacks from native tribes, disease, etc.[33] The story of Travis drawing a line in the sand and/or Crockett killing Mexicans with his bare hands are myths that were created long after the battle took place.[34]

A more accurate account of the Alamo was written by Vicente Filisola, who had been among the attackers on March 6, 1836; his account gives little credit to Santa Anna's judgment as a military commander. What is surprising from this eyewitness account is Travis' offer to surrender on the condition that his life and lives of his men be spared.

> On this same evening, a little before nightfall, it is said that Barrett Travis, commander of the enemy, had offered to the general in Chief by a woman messenger, to surrender his arms and the fort with all the materials upon the sole condition that his own life and the lives of his men be spared. But the answer was that they must surrender with discretion, without any guarantee, even of life, which traitors did not deserve...[35]

Vicente Filisola further states that most of their casualties were by their own men, who upon firing from the rear with the low range muskets, struck the backs of their own men:

> The attack was extremely injudicious and in opposition to military rules, for our own men were exposed not only the fire of the enemy but also to that of our own columns attacking the other fronts; and our soldiers being formed in close columns, all shots that were aimed too low struck the backs of our foremost men. The greatest number of our casualties took place in that manner; it may even be affirmed that not one-fourth of our wounded were struck by the enemy's fire, because their cannon owing to their elevated position, could not be sufficiently lowered to injure our troops after they had reached the foot of the walls...The official list of casualties, made by General Juan de Andrade shows: officers 8 killed, 18 wounded; enlisted men 52 killed, 233 wounded. Total 311 killed and wounded. A great many of the wounded died for want of medical attention, beds, shelter, and surgical instruments...The whole garrison (Alamo) was killed except an old woman and a Negro slave for whom the soldiers felt compassion, knowing that they had remained from compulsion alone. There were 150 volunteers, 32 citizens of Gonzales who had introduced themselves into the fort the night previous to the storming, and about 20 citizens or merchants of Bexar. [Total 202][36]

After victories in the Alamo, Goliad and a skirmish with Houston's army, Santa Anna made an incredible blunder. He failed to place sentries while his army was taking a siesta on April 21, 1836. The attack was literally a slaughter of Mexican forces. Few prisoners were taken. Those who surrendered "were clubbed and stabbed, some on their knees..."[37]

What followed was a steady stream of men, money and supplies for the invasion of Texas. Mexico's Minister to the U.S. protested the arming and shipment of troops and supplies to the Mexican territory. By 1844, James K. Polk, an advocate of expansionism won the Presidency by a small margin and shortly thereafter ordered General Zachary Taylor to go into disputed territory with the aim of provoking an attack, leaving a small army behind to come "to the rescue."[38] The U.S. provoked the war leveling the Mexican city of

Matamoros, robbing Mexicans of their cattle, corn, stealing their fences for firewood, drinking and killing innocent inhabitants of the town. George Gordon Meade later recorded:

> They (the volunteers) have killed five or six innocent people walking in the street, for no other object than their own amusement...They rob and steal cattle and corn of the poor farmers and in fact, are more like a body of hostile Indians than civilized Whites. Their officers have no command or control over them...[39]

American troops destroyed every city they entered. Anglo volunteers had no respect for anything as they desecrated Churches abusing priests and nuns. Military executions were common particularly against Irish Catholics. Chamberlain in his *Confessions* records the atrocities:

> ...We found a "greaser" shot and scalped but still breathing; the poor fellow held in his hands a rosary and a medal of the "Virgin of Guadalupe"...shouts, curses and cries of women and children...on the rocky floor lay over twenty Mexicans, dead and dying in pools of blood...Most of the butchered Mexicans had been scalped; only three men were found unharmed. A rough crucifix was fastened to a rock, and some irreverent wretch had crowned the image with a bloody scalp...[40]

General Taylor stole over one million dollars from the Mexican citizenry by force of arms but also, to the chagrin of Mexicans, let "loose on the country packs of human bloodhounds called the Texas Rangers" ; the infamous Texas Rangers' hate towards Mexicans is now well documented. Their brutality is exemplified by the following account:

The place was surrounded, the doors forced in and all the males capable of bearing arms were dragged out, tied to a post and shot...Thirty-six Mexicans were shot at this place, a half hour given for the horrified survivors, women and children, to remove their little household goods, then the torch was applied to the houses, and by light of the conflagration the ferocious Tejanos (Rangers) rode off to the fresh scenes of blood...[41]

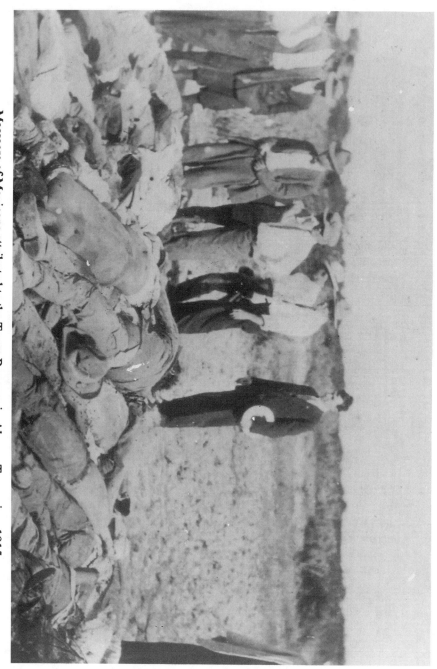

Massacre of Mexicans attributed to the Texas Rangers in Alamo, Texas circa 1915.

JUAN NEPOMUCENO CORTINA: REBEL FOR JUSTICE

By the 1850's Texas Anglo-Americans had built an oligarchy in which class was largely based on race, culture and religion. Mexican-Americans had been denied the opportunity to acquire property, to have political control and have equal rights under the law. Frontier lawlessness, wars and general corruption of civic administration obviated justice for the Mexican-American underclass. According to Taylor, the Spanish speaking Mexicans/Tejanos had no other recourse but to attempt to survive outside the law.[42]

Too often past historical studies have relied on prejudicial sources, usually the inflictors of oppression e.g. the Texas Rangers who harbored hatred toward Mexicans, their culture and religion; as a consequence, it is not surprising that any rebel that created a defense of natural rights was labeled a bandit. Such a case was observed by attorney J.T. Canales of Brownsville, Texas in his objective analysis of Juan N. Cortina. In an address to the Lower Rio Grande Valley Historical Association, he notes the negative, stereotypical epithets given to Cortina by well established writers: J. Frank Dobie, Walter Prescott Webb, Carey McWilliams, Charles Goldfinch and Lyman W. Woodman. The aforementioned refer to Cortina as "bandit" and "a thief," as the "red robber of the Rio Grande", as "the black sheep of his mother's otherwise commendable flock"; as "the scourge of the Lower Rio Grande Valley" and as "the rogue of the Rio Grande."[43] According to Canales, there is a thin line between bandit and hero; it often depends upon one word...success. He cites Robert Emmet who is now considered a hero and patriot in Ireland but was hanged as a bandit by the British government. Father Hidalgo y Costilla, was at first disgraced, excommunicated, then shot as a bandit; now he reigns as a hero and father of his country. Benjamin Franklin once said: "Gentlemen, we must hang together or else we will hang separately" i.e. those that survive are sometimes patriots; those who are hanged are often bandits.[44]

The question of definition is raised by Acuña referring specifically to Ed Hobsbawm and his work entitled *Primitive Rebels: Studies in Archaic Form of Social Movement in the 19th and 20th Centuries* defines the Mexican with a historical context: "taking Mexican banditry in the context of history, it represented 'in one sense...a primitive form of organized social protest, perhaps the most primitive we know.'"[45] While this definition may fit some e.g. Tiburcio Vásquez, it does not fit the model of Juan N. Cortina, since Cortina had an ideology and a military type organization that led warfare against the abusive establishment. As a whole, both are rebels in defense of sacred principles i.e. family, honor, home, land, religion; both are courageous in light of danger; both challenge the corrupt and inequitable systems that pass as law; both challenge the double standard that is applied to the underclass or subordinate group. The difference is in the sophistication of technique, in the organizational and tactical approach to the problem. Here, Juan N. Cortina rises above the rest in view of his accomplishments as a leader of men. Cortina was not only an officer but a commander of military forces fighting the French in Mexico. He had been recognized and had the full confidence of President Juárez; he, moreover, distinguished himself by being governor of the state of Tamaulipas. His integrity and good education was praised even by his enemies. Col. J.S. (Rip) Ford, who himself admits he did the best to kill Cortina in 1859, said the following about the military commander at Matamoros:

> In regard to the manner in which Cortina treated citizens of the United States, and of Texas, while he was in power in the state of Tamaulipas, it was worthy of remembrance. There were Americans in Matamoros known to have been personally unfriendly to Cortina, and he treated them kindly and honorably.[46]

Webb admits the victimization of Mexicans by the law and the double standard, which merely planted the seeds for rebellion for the champion of the people to redress the inequities of Anglo-American abuse:

> The Mexicans suffered not only in their persons, but in their property. The old land holding Mexican families found their titles in jeopardy and if they did not lose in the courts they lost to their American lawyers...Both high and low (classes) were ready to support a champion of Mexican rights; one that would throw off American domination, redress grievances and punish

their enemies. Just such a champion arose in the person of Juan Nepomuceno Cortina.[47]

Cortina's life as a defender of the poor and the weak begins on July 13, 1859 after "Cheno" Cortina had taken his morning coffee at the Brownsville Market Place. Riding home, he saw the city Marshall Bob Shears unmercifully pistol whip a drunken Mexican. The victim had previously worked for Cheno's mother. When Cheno Cortina offered to take responsibility for the offender, Shears replied: "What is it to you, you damned Mexican?" After firing a warning shot to no avail, Cortina shot the Marshall in the shoulder, rescuing the abused victim. To Prescott Webb, he rode off "in the grand style of...a Mexican vaquero on a holiday."[48]

However, to Cheno Cortina, a highly devout Christian and man of high principles and ethics, it was his Christian duty to come to the rescue of the poor and the meek. This can be readily seen in his proclamation to the Mexican Americans of South Texas issued on November 23, 1859 from his stronghold at the Rancho Del Carmen in Cameron County:

> Mexicans! When the state of Texas began to receive the new organization which its sovereignty required as an integral part of the Union, flocks of vampires, in the guise of men, came and settled themselves in the settlements, without any capital, except for the corrupt heart and the most perverse intentions. Some brimful of laws, pledged to us their protection against the attacks of the rest; others assembled in shadowy councils, attempted and excited the robbery and burning of the horses of our relatives on the other side of the river Bravo (Rio Grande); while others, to the abusing of our unlimited confidence, when we entrusted them with our titles, which secured the future of our families, refused to return them under false and frivolous pretexts...Many of you have been robbed of your property, incarcerated, chased, murdered and hunted like wild beasts, because your labor was fruitful, and because your industry excited the vile avarice which led them...Mexicans! Is there no remedy for you? Inviolable laws, yet useless, serve, it is true, certain judges and hypocritical authorities, cemented in evil and injustice, to do whatever suits them, and to satisfy their vile avarice at the cost of your patience and suffering; rising in their

frenzy, even to the taking of life, through the treacherous hands of their bailiffs...Mexicans! My part is taken; the voice of revelation whispers to me that to me is entrusted the work of breaking the chains of your slavery and that the Lord will enable me, with powerful arm, to fight against our enemies...On my part, I am ready to offer myself as sacrifice for your happiness; and counting upon the means necessary for the discharge of my ministry...[49]

The fact that Cheno Cortina fought as a Mexican commander against the French does not detract from his fidelity and love for what became Texas in South Texas. Cortina's family were of the original settlers of Carmargo and rightful grantees of the Espíritu Santo Grant where the city of Brownsville is now located. When the Treaty of Guadalupe Hidalgo was enacted, the Cortina family became American citizens. Canales attests that there is no record that any of the Cavazos or Cortinas even formally repudiated their American citizenship; but there is abundant evidence that they considered themselves American citizens i.e. Cortina's full brother José María Cortina was elected Tax Assessor of Cameron County and Juan Cortina himself actively participated in the election of county officers in Cameron County. His half brother Sabas Cavazos, always considered himself an American citizen. In fact, Cortina backed the filibustering expeditions led by José María Carbajal in 1851 which were financed by local Anglo merchants who wanted to separate the Rio Grande Valley from Texas to form the Republic of the Sierra Madre. Much of disreputable allegation of Cortina as a bandit begins early with a business partner described as a nefarious German (Adolphus Glavecke), who had a personal vendetta against Cortina. In the spring of 1859, after defending the abused and pistol whipped drunken Mexican and with no possibility of a fair trial, Cortina prepares to leave for Mexico. In his disgust with Anglo-American unethical practices, he rides into Brownsville and raises the Mexican flag. Here he was accused of plundering the city but the record shows that he did not rob or steal in the Brownsville raid of September 1859:

When he raided Brownsville September 28 and 29, 1859,...he did not rob or steal when he had the city at his mercy--even the affidavit of his sworn enemy Adolphus Glavecke...does not charge him doing that. The record shows he bought and paid for the arms and ammunition he got for his men at Alexander Werbiski's Store, which he would not have done had he been a bandit...Cortina maintained throughout that he had entered Brownsville only to bring retribution to those whose punishment had long been delayed. There is no evidence that any plundering took place...In Cortina's proclamation...he pointed out that certain men in Brownsville had formed a league to persecute and rob those of Mexican origin and that, since the machinery of government was largely in their hands, the Mexicans had finally decided to take matters into their own hands and bring to justice those who had gone unpunished for a long time. He named four of the five men killed, as being in that class and regretted the others had escaped...[50]

Among the Anglo-American abusers killed were William P. Neal and George Morris, both of whom had murdered innocent Mexicans without any interference of the law.

Seeking revenge, the authorities in Brownsville arrested Tomás Cabrera, a friend of Cortina and without the benefits of a trial as the law required, was allowed to be taken out of jail and hung by "an unknown and lawless mob." Cortina responded to his friend's arrest by demanding the old man's release; when unsuccessful, he engaged in battle against both the Brownsville militia and the Mexican army at Matamoros and defeated them in battle as well as the Texas Rangers shortly thereafter. After issuing his proclamation and his victories over the oppressive political machine of Cameron County, Cortina became big news in the U.S. newspapers, with hyperbole as the main journalistic technique. Sensationalism and outright fabrications became standard print. More in perspective was the report by Robert Taylor, a commissioner sent by Houston to investigate matters on the border: "I am sorry to say a good many of the latter (Anglos) in fact some of them who have been burning and hanging and shooting Mexicans without authority by the law are more dreaded than Cortina."[51]

By 1870, vigilantes had taken the law into their own hands spreading terror to the Mexican American population using Cortina as an excuse for their atrocities. By 1874, the Texas Rangers with six

Juan Nepomuceno Cortina in Santa Rita, Texas

mounted battalions of seventy five men each conducted a race war against Mexicans that continued throughout the region. Although unsuccessful against Cortina, the U.S. then brought pressure to the Mexican government who subsequently jailed him on charges of cattle rustling, and when the General and Dictator Porfirio Díaz seized power, Cortina was exiled to Mexico City. Dictator Díaz as an oppressor of the poor and a representative of the colonial oligarchy (Spanish elite and Catholic Church) gave Anglo investors a carte blanche to exploit enormous tracts of land in (previously stolen from Amerigenous communities) including mineral and other natural resources. It was not until 15 years later (Spring, 1890) that Juan Nepomuceno Cortina returned to the border where he was received with great admiration and affection by the Spanish-Speaking populace. In the end, Juan N. Cortina must be seen a man of great integrity and honor, notwithstanding moral and ethical rectitude. Cortina wanted to see peace and democracy to his beloved area in South Texas where Mexican-Americans and Anglo-Americans could function as brothers in true Christian spirit. His proclamation, in which he declares his ministry to protect the poor is to be sustained on the following basis: (1) a society in Texas in which tyranny will be eliminated with the goal of improving the unhappy condition of Mexican residents, (2) a society in which the articles of the Constitution must be enforced and (3) the Mexicans in Texas must place faith in "the good sentiments of the governor elect of the state, General Houston and trust that upon his election to power he will begin with care to give us legal protection within the limits of his powers." The last paragraph of his proclamation underscores his moral/ethical/spiritual intentions: "Mexicans! Peace be with you! Good inhabitants of the state of Texas, look on them as brothers, and keep in mind that which the Holy Spirit saith: 'Thou shalt not be the friend of the passionate man; nor join myself to the madman, lest thou learn his mode of work and scandalize thy soul'"[52]

U.S. POLITICAL AND TERRITORIAL AMBITIONS

Polk's plan from the beginning was clear. It was a campaign that was planned in three stages: (1) Mexicans would be cleared out of Texas, (2) Anglo-Americans would occupy California and New Mexico and (3) U.S. forces would march into Mexico City to force the Mexican government to make peace on Polk's terms.[53] In the end the United States took over one million square miles of Mexican lands justifying its invasive actions through the Puritan idea of Manifest Destiny which presupposes the establishment of the City of God on earth and that it is not only the duty of those chosen people predestined for salvation but is also the proof of their state of grace. This belief carried over to the Anglo-American conviction that God had made them custodians of democracy with the predestined mission of spreading its principles. It was the belief among many citizens that God had destined them to own and occupy all the land from ocean to ocean. This attitude of righteousness was also used by the Spanish with the cross in one hand and the sword in the other. It is an old medieval idea used in crusading that gives a righteous justification and blessing to invade, plunder and steal from the original inhabitants of lands. It is this aggression that violates the basic principles of Christianity. It is a hegemony of the majority society to the different groups i.e. people representative of color, race or ethnicity. There is curiously within what Gramci calls the urban and rural intellectuals a Hegemonic process that has at its roots a prejudicial ethnocentric posture. It is this posture that allowed the U.S. Congress to omit Article X of the Treaty of Guadalupe Hidalgo. The omitted article X had comprehensive guarantees protecting "all prior and pending titles to property of every description."[54]

In addition to the hatred and distrust of all things Mexican, Anglo Texans were aggravated by their run-away African-American slaves. It is estimated that 4,000 fugitive slaves made their way into Mexico. Mexico was blamed for encouraging slaves to escape. When several expeditions were financed to recover the slaves, it merely added to the existing border tensions. Anglo Texans' anger soon included all Mexicans as suspects in aiding African-Americans and were, therefore, subject to attack.[55] Texas constitutional law was racist in view that it aided in the oppression of Mexicans by excluding them of citizenship or ownership of property particularly those who had refused to participate in the Texas revolution.

Historians like Prescott Webb became an apologist for the Texas Rangers in view of his bias and admiration for the group. Recent scholars like Americo Paredes, Llerena B. Friend and Larry McMurtry show Webb's flaw in attitude, a mixing of homage with history, an inability to recognize the brutality and violence of these men. In a letter written by Enrique Mendiola, (whose grandfather owned the ranch that the Texas Rangers under McNeely, mistakenly attacked), notes that many of the so called Mexican bandits were actually people who were trying to recover cattle stolen from them by Anglo Texan 'Robber Barons': "Most historians have classified these men as cattle thieves, bandits etc...but most of them, including General Juan Flores, were trying to recover their own cattle that had been taken from them when they were driven out of their little ranches in South Texas. They were driven out by such men as Mifflin Kennedy, Richard King and (the) Armstrongs."[56] The Texas Rangers were representatives of Anglo-Texan ranchers and merchants who controlled the Rio Grande Valley. Law and order meant keeping the Anglo-Texan oligarchy in place. Violence was the means to the end of maintaining a hold on commercial interests and a closed social structure that placed Mexicans at the bottom of the social ladder. Thus, the Texas Rangers facilitated the domination of the area by a handful of unscrupulous and brutal men who corrupted local and state authorities. To gain control, these men assassinated the opposition, stole lands and homes and appropriated other peoples' cattle. The land and wealth soon passed to the Anglo-Texas oligarchy. By 1860, they completely dominated the Texas economy. These Robber Barons (Richard King, Charles Stillman, Mifflin Kennedy among others) made their fortune by stealing of cattle and land through hired cattle rustlers in addition to acquiring property through crooked lawyers. King made his money as a smuggler and was often accused of cattle rustling and murdering small land owners to get their land, paying bonuses to the Texas Rangers.[57] What started out as peaceful settlements along the "border" by Ecandón Spanish grants in the 18th century, was overrun by Anglo adventurers and soldiers of fortune seeking gold, a process that lasted for 200 years.[58] According to David Montejano, the attitudes of prejudice were the product of bitter warfare plus the long history of prejudice against natives and blacks; the behavior of the dominant class was reflected by references to economic status and specific interests. The cattle barons established an economic, social and political feudalism changing the complexion of the landowning class. The farm working class remained tied to the land through non-market criteria, violence and coercion; thus Mexicans became labeled as inferior.[59] By 1839 many Mexican families were forced to abandon their homes and lands; these include Victoria, Refugio, Goliad and Nacogdoces. Mexican livestock was declared public property; thus began raids by reckless young men (called cowboys) as such Anglo-American banditry became legal.[60] Another tactic used to acquire land was through marriages; this became a good way to amass large tracts of property in addition to gaining recognition, protection and status.

In the rest of the southwest, the pattern of invasion and expansionism continued circa 1840-1860. With regard to New Mexico, much has been expounded on the myth that New Mexicans became a willing enclave of the U.S. due to the bloodless conquest of New Mexico. This idea seems to have originated and shared by some early New Mexican writers and merchants who belonged to an elite class. Most of the 60,000 people in New Mexico were not enthusiastic about the U.S. invasion of their land.[61]

Hostilities began when Stephen Kearney led an army through New Mexico. U.S. loyalists in Taos supporting the Texas cause formed the American party. In 1841, General Hugh McLeod entered New Mexico with about 300 Texans and 6 military companies, only to be met and defeated by Governor Manuel Armigo's militia. This prompted outrage on the part of New Mexicans in view that a mob subsequently invaded the house of the U.S. Colonel Manuel Alvarez. Such was the protest that the U.S. government was accused of complicity to which the government then responded with open hostility.[62] Texas retaliated with invasive attacks between 1842 and 1843. Colonels A. Warfield and Jacob Snively raided and plundered Mora and caravans, killing innocent people indiscriminately. Anti-American feelings were intense particularly after Zachary Taylor attacked northern New Mexico. In June 1946, Stephen Watts Kearny prepared 3,000 army regulars of the west with the intent of occupying Mexican land from New Mexico to California. His ultimatum to Governor Armigo to surrender carried additionally, the inference of suffering the consequences. After capturing Las Vegas, New Mexico, surprisingly he met no resistance from Armigo en route to Santa Fe. Armigo had fled without defending the capital. It is surmised that Armigo accepted a bribe of $30,000 in view that

Magoffin submitted a bill to Washington for "New Mexico expenses" of which he received $30,000. Later, Magoffin boasted that he bribed Armigo.[63] Kearney's proclamation stating the province of New Mexico as a permanent possession of the U.S. was in violation of international law since the Treaty of Guadalupe Hidalgo is still two years away from being a reality. Resistance to the invasion mounted as New Mexicans, like Tomás Ortiz, Colonel Diego Archuleta, Padre Antonio José Martínez and Reverend Juan Felipe Ortiz conspired to revolt. However, the plot was uncovered by then Governor Bent (from the Taos American Party) who described New Mexicans as "mongrels to Anglo American rule." At the level of the masses, Pablo Montoya, a Mexican campesino and Tomasito Romero, a Pueblo Native American, led the resistance, attacking and killing Bent and five other members of the American Party on January 19, 1847. Resistance was also recorded in Arroyo Hondo and other communities. McWilliams cites the slaughter of New Mexican rebels and Pueblo Native Americans by Colonel Sterling Price: "About 150 Mexicans were killed; some twenty five or thirty prisoners were shot down by firing squads and many of those who surrendered were publicly flogged. Colonel Price's troops are said to have been so drunk at the time that the Taos engagement was more of a massacre than a battle".[64]

While the invasion was unjustifiable, there were some faults in the Mexican system. As in Mexico, the Spanish social structure was vertical as it was in the Middle Ages. It was the few that enjoyed the privileges at the top much like the nobles of medieval times. The masses (serfs in the Middle Ages) were exploited, both the Hispanic as well as the Native Americans. It was the elite who owned large tracts of land who exploited its workers and thus "participated in the enslavement of non-sedentary Indians."[65]

Still, there was a sharing of communal grants and Pueblo Native Americans did enjoy specified rights. Since there was relative harmony, miscegenation took place among the Hispanics and the Native-Americans. In terms of the "land-grab" in New Mexico, the method of acquisition was the same as with Texas; however, life was more rooted, villages more extensive. When Anglo-Americans moved in to enjoy the spoils of conquest, they formed an alliance with the elite Mexican/Hispanos controlling government and administering its laws to gain political economic and social hegemony. Since there was a direct political pipeline to Washington Anglo-Americans used this advantage as executive, judicial posts and other state offices went to Anglo-Americans who were recommended to the new political machine. The Hispanic *ricos* through their alliance with the Anglo-Americans helped maintain the political oligarchy and thus control the legislature. However, since Anglo Americans controlled the banks and economics, it forced many small farmers into bankruptcy and forfeiture of lands.

The Catholic Church also underwent substantial change in its leadership. The day of liberal people oriented philosophy as exemplified by Padre Antonio José Martínez, became a thing of the past. After 1850 control of the Church passed to an Anglo-American hierarchy, an alien clergy that related to the power structure and the elite as opposed to the masses. Eventually Padre Martínez was persecuted by the Church, denied communion; his follower, Father Gallegos, similarly was excommunicated to set an example for new priests. Since the Church was careful to select French, German and Belgian priests for service in New Mexico. Other New Mexican heroes emerged in the resistance movement. After the invasion of Socorro by Anglo Texans, Elfrego Baca, a deputy sheriff arrested a Texas and single-handedly held off the Anglo Texans for a day and a night. Similarly Sóstenes L'Archevêque, born in Santa Fe became famous for his notches in his gun. Much of his vendetta is the result of his father being shot down by Anglo-Americans in Sapelló, New Mexico. It is said that he had two more notches than Billy the Kid. Much to his surprise, his death came as part of a trap set by his own people. It was thought that by doing so, they could prevent wholesale retaliations.[66]

Arizona like Texas and New Mexico had two distinct societies; 1848-1849 serves as a marker in view that many Anglo Americans appear to have passed through the area and became interested in the Mesilla Valley, south of the Gila River largely for its mineral wealth. As in Texas and New Mexico, early Anglo American residents of Tucson quickly married "Spanish" ladies and acquired land, titles and respectability. Thus, before 1848, there was, according to McWilliams, no racial or ethnic animosity and were "on the most friendly terms; neither race scorned the other."[67]

The conflict begins shortly after the mining strikes around Tombstone. Acuña argues that historians have been captives of their sources and thus naïve of the political and economic motives of the Anglo-Americans. The Gadson Purchase in 1854 was not solely for the purpose of building a railroad. Mining had existed as early as 1736 near Nogales and a San Francisco company had worked on a copper mine in the Sonoita region since 1855.[68] Building a railroad through this land necessitated economically, the Sonoran part of Guaymas. When Mexico was unwilling to part with its southern area, Gadson, knowing the mineral potential of southern Arizona and New Mexico, began to coerce and threaten Mexican ministers into selling the land.[69] When Mexico ceded over 45,000 square miles of which 35,000 was in southern Arizona, it became clear that the railroad route was no longer feasible and that it was the political and economic motive that was underlying the process of expansionism.

Another problem was the demand for beef cattle, particularly after the campaigns against the Apache natives. Like in Texas and New Mexico, the "Texas cowboys," described as outlaws by many began to raid and pillage Mexican ranches along the border. These Texas outlaws numbered in the hundreds and included the Clanton gang killing Mexicans indiscriminately and "in a negligent way."[70]

Another cultural difference was sheep interests for the Mexicans vis a vis cattle interests for Anglo Americans. These callings, according to Wellman, "fostered the mutual distrust and dislike which the races held for each other."[71] Hence, the hatred of cattlemen for sheepmen was in most cases, a hatred of Anglos for Hispanos. Like Texas and California, Arizona had a long record of Mexican lynchings. Lynchings were recorded and defended by the establishment in Phoenix, Tucson, and Bisbee during the 70's and 80's. Such was the resentment and prejudice against Mexican Americans that ordinances were enacted outlawing Mexican Fiestas in Arizona. These Mexican lynchings, moreover, continued into Colorado and California.[72] Central to the building of a power structure based on race, religion and culture is the exploitation of the minority masses; these formally primary citizens are now the secondary labor force of the new Anglo-American Hegemonic process. Arizona's rugged climate, lack of transportation and frontier conditions made it a natural place for the exploitation of Mexican labor. Sonora, Mexico was seen by the new Hegemonic order as essential for economic prosperity. This Mexican state had a good supply of Mexican manual laborers and miners. And because they were Mexican, the wage scales were lower. Anglo-Americans in Arizona encouraged Apaches to raid Sonora in order to "weaken" it,making it vulnerable for annexation (2) drive out Sonoran citizens, to seek refuge in Arizona and (3) provide cheap labor in Arizona. It was Charles D. Poston, owner of the Sonora Exploring and Mining Company, who made a treaty with the Apaches. The Apaches were instructed not to disturb the Anglo Americans' interests and in return, they would not interfere with the Apaches' trade with Mexico."[73] Acuña cites that not everyone agreed with the policy of genocide by proxy. An editorial on *The Weekly Arizonian* (April 28, 1859) condemned the use of Apaches to annihilate Sonorans: "It is, in fact, nothing more or less than legalized piracy upon a weak and defenseless state, encouraged and abetted by the United States government."[74] Anglo-Americans who supported annexation of Sonora "without Mexican designs" were racists who saw Mestizos as half breeds not adequate for assimilation into a superior Anglo-Saxon dominant group.

With Anglo-American interests monopolizing the economy and the government, access to capital became difficult. The result was the creation of two societies: (1) Mexicans relegated to manual labor and the lowest jobs and (2) a privileged entreprenual class who owned and managed big money. The few elite/middle class Sonorans cooperated with the Anglo-Americans. Owners of large tracts of land, Anglo marriages into wealth related Mexican families was common in the beginning circa 1860's. While it is true that there were few "white" women, Anglo-American men needed the Mexicans for economic reasons as well as protection against the Apaches. It is interesting to note that as soon as railroads brought "white" women into the territory and the Apache threat was minimized, intermarriage became totally unacceptable.[75]

What was created by the Spanish colonial, i.e. caste system, peonage and color racism, was continued by the Anglo American. While it did become illegal soon after slavery was abolished, it continued well into the XX century as evidenced in the mid-century by the Bracero exploitation.[76] This era also marks the beginning of a pattern that Barrera calls a subordinate ascriptive class. Among the ways it was incorporated into the American political/economic system was by (1) relegating Mexican-Americans as a captive labor force, (2) creating a dual wage structure, (3) occupational stratification, (4) creating a reserve labor force and (5) using the ascriptive class as a buffer in times of economic dislocation.[77]

While Barrera refers to Chicanos between 1900-1930, there is evidence that the double wage standard and other characteristics aforementioned in his research were in place in the 1850's through the end of the century.[78] As machines replaced Mexican Americans in mining and agriculture, this captive labor group became seasonal and/or when farm workers were needed. After losing their land they were forced into wage labor in agribusiness, ranching and mining. Beyond Sonora as a labor supply pool, El Paso became a clearing house for Mexican labor in spite of the prohibition of Mexican contracted labor in the 1880's. Due to the need for cheap labor, the U.S. government did not enforce its own prohibition of contractual Mexican labor. It allowed, in fact, the exploitation of Mexicans and the protection of Anglo-American capitalist interests. It left a large pool of poor Mexicans without rights of citizenship, within the existing *patrón/peon* relationship. As in the case with the Spanish colonial economic oppression when the American born *criollos* challenged the *gachupines* (Spanish), the few Mexican elite responded to outright cultural genocide and racism by forming *La Alianza Hispanoamericana* on January 14, 1894. The need for a protective alliance organization was stimulated by both economic as well as cultural reasons. Their role soon took the character of trade union organizing and was more successful in mining than in agriculture or ranching. Within a decade of its founding, it had voted to admit women to pull membership in the organization.[79] While union officials attempted to restrict Mexican immigration, Anglo American mining interests used undocumented Mexicans as scabs. The Anglo American oligarchy maintained its hegemony, jealously guarding its privileges, while at the same time viewing all Mexicans as culturally and intellectually inferior, ergo, its designation as cheap labor. Still, the seeds for the Mexican -American were planted near the end of the century and were to the starting point for future XX century cultural /political resistance movements.

The pattern of invasion/occupation in Texas, New Mexico and Arizona by Anglo-American settlers continued in similar fashion in California. Just like the Spanish invasion and/or attack of the Antilles was followed by the mainland, so likewise, did the Anglo Americans establish a pattern of strategic political, economic and cultural hegemony. The Spanish-speaking residents even prior to 1821 were called *Californios*. As a group, the landed elite maintained a ranch economy with lower socio-economic class Mestizos mulattos and Native Americans forming the labor pool. Prior to 1841 foreigners coming into California generally assimilated into Mexican society and like the pattern established from Texas to Arizona, intermarried acquiring large tracts of land, and a position of respect in society. As hostilities intensified from 1843 to 1846, negative images of Mexicans, prejudice and fear became the predominant characteristics in the minds of Anglo Americans. The U.S. government followed its pattern of acquisition of land through coercion and attempted bribery of Mexican officials. Following the goal of expansionism, exploratory expeditions were discharged and in the case of California, under the leadership of the dubious character of John C. Fremont. Fremont completed these expeditions fomenting discontent among the *Californios* in view of his heavily armed contingent. From the Presidency James K. Polk's ambitions served the goals of Manifest Destiny as he conspired to take California. Leonard Pitt in his work *The Decline of the Californios*, soberly views the past glorifications by historians of Freemont's Bear Flag Rebellion as naïve; rather he places credence on the scholarly works of Hubert Howe Bancroft, Josiah Royces and Bernard de Voto who clearly saw the United States conniving rather cynically to acquire California and like Zachary Taylor in Texas, provoke the native Californians into a dirty fight.[80] Resistance came in the person of José María Flores, a former Mexican officer and General Andrés Pico, brother of the exiled Governor. Both had resounding victories albeit poorly equipped. However, the effort was insufficient against great odds i.e. a fleet of warships, marines, infantry and cavalry. The local war ended with the signing of the Treaty of Cahuenga on January 13, 1847. Ironically many *Californios* were relieved and saw the occupation favorably. It represented the end of the old repressive order. On the other hand, Anglo American "Bear Flaggers" had terrorized the Mexican and Native American populace, taking cattle, looting homes, wounding or murdering innocent people. Kit Carson in a scouting party was said to have killed several unarmed Mexicans, killing an old man for mere pleasure.[81]

Californios, like South Texas Mexican/Tejanos, had a distinctive middle class/elite group that had inherited from the Spanish colonial tradition the cacique/patron/peon system; essentially it was a quasi feudal/serfdom system, that relegated the masses to the exploitation by the few landed estate minority. These have been referred to as the *ricos* and *gente de razón*. The latter is particularly colonial and expresses a number of assumptions which can be traced back to medieval times. One of the implications derived is that you are not of "Indian" blood, thus you are not without reason. It is the others that are seen as barbaric, uncivilized as unintelligent children without reason. Thus, comfortable colonial *Californios* were happy to go back to rancho life including the persecuted Alvarado and the exiled governor Pico. To the misfortune of the *Californio*, the war had caused great economic hardships; ranches were destroyed leaving the Californios with serious financial obligations. Creditors ascended to foreclose many large ranches like the Rancho Mariposa owned by Alvarado. As was the case in Texas, Mexican-Americans had no choice but to sell cheaply.

Acuña notes that the newcomers depended almost totally on the market place and the transaction of capital. It depended on the exploitation of resources stimulating growth of factories in the northeast. Thus, the *rancho* economy was replaced by this new order which created simultaneously a very large and poorly paid wage force.[82] By 1849, eight Californios became delegates to the political convention; they were in a position to champion the rights of the masses but elected as middle class/ elite *Californios* to seek only their own interests and protection. This is typical of colonial mentalities that originate from the propertied class and is inculcated culturally into the exploitation of the masses and the acquisition of material wealth: "1849 marks the year of gold rush with 80,000 Anglo Americans, 8,000 Mexicans, 5,000 South Americans and several thousand Europeans increasing greatly to a quarter of a million by 1852".[83]

Much to the chagrin of the *Californios* the Anglo American newcomers refused to acknowledge any real distinctions between Latin Americans. Whether from California, Chile, Peru or Mexico, whether residents of one week or twenty, the Spanish speaking were categorized together as "interlopers" or "greasers." Mining, money and greed added to the difficulties experienced by the Spanish-speaking Californians. They became the scapegoats for Anglo American miner's failures. White Anglo American merchants resented the success of Mexican peddlers and mule dealers. Soon laws were passed to prohibit Mexicans working in mines. This idea appears to be first circulated by General Persifor Smith in a circular published n 1849. Racist stereotypes were already being voiced by legislatures e.g. G.B. Tingkey of Sacramento. The final solution proposed by Texan white supremacist Thomas Jefferson Green was to tax foreigners. The tax as can be surmised was intended primarily for Mexicans and other Spanish speaking groups.[84] McWilliams attests that shortly after the foreign tax was passed, "a mob of two thousand American miners descended on Sonora firing at every Mexican in sight. The camp was burned to the ground and a hundred or more Mexicans were rounded up and driven into a corral or stockade. During the week that the rioting lasted, scores of Mexicans were lynched and murdered...,"[85] As a result, Mexicans were forced to abandon their claims fleeing to the southern part of the state. Within these persecuted miners was the famous Joaquín Murieta, who later rebelled against injustice and was labeled by the Anglo American populace as a bandit. Of the most famous lynchings is the case of a Mexican woman who was three months pregnant, referred to by folklore as Juanita. Her real name was Josefa, of good character and above average of camp women in those days. Josefa was involved in an argument with a drunken miner who broke down the door of her home and her companion José. In the ensuing argument the American miner called her a prostitute among other verbal abuses. When the Anglo American miner refused to pay for the door and continued to insult her in her own home, Josefa fatally stabbed him. A kangaroo court was quickly held and Josefa was condemned to hang and her companion José, was banished. It is interesting to note that Senator John B. Weller was present in town and did nothing to stop the hanging. After 2,000 people witnessed the hanging, lynching of Mexicans became commonplace and the justice and democracy of Anglo Americans became known among the Spanish-speaking as *Linchocracia*.[86]

Crimes of violence had been almost unknown in California prior to the Anglo American invasion/conquest. It was the lawlessness of the newcomers with greed in their minds and with no government to curb the predilection for violence and direct action that soon caused the persecuted lower socio-economic classes to rebel for injustices provoked in their own land. McWilliams states: "Injustice rankles, and they were often treated by the rougher American elements as aliens and intruders, who had no right in the land of their birth."[87] Leadership in the Resistance movement became apparent in the persons of Tiburcio Vásquez, Joaquín Murieta, Louis Bolvia, Antonio Moreno, Procopio Soto, Manuel García, Juan Flores and Pancho Daniel among others.[88] The origin of rebellion is clearly one of defense. After years of unmitigated abuse and lynchings, the strong fight back. There was deep resentment and vengeance in the hearts of many rebels who stood their ground on ancient principles of family, respect and land. Hired guns of vigilante groups persecuting and killing Mexicans was a pattern already established by the Texas Rangers. Tiburcio Vásquez was reacting to the vigilante activities but also to the socio-cultural hegemony that was taking place by an invading and arrogant Anglo American populace. Vásquez explained his actions: "A spirit of hatred and revenge took possession of me. I had numerous fights in defense of what I believed to be my rights and those of my countrymen. I believed we were being unjustly deprived of the social rights that belonged to us."[89]

What was banditry in the eyes of Anglo American newcomers, was seen as justification to the practice of lynching Mexicans. McWilliams contends that what started out as a form of vigilante punishment for crime degenerated to an outdoor sport in southern California (as had been witnessed in south Texas by Texas Rangers).[90] In the late 50's and 60's, lynchings were so common that in Los Angeles, newspapers scarcely bothered to report the details. By the mid 50's California had more murders than the rest of the states combined, with the last lynching reported in 1892. With the execution of Tiburcio Vásquez, racial tensions increased and the elite *Californios* became concerned about a racial war. However, two factors quelled any further uprisings: (1) the Catholic Church, cooperating with the conservative elites (as in New Mexico) campaigned for the Americanization of the masses. It's hierarchy placed European and Spanish priests in the respective Spanish-Speaking parishes, in an effort to control the plaza in Los Angeles and to dispel any rebellion against authority and (2) by the beginning of the last decade of the XIX century, the railroad ended the dominance of the Mexican population. While the Mexican population increased slightly, the Anglo-American population increased ten fold.[91]

The Spanish-speaking became the minority, drifting into the bottom of the socio-economic ladder. McWilliams acknowledges the brutal physical attack followed by economic attrition of a cultural minority which is annexed to an alien culture and way of life. However, he speaks of a spiritual defeatism which affects individual ambition and their culture.[92] While the Spanish-speaking may have been victimized economically and educationally, it is clear that they have not been defeated spiritually in view of the cultural and linguistic cohesiveness that has maintained a Mestizo culture intact within the parameters of mainstream America.

ENDNOTES

[1] The Random House Dictionary of the English Language (N.Y.: Random House, 1987), p. 488.

[2] Funk and Wagnalls New Standard Dictionary of the English Language (N.Y.: Funk and Wagnalls Co., 1968), p. 629.

[3] Antonio Gramci: *Selections from the Prison Notebooks of Antonio Gramci;* ed. trans. Quintin Hoare, Geoffrey Nowell Smith (N.Y.: International Publishers, 1989), pp. 14, 353.

[4] I refer here to Antonio Vigil's book written in the 1960's entitled *The Coming of the Gringo (Ay vienen los gringos) and the Mexican-American Revolt* (N.Y.: Vintage Press, 1970).

[5] The extensive corpus of literature in the field of anthropology, archeology, history and art history is replete with biased distortions of Pre-Columbian reality. This is due to the use of Post-Conquest censored codices which were under the supervision of the Inquisitional ecclesiastical councils for a period of 300 years in Latin America. See my article entitled "Aztec Myths and Cosmology: Historical-Religious Misinterpretation and Bias," *Wicazo Sa Review,*(Spring, 1995). pp. 1-24.

[6] See William Robertson's *History of America* (London, 1777) reprinted in New York by J. Harper, in 1832. It is not surprising that Prescott (*Conquest of Mexico*, 1843) was influenced by this source of traditional prejudices and vague premonitions in view of Prescott's biased notions of mestizo culture.

[7] See my article entitled "Aztec Conchero Dance Tradition: Religious and Cultural Significance," *Wicazo Sa Review*, (Spring, 1994). p. 63.

[8] Arnoldo Carlos Vento, *Tres Civilizaciones del mundo medieval: crítica, análisis y crónicas de las primeras cruzadas* (Lewiston,N.Y.: The Edwin Mellen Press), In Press.

[9] A. Vigil, *The Coming of the Gringo and the Mexican-American Revolt*, p. 48.

[10] Ibid., p.

[11] A. Gramci, *Prison Notebooks*, p. 20.

[12] Raymond Paredes. "The Origin of Anti-Mexican Sentiment" *New Directions in Chicano Scholarship*. ed. Ricardo Romo, Raymond Paredes(San Diego: Chicano Studies Monograph Series, 1978) p. 141.

[13] Vigil, pp. 53-55.

[14] Paredes, "The Origin of Anti-Mexican Sentiment," p. 145.

[15] Bartolomé de las Casas, *Brevísima historia de la destrucción de las Indias*(Mexico: Metro, 1974) pp. 19-20.

[16] Arnoldo Carlos Vento. "Aztec Myths ...2p.

[17] See J. Elliot, *The Old World and the New,* 1492-1650 (Cambridge: England: Cambridge University Press, 1970) p. 1-53.

[18] Mather set out to learn Spanish along with Sewell who published a Protestant pamphlet in Spanish entitled "La Fe del Cristiano."

[19] Paredes, Raymond, *Origins,* p. 154.

[20] William Robertson's first printing of *The History of America* was in London in 1777; it was subsequently reprinted in New York (J. Harper) in 1832.

[21] Paredes, Raymond, *Origins,* p. 158.

[22] Rudolfo Acuña. *Occupied America: History of Chicanos* (N.Y.: Harper and Row, Publishers, 1981), pp. 3-4.

[23] McWilliams, Carey. *North from Mexico* (N.Y.: Greenwood Press, 1968), p. 84.

[24] Van Alstyne, Richard. *The Rising American Empire* (N.Y.: Norton, 1974), p. 101.

[25] Acuña, R. *Occupied...* p. 6 cites Nathaniel W. Stephenson *Texas and the Mexican War: A Chronicle of the Winning of the Southwest* (N.Y.: U.S. Publishing, 1921), p. 52; also Eugene C. Barker, *Mexico and Texas 1821-1835* (N.Y.: Russell and Russell, 1965), p. 128. Additionally, Carlos Castañeda *Our Catholic Heritage in Texas,* 1519-1933, vol. 6, p. 234.

[26]Castañeda, Carlos. *Our Catholic Heritage,* p. 234. See also Gene M. Brack, *Mexico Views Manifest Destiny, 1821-1846: An Essay on the Origins of the Mexican War* (Albuquerque: University of New Mexico Press, 1975), pp. 67-68, for additional information of Butler's lack of scruples.

[27] Of the companies most responsible for the sale of "landscrip" were The Galveston Bay and Texas Land Company and the Nashville Company.

[28] Acuña, *Occupied...*p. 7.

[29] Ibid., p. 9.

[30] Vigil, *The Coming...* p. 72.

[31] Ibid., p. 73.

[32] Ibid., p. 74.

[33] Acuña notes Santa Anna's men had archaic muskets with a range of only 70 yards in the open field while the well equipped Anglo-Texans had rifles with a 200 yard range plus twenty-one cannons to the Mexicans' eight or ten. p. 9.

[34] See Walter Lord, "Myths and Realities of the Alamo," *The American West*, 5, no. 3 (May, 1968), pp. 18-24.

[35] See *A Documentary History of the Mexican Americans*, Wayne Moquín, Charles Van Doren, Feliciano Rivera eds. (N.Y.: Praeger Publishers, 1972), p. 160. Original source of this eyewitness account is reproduced by Amelia Williams, "A Critical Study of the Seige of the Alamo and the Personnel of its Defenders," *Southwestern Historical Quarterly*, (July 1933).

[36] Moquín, Van Doren, Rivera eds. *A Documentary History...*, p. 161.

[37] Carlos Castañeda, *Our Catholic Heritage in Texas, 1519-1933* vol. 9 *The Church in Texas Since Independence, 1836-1950* (N.Y.: Arno Press, 1976), p. 5.

[38] Vigil, Antonio. *The Coming...*, p. 77.

[39] Acuña, citing William Starr Meyers, ed. *The Mexican War Diary of General B. Clellan*, vol. I (Princeton: Princeton University Press, 1917), pp. 109-110.

[40] Samuel E. Chamberlain, *My Confessions* (N.Y.: Harper and Row, 1956), pp. 75, 87-88.

[41] Ibid., p. 176-177.

[42] See Paul S. Taylor, An American-Mexican Frontier (N.Y.: Russell and Russell, 1971), p. 49.

[43] J.T. Canales, Juan N. Cortina: Bandit or Patriot? (San Antonio: Artes Gráficias, 1951), p. 4.

[44] Ibid., p. 4-5.

[45] Rudolfo Acuña...*Occupied*...p. 33. See also E.J. Hobsbawm, *Primitive Rebels: Studies in Archaic Forms of Social Movement in the 19th and 20th Centuries* (N.Y.: Norton, 1965), p. 13.

[46] J.T. Canales, *Juan N. Cortina*...p. 15.

[47] Adela Sloss-Vento, *Alonso S. Perales: His Struggle for the Rights of Mexican Americans* (San Antonio: Artes Gráficas, 1977), p. 4, citing Dr. Walter Prescott Webb, *The Texas Rangers* (Cambridge: Riverside Press, 1985).

[48] J.T. Canales, *Juan N. Cortina*..., p. 10.

[49] Wayne Moquin, Charles Van Doren, Feliciano Rivera, eds., *A Documentary History of Mexican Americans* (N.Y.: Praeger, 1972), pp. 207-209. Original text is from 36 Congress, I Session, House Executive Document No. 52 "Difficulties on Southwestern Frontier," pp. 79-80.

[50] J.T. Canales, *Juan N. Cortina*..., p. 11. See also Charles W. Goldfinch, *Juan N. Cortina, 1824-1892* (Brownsville: Bishop Print Shop, 1950). (thesis)

[51] Cited by Acuña p. 37. Original quote from Evans, p. 127.

[52] W. Moquin, C. Van Doren, F. Rivera eds., *A Documentary History...* p. 209.

[53] Acuña, R., *Occupied...*p. 12.

[54] See Lynn I. Perigo, *The American Southwest* (N.Y.: Holt, Rhinehart and Winston, 1971), p. 176.

[55] Acuña citing Ronnie G. Tyler "The Callahan Expedition of 1855: Indians or Negroes?" *Southwest Historical Quarterly,* 70, No. 4 (April, 1967), p. 575, 582.

[56] Letter cited by Llevena B. Friend, "W. P. Webb's Texas Rangers," *Southwestern Historical Quarterly* (January, 1971), p. 321.

[57] Acuña, *Occupied America,* p. 33.

[58] Virgil N. Lotts, Mercurio Martínez, *The Kingdom of Zapata* (San Antonio: Naylor Company, 1953), p. 1.

[59] David Montejano *Anglos and Mexicans in the Making of Texas 1836-1986* (Austin: University of Texas Press, 1987), pp. 2-11.

[60] Ibid., p. 30.

[61] It was Fray Angélico Chávez, a prominent New Mexican Catholic priest who wrote of its citizens as true and loyal American citizens. No doubt this was shared by prominent elitist *Hispanos* whose middle class attitudes can be compared to the South Texas *Tejanos* and the *Californios.* See David Weber, ed. *Northern Mexico on the Eve of the United States Invasion* (N.Y.: Arno Press, 1976). Also Howard R. Lamar, *The Far Southwest, 1846-1912: A Territorial History* (N.Y.: Norton, 1970), p. 30.

[62] Rodolfo Acuña, *Occupied...*p. 49. Acuña cites Ward Alan Minge, *Frontier Problems in New Mexico Preceding the Mexican War, 1840-1846* (Albuquerque: University of New Mexico Press, 1965), p. 53.

[63] L. Perrigo, *The American...*p. 164. See also Ralph Emerson Twitchell, *The Conquest of Santa Fe 1846* (Española, NM: Tate Gallery Publications, 1969), p. 52.

[64] Carey McWilliams, *North from Mexico,* p. 118.

[65] See the work of Daniel T. Valdés, *A Political History of New Mexico,* rev. ed., p. 5. Acuña states form this source that in 1780 , one hundred and ten *rico* (elite) families controlled 36,500 debtor and non-debtor peons in addition to 400 military personnel.

[66] See C. P. Loomis, *Sociometry,* (February, 1943). Also Manuel Gamio, *Mexican Immigration to the U.S.,* pp. 208-216.

[67] McWilliams, C., *North...*p. 125. The citation originally belongs to Dr. Frank C. Lockwood; 1943 and "Race Relations in New Mexico," pp. 208-216.

[68] Acuña, Rodolfo. *Occupied*...p. 73. See also Hubert Howe Bancroft *History of Arizona and New Mexico* (Albuquerque: Horn and Wallace, 1962), pp. 493, 496, 498; also Howard R. Lamar, *The Far Southwest, 1846-1912: A Territorial History* (N.Y.: Norton, 1970), p. 417.
[69] See J. Fred Rippy, "A Ray of Light on the Gadson Treaty," *Southwestern Historical Quarterly*, 24 (January, 1921): p. 241
[70] See Paul I. Wellman *The Trampling Herd*, (1939).
[71] Ibid.
[72] Documentation regarding lynchings in Arizona is in *New Mexico Historical Review* vol. 18; for Colorado, see Gamio, p. 213.
[73] Howard R. Lamar *The Far*...p. 419. See also Charles D. Poston, "Building a State in Apache Land," *Overland Monthly* 24 (August, 1894): p. 204.
[74] Rodolfo Acuña, *Occupied*...p. 76.
[75] See Sylvester Mowry, *Arizona and Sonora* (N.Y.: Harper and Row, 1864), p. 35.
[76] Adela Sloss-Vento, *Alonso S. Perales: Struggles for the Rights of Mexican Americans* (San Antonio: Penca Press, 1977), p. 48-50.
[77] Mario Barrera, "Class Segmentation and the Political Economy of the Chicano," (1900-1930)., *New Directions of Chicano Scholarship*..pp.169-170.
[78] Evidence of the dual wage standard is cited by Acuña from *Report of Frederick Brucknow to the Sonoran Exploring and Mining Company upon the History Prospects and Resources of the Company in Arizona* (Cincinnati, Ohio, Railroad Record, 1859), pp. 17-18. Also cited in the *Fourth Annual Report of the Sonora Exploring and Mining Company*, March, 1860 (N.Y.: Minns, 1860), pp. 12-14.
[79] Mario T. García, "Obreros: The Mexican Workers of El Paso, 1900-1920," (originally for dissertation University of California at San Diego, 1975), p. 24.
[80] Leonard Pitt *The Decline of the Californios: A Social History of the Spanish Speaking Californians, 1846-1890* (Berkeley: University of California, 1970), p. 26. Most of the information of the second chapter concerning war and annexation (1846-1848) is from Hubert Howe Bancroft, *History of California* (San Francisco: 1886), V 1846 to 1848; George Tays, *Revolutionary California: The Political History of California from 1820 to 1848* (rev. ed.; Ph.D. dissertation, University of California at Berkeley, 1943); Bernard de Voto, *The Year of the Decision, 1846* (second edition; Boston, 1961) and Otis A. Singletary, *The Mexican War* (Chicago, 1960).
[81] Leonard Pitt, *The Decline*...p. 30.
[82] Rodolfo Acuña, *Occupied*...p. 98.

[83] See Doris Marion Wright, "The Making of Cosmopolitan California: An Analysis of Immigration, 188-1870," *California Historical Society Quarterly*, XIX (December, 1940), pp. 323-343; also in XX (March, 1941), pp. 65-79.

[84] See Richard Morefield, "Mexicans in the California Mines, 1848-1853," *California Historical Quarterly* 24 (March, 1956): 38.

[85] Carey McWilliams, *North...*p. 128.

[86] See William B. Secrest, *Juanita: The Only Woman Lynched in the Gold Rush Days* (Fresno, California: Saga West, 1967), pp. 8-29; also Secrest in *El Clamor Público*, (April 4 and 16, 1857).

[87] Carey McWilliams, *North...*, p. 130.

[88] For a detailed description of rebel activities, see Chapter X entitled "Cow Country Bandidos, 1856-1859," in Leonard Pitt's *The Decline...*pp. 167-180.

[89] Quoted by both McWilliams and Acuña, original source is Robert Greenwood, *The California Outlaw: Tiburcio Vásquez* (Los Gatos, California: Talisman Press, 1960), p. 12.

[90] Carey McWilliams, *North...*p. 130.

[91] See Richard Griswold del Castillo, *La Raza Hispano-Americana*: "The Emergence of an Urban Culture among the Spanish Speaking in Los Angeles, 1850-1880," (Dissertation, University of California at Los Angeles, 1974), p. 66.

[92] Carey McWilliams, *North...*p. 132.

PART II

THE XX CENTURY
MESTIZO/ CHICANO

CHAPTER V

MEXICAN/ CHICANO ADAPTATION,
RACISM & RESISTANCE

THE BACKGROUND : 1890-1939

After 1890, immigration from Mexico began to be felt in the Southwest, particularly between 1910 and 1920 when Mexico was in the throes of revolution, as the dictatorship of Porfirio Díaz was overthrown and various political factions fought for power. It was during Diaz's regime that *campesinos* lost their lands. It is estimated that 90% of the people of Mexico found themselves landless through the positivistic reforms that put most of the land into the hands of the wealthy and foreign speculators. Since the 1880's , Mexican labor was extensively used in the construction of the Southern Pacific and Santa Fe lines in the Southwest. Mexicans comprised seventy percent of the section crews and ninety percent of the principal western lines. As they extended northward to Kansas, Nebraska and Chicago, settlements grew along the lines. The colonies were the outgrowths of labor camps. Seasonal in nature, the rail lines fed workers to other industries and consequently was continually recruiting additional workers in Mexico. The wages earned by Mexicans were a dollar a day, considerably below similar labor on middle western and eastern lines.[1] After 1905, Mexican labor extended through Colorado, Wyoming, Utah, Montana, Idaho, Oregon and Washington. The mining booms of the 1880's and the 1890's, the expansion of railroads, the exclusion of the Chinese in 1882, the tariffs on sugar, the new specialized farming equipment requiring seasonal labor and the Reclamation Act of 1902 contributing to irrigation of large tracts of land, all motivated the migration northward. By 1910, 222,000 new settlers had entered with estimates ranging as high as 500,000.[2] As early as 1890 Mexican labor had been following the harvest of cotton in the cotton producing fields of east Texas. As mechanization increased, Anglo-Texans began to substitute transient Mexican labor for African-American and poor white sharecroppers and tenants. Edward David saw a meeting of feudalism and the plantation system[3] and from this meeting came the large scale farming based on migratory labor. Mexicans were quickly blamed for the disappearance of rural schools and churches since poor white sharecroppers were replaced by Mexicans. Clearly, Mexicans were not the cause in view that they were recruited for employment. Recruitment continued to Arizona (7,269 in 1919), the Mesilla Valley of New Mexico, the Imperial Valley and the San Joaquín Valley of California.[4]

In South Texas, the new era had come into place. Montejano cites several factors that led to the demise of ranch society: "The homesteads of Kansas and Nebraska had been exhausted, fertile Indian land had already been overrun, and thousands of midwestern farmers were seeking large tracts of land they could not possibly buy at home. The technological advances of the day--dry farming techniques, irrigation systems, the refrigerated rail car--now made the successful pursuit of intensive farming in the semi-arid southwest possible."[5] Jovita González depicts the situation between Anglo-Americans and Mexican Americans along the border as determining race relations. She alludes to "Mexicans" treated as an inferior race, segregated in their own quarters and refused admittance at restaurants, movies, bathing beaches, etc. The old Mexican middle class elite families were bitter about the changes. Montejano cites Jovita González who recorded the feelings of an established middle class Mexican-American:

> We, Texas-Mexicans of the border, although we hold on to
> our traditions, and are proud of our race, are loyal to the
> United States in spite of the treatment we receive by some of
> the new Americans. Before their arrival, there were no racial
> or social distinctions between us. Their children married
> ours, ours married theirs and both were glad and proud of
> the fact. But since the coming of the "white trash" from the
> north and middle west we felt the change. They made us feel
> for the first time that we were Mexicans and they considered
> themselves our superiors.[6]

The Anglo-American new comer did not distinguish between the aristocratic or middle class old Spanish families and the landless Mexican campesino/peon. Now a Mexican-American was simply a Mexican in the pejorative sense. This lack of respect for Mexican culture invariably led to civil abuses and deaths of the now underclass Mexican-American. A Spanish-Speaking sheriff explained the situation candidly: "A large share of the border troubles could be explained by the reckless manner in which undisciplined "pistol toters" Rangers and other civil officers have been permitted to act as trial judge, jury and executioners."[7]

By 1915, Texas-Mexicans cornered and abused, created an armed insurrection in which hundreds of incidents were recorded. The insurrection was the work of the Plan de San Diego which called for the independence from Yankee Tyranny and an independent republic to consist of Texas, New Mexico, Arizona, Colorado and California. Anglo-American Texans speculated on ties to Mexican revolutionary leaders either Victoriano Huerta or Venustiano Carranza; others saw a German connection or just plain banditry. After an attack on the Las Norias Division of the King Ranch by sixty Mexican raiders carrying a red flag with the inscription "igualdad e independencia" (equality and independence) the Texas Rangers began a manhunt killing 300 Mexicans according to citizens and army officers.[8] Many Mexican and Mexican-Americans fled to Mexico seeking refuge while Anglo-Americans left for Corpus Christi or San Antonio. By 1916 state militia from Virginia, Iowa, Illinois, the Dakotas, Minnesota, Indiana, Nebraska, Louisiana and Oklahoma were ordered to the Valley. It is estimated that 50,000 combat ready soldiers were stationed in the Lower Rio Grande

Mexican-American/Chicano Migrant Families going to the *Piscas al Norte*

Valley. Peace was eventually established with the cessation of protest notes and the threat of an American attack and bombardment of Matamoros. During this conflict, as many as 5,000 Mexicans were killed in the Valley.[9]

While it is clear that Texas Rangers hated Mexicans and saw themselves as the pillars of justice, their function as officers went beyond into outright civic lawlessness. From reports of army officers, there seemed to have been an unspoken campaign of extermination of Mexicans. It was often heard "We have to make this a white man's country." Many well established and landed Spanish-Speaking natives of Texas of Mexican origin were driven away by Texas Rangers who told them, "If you are found here in the next five days you will be dead." Thus they were forced to abandon their property or sell at almost any price.[10] Sometimes the seizures were accompanied by the formality of signing bills of sale--at the point of a gun.[11]

Thus, the inclusion and dominance by the northern newcomers assumed an acute racial character, breaking old communal ties and replaced them with a new materialism and Hegemonic social structures. The underclass Mexicans/Mexican-Americans became a captive labor group and with that came the labor smuggler who developed a lucrative racket with Mexicans. This smuggler was commonly referred to as a coyote who crossed the border not only to organize crews but to get them across to the U.S. in violation of immigration regulations. This was accomplished by arranging the undocumented workers to jump the fence, conceal them in trucks or by finding the Rio Grande at night. Once across, they were turned over to a labor contractor called an *enganchista* who then sold each for fifty cents to a dollar to agricultural, railroad or mining employers. The employers were charged a fee for the supply of laborers; the contractors charged the workers for transportation and subsistence en route. Sometimes crews were stolen at force of arms to resell to another employer.[12]

While the Mexican workers dominated in numbers with regard to vegetables, fruit and truck crops (up to eighty-five percent), they were certainly recognized as *betabeleros* or workers in the *piscas* (harvests-usually cotton). Originally the sugar beet companies used trains to haul Mexicans but later it was handled by Mexican truckers and contractors. Most of the trucks were stake trucks not intended for passenger transportation. Most often 50-60 Mexicans were huddled like animals with only a tarpaulin thrown over their heads to conceal them. The trip standing lasted forty to fifty hours. Once employed, they could only expect exceedingly low wages, miserable health and housing conditions, child labor sickness and disease. Large employers deliberately isolated Mexicans, discouraging all outside contracts, limiting there to certain categories of work. This severely limited opportunities for acculturation, personal and economic advancement. During times of depression, Mexicans became the scapegoats, a pattern of repression that was to be repeated in the rest of the XX century. Capitalist interests welcomed Mexicans as temporary laborers but not as residents. The *Partido Liberal Mexicano* threatened many Anglo-Americans who believed Mexicans were about to revolt. The Los Angeles based *magonistas* encouraged labor organization among Mexicans, supporting the AFL's appointment of Juan Ramirez as the organizer in 1910-1911 as well as the formation of the *Jornaleros Unidos.*[13] When the economy dissipated in 1921, a depression caused heavy unemployment; once again, Mexicans were the scapegoats. Corporate interests felt no obligation to thousands of Mexicans left stranded and destitute. Acuña cites a passage out of the Mexico City newspaper *El Universal* stating, "when they arrived at Phoenix, a party of Mexican workers were taken to Tempe and introduced to a concentration camp that looks like a dung heap."[14] The scene was repeated in Kansas City, Chicago and Colorado. In Ranger, Texas, terroristic Anglo-Americans dragged a hundred men, women and children from their tents, beat them and ordered them out of town.[15]

By 1929, the Great Depression had reduced Mexicans considerably. In one decade the entering population decreased from 238,527 to only 8,737. Special bills were introduced to restrict immigration of Mexicans on the basis of widespread unemployment, racial undesirability and un-Americanism. Between 1931 and 1934, thousands of Mexicans/Chicanos, many of them U.S. citizens, were sent back. It is estimated that as many as half a million found themselves back in Mexico. About one third were repatriated and some sixty percent of whom had children born in the U.S. to

Chicanos the term repatriation was merely a euphemism for deportation.

In South Texas, political power was in the hands of cliques of merchants, lawyers and big landowners. Loyalty and allegiance was expected from the poor and dependent workers. Generally, the two parties consisted of Reds and Blues, the former for Republicans and latter for Democrats. Distinctions were not clear between the two; essentially it took on the character of power politics, personal enmity and hatred and rival bossism. It was not unusual for political bosses to use names of dead citizens or bring in a truckload of undocumented workers from Mexico to insure victory.

As Texas moved into modernity in the 20's, socially it was characterized by wage-laborers, impersonal contracts and a rational market orientation. Moreover, it was characterized by segregationist policies which resembled the colonial Spanish caste system. Mexicans had to maintain separate quarters with regulated interracial contact. In the Rio Grande Valley the string of small communities stretching from Mission to Brownsville were divided into Mexican and American towns; it was highway 83 and the railroad tracks that served as the dividing line. This not only affected business but entertainment as well. Most important was the school segregation. Chicano/Mexican American school children never got to associate with Anglos until high school and the latter was usually not easily attained due to the oppressive system affecting Mexicans/Chicanos. From this emerged Mexican schools as early as 1902 and the practice continued even into the forties.[16]

> The patterns of segregation in the farm society did not have a clear single path; rather, as Montejano suggests, had different tendencies, directions even within the context of supremacy: There were in other words, various strategies for handling inferior races; which strategy was favored depended on the particular economic interests of class segments within the Anglo community. For growers and their allies, development meant importation and repression of Mexican laborers; for Anglo working farmers and wage laborers, development meant containment and exclusion of Mexicans... A third tendency emerges if the situation of the retailer dependent on the Mexican trade is considered. Such businessmen were concerned about

developing an internal market...a separate development... merchants always followed their best interests when it came to political matters.[17]

Thus the degree of racism depended on the extent of class composition of the Anglo-American community.

MEXICAN/CHICANO RESISTANCE MOVEMENTS IN THE SOUTHWEST

Mexican immigrants and Mexican Americans came to realize that the occupations given to them and the conditions under which they worked meant they were regarded as an inferior race. The Spanish-speaking communities felt the need to organize in self protection from Texas to California. One of the early strikes occurred in the panhandle in 1883 by several hundred cowboys. It is called the first attempt to form a union by "agricultural" workers in the United States. Part of the strike call was signed by Juan Gómez. In 1903, Mexican and Japanese workers went on strike in Ventura, California. In 1927 the *Confederación de Uniones Obreras Mexicanas* established in southern California, organized in twenty locals throughout the region. This organized labor union effort led to thousands of Mexican workers walking out of berry, onion and celery fields. Strikers were often seriously wounded by police and had difficulty in securing medical aid. Growers concurrently, spent thousands of dollars in the employment of armed guards recruited for strike breaking detective agencies. The strikes in California in the thirties were exacted also in Arizona, Idaho, Washington, Colorado, Michigan and the Lower Rio Grande Valley in Texas. And in every case, strikes were broken by the use of violence and was followed with deportations. Mexican workers for the most part acted alone without the support of organized labor i.e. CIO or AFL.

Previously Anglo-American critics had argued that Mexicans/Mexican Americans were not assimilable; yet in two decades, they learned to protest in typically American fashion against "white trade only" signs in business establishments, segregation in seating arrangements in cinemas, residential restrictions to real estate, segregation in the school system and discrimination before the law. In New Mexico, several thousand coal miners employed by the Gallup-American Company went on strike, the area subsequently placed under martial law for six months.

When eviction writs were ordered, a bloody riot ensued. Hundreds of workers were arrested but news of their struggle reached Santa Fe and Taos where writers and artists flocked to Gallup to aid the struggle of the miners. It was here that a miner from Chihuahua organized the *Liga Obrera de Habla Española* which attested to a membership of 8,000. In the end, criminal proceedings were dismissed and strikers were able to win relief rights. Unfortunately, Jesús Pallares, the founder of the workers league was arrested and deported to Mexico. In addition to labor movements the Spanish-speaking also created civic organizations that dealt with citizenship and the civil liberties of all Mexican-American citizens. Early in the XX Century mutual aid societies or organizations known as *mutualistas* formed everywhere there were Spanish-speaking populations; their aim was to protect the needs of the Spanish-speaking in fellowship, security and recreation. Their motto was *Patria, Unión y Beneficiencia*, a unifying symbol that spread from the southwest to the mid-west in a variety of organizations that ranges from apolitical to reformist, to radical. These organizations were numerous representing both moderate/middle class activities as well as activist-radical pursuits. A common problem was (and still is) intra- and intergroup fights. Power/leadership problems stemming from the "*chingón* complex" often lead to splits and/or disappearance of organizations. By the twenties, second generation Mexican Americans/Chicanos began to move away from the more "Mexican" mutualistic societies and created a number of organizations that were oriented toward citizenship and civil rights. These were aimed at American born or naturalized Spanish-speaking citizens. The orientation was not assimilation although many of its members were college educated i.e. lawyers, doctors, engineers; thus their orientation was social, economic, political and educational. They include *El orden de los Hijos de America* established in San Antonio in 1921, *the Knights of America* and the *Sons of America* (Corpus Christi). The key organization of national significance was the invention of attorney Alonso S. Perales of San Antonio, Texas. His mission begins in 1919 while riding the train to attend Washington State University; here he saw an Anglo-American commit a cowardly crime to a defenseless Mexican. From that day on he knew he had found his aim in life, to defend the rights of the

Spanish-Speaking. He conceived very early the idea of coalescing existing organizations and forming a league that would represent the ideals for leadership and defense of *Mexicanos* throughout the state. Adela Sloss-Vento states in her work on Alonso Perales:

> The unity of Mexican-American citizens was the dream of Attorney Perales, a man of high moral ethics and principles who did not believe in compromising his priniciples for material gain. Rather than taking the easy road to financial and political success, he chose rather to struggle for the rights and advancement during his lifetime of his Raza.[18]

Miss Sloss-Vento further states in her conclusions that Alonso S. Perales encouraged unity among Mexican-Americans in Texas:

> He felt the Mexican-Texano should organize and unify so that he too could enjoy all the rights and privileges as the Anglos. He saw part of the solution in the education of the Mexican-American youth. He felt it was imperative that the youth be provided with the educational facilities and opportunities for advancement for a better tomorrow...[19]

With these perspicacious goals in mind, he formed *The League of Latin Americans* in Harlingen, Texas on August 14, 1927. He established eight councils in Harlingen, Brownsville, Laredo, Peñitas, McAllen, La Grulla, Encino and New Gulf Texas. It should be noted that the organizations *Sons of America* and *Knights of America* of Corpus Christi sponsored by Mr. Bernardo Garza did not join in the formation of the new league, although he was extended a personal invitation by Perales. A year later Perales was called upon by Washington to serve on several diplomatic missions in Cuba and Nicaragua. Writing from Managua, Nicaragua, Perales pleads with Mr. Bernardo Garza to persuade the two organizations Sons of America and *Knights of America* to join *The League of Latin Americans* stating further that he would be pleased if he (Bernardo) were to be elected President General of the league in the coming convention. In Mr. Garza's response, he graciously declines stating, "I would rather see the high position of President General fall upon a more intelligent person like you, Idar, Canales or some other. My intentions are good but I lack the education to be at the point of such an organization..."[20] While Perales was for unity, J.T.. Canales was skeptical regarding the admission of the Corpus Christi councils stating that they had not earned their mark in socio-civic affairs in defense of Pro-Raza pursuits.[21]

On the 19th of February, 1929, the Corpus Christi councils joined the League and later reorganized adding "United" to the original name ergo *League of United Latin American Citizens*. As has been pointed out previously, there has always been among the Spanish-Speaking power struggles often to the demise of many organizations. Often it is personal and individualistic but sometimes it is ideological. No sooner had the League been established; a rash of criticism and attacks were levied at Alonso Perales and J.T.. Canales. The problem here appears to be one of the Mexicans vs. Mexican Americans. Those that were critical were nationalists or Mexican officials working out of the U.S. e.g. *Consul General* of San Antonio. In defense, Perales states, "It is not strange that the consulates try to control Mexican-American organizations that are founded in the U.S. for their own political and anti-clerical propaganda and to exclude certain refugee elements, but what seems contradictory is that the *Consul General* of San Antonio is displeased for not obtaining control of Mexican-Americans who in any form have anything to do with the politics of Mexico."[22] It was not the intention of Perales to move toward assimilation and a departure of Mexican culture but rather a re-orientation towards education and leadership for the creation of newer generations who would not have to suffer the indignities of an inferior position. In his defense of J.T. Canales, he points to his integrity, a member of a highly respectable and distinguished family, a man of culture and liberal ideas, his love for his *Raza*, a member of Congress where he denounced the Texas Rangers for crimes committed to Mexicans... A person who risked his life and by his own choice his political position...his father was also appreciated for his integrity and love toward the Mexican people."[23]

The league eventually spread to twenty one states with its main strength centered in Texas. It is true that it promoted true and loyal citizens, the learning of English as important through the leadership of Bernardo Garza but the initial idea of Perales was to have a *Raza* that was educationally prepared to take on as citizens and leaders, the problems and inequities of this country. By inference it suggested "beating them at their own game" in order to rectify social, political, economical and educational discrimination. In my view both the mutualistas and the new Mexican American civic organizations (LULAC, GI Forum, etc.) aided in the unity and defense of the Spanish-Speaking. The mutualistas must be praised for their efforts on the local and regional levels. LULAC was an extension, a new approach that saw unity on a state and national level. Acuña candidly cautions that "Although it has become popular to criticize LULAC's middle class, integrationist approach, it should not be evaluated by present standards. Men like Alonso S. Perales and J.T.. Canales courageously defended the rights of Mexican in the United States. For years, LULAC was the only organization with a nationwide network. It also cut reliance on the Mexican consuls and concentrated on U.S. issues.[24] Integrationalist here does not mean assimilation as witnessed by the articles 7, 9, 11 and 22 of the LULAC constitution:

> We solemnly declare once and for all to maintain a
> sincere and respectful reverence for our racial origin of
> which we are proud... We shall destroy any attempt to
> create racial prejudices against our people and any
> infamous stigma which may be cast upon them, and we
> shall demand for them the respect and prerogatives which
> the constitution grants to us all...we shall denounce every
> act of peonage and mistreatment as well as the
> employment of our minor children of scholastic age.[25]

While the league denied it was a political organization, it left the door open for development of a national and political organization who would protect in the courts, the rights of the Spanish-Speaking in the United States. Very early, it established a fund for "mutual protection and for the defense of those of us who may be unjustly persecuted and for the education and culture of our people."[26]

The question of racism in the structuring of a new order merits consideration. Montejano refers to newcomer ethnocentrism and old time Texan prejudices as powerful influences in the shaping of the farm order. He contends that the new society with new class groups and class relations had a capacity to generate "indigenous" rationales for the ordering of people and that the specific mechanisms of separation could be best understood in terms of the division of labor in the farm order.[27] This new order expressed a social hierarchy where wood frame houses with paved streets and sewers were found in the Anglo-American neighborhood while the Mexican towns were represented by corrugated tin shacks, dirt roads and outdoor privies. Racial superiority by the Anglo-American called for the Mexican to assume a certain posture and a respectful tone; public buildings were considered "Anglo territory," Mexican women were to shop only on Saturdays during the early hours; Mexicans were allowed only counter and carry out service in Anglo-American cafés and all Mexicans were expected to be back in their Mexican town by sunset. This created two separate and distinct communities within Texas. Educational segregation usually extended to the fifth grade or sixth grade since, as administrators and growers noted, because "Mexicans rarely go that far." By the 20's, this no longer was true as the segregated school system expanded and Mexican junior and senior high schools began to appear.[28]

Specifically the Anglo American's prejudice stemmed from the notions of class and color. Generally, Mexicans were looked at as cross-breeds, off color race that could never be equal to whites; a Mexican no matter how educated, could not be as good as a white man because "God did not intend him to be...He would have made him white if He had."[29] Mexican inferiority, while generally an Anglo American colonial racial attitude, took on specific views in Texas. The older native Anglo-Americans related to ideas of hatred towards Mexicans as a result of the U.S.-Mexico war whereas transplanted southerners with an ingrained color prejudice, saw Mexicans as they had done with black labor; some midwesterners saw Mexicans as "domesticated Indians."[30] Newcomers to the area were also concerned with hygiene and notions of germ theories. Mexicans were seen as filthy, unsanitary, their habits repulsive to the Anglo-American newcomer who had been inculcated with anti-germ theories for generations. Montejano appropriately categorizes the meaning of "dirty Mexicans." "Dirty" as used by Anglo-Americans here could be used as synonym for dark skin color and inferiority; it could mean the position of a lowly farm laborer or the horrible living conditions of Mexican towns.[31]

It should be pointed out, that Anglo-American controlled cities relegated Mexicans to virtually no facilities in their side of town, expecting simultaneously for them to pay taxes. Mexican housewives strived for neatness and cleanliness but only so much was possible considering the conditions given them. and when diseases like diphtheria and tuberculosis broke out, it was due to a great extent to the impoverished and deplorable conditions afforded to Mexican towns. This, coupled with undernourishment, broke down immune systems which led to disease among the poor.

McWilliams speaks of Mexican settlements as *colonias* varying in size of small homes or shacks to communities of four to 10,000 people. Most are located in unincorporated areas adjacent to a town or city usually the other side of the railroad track, a bridge, a river or a highway. Economic factors often determine sites i.e. low land values, cheap rents, low wages, little or no facilities. Most were unplanned, or outgrowths of labor camps. These more appropriately were satellites which were conveniently distant from the parent community. These *colonias* bring about social and psychological isolation breeding resentment and frustration, for being unable to break out of the cycle of poverty and the *colonia* complex.[32]

When Mexicans and Mexican-Americans began the migrant stream into the middle Western states, they came into much sharper and fuller contact with Anglo-American culture than in the racist Southwest. For those that did not harvest the crops from Ohio to Washington state, there were opportunities, particularly in Chicago and Detroit in the highly mechanized industries. *Solos* or single men numbering about one third of the labor force, intermarried and settled in Mexican communities.[33] Rather than seen as indigenous peoples or racial minorities, they were seen more as immigrant groups. In Los Angeles, San Antonio and El Paso, Texas house courts multiplied as Mexican housing became acute. The eastside of Los Angeles and pocket settlements i.e. Chávez Ravine, Happy Valley, *El Hoyo*, began to spread into old Mexican settlements.

By 1942, after the Japanese had been excluded from the West Coast, Mexicans once again became the scapegoats to the print media as Mexican crime and delinquency was overblown and anti-

Mexican sentiment began to flourish in a full scale offensive against the Mexican minority. Such was the "Case of the Sleepy Lagoon" in which fights between two gangs took place. The next day the body of a young man was found to which the autopsy surgeon noted that the death may have been by repeated hard falls on the rocky ground, similar to those seen on victims of auto accidents. What is strange is that none of the boys that were there the day before were called as witnesses and the old gravel pit was quickly dubbed "The Sleepy Lagoon"; the presses creating fanatic orchestration of crime and mystery quickly led the police to arrest seventeen youngsters in the largest mass trial for murder in the U.S. These boys were subsequently questioned, handcuffed to chairs and beaten for information by the police. The young defendants were not allowed to get haircuts or packages of clean clothes by orders of the prosecutor. The case was tried before a biased and prejudiced judge and conducted by a prosecutor who pointed to their manner of appearance as reasons for guilt; the atmosphere was out of intense community-wide prejudice which had been the product of the Hearst newspapers characterized by sensationalism, crime mongering and Mexican baiting. Following the expected conviction, the case was appealed and on Oct. 4, 1944, the District Court of Appeals in a unanimous decision reversed the conviction for lack of evidence. This marked the first time in the history of Los Angeles that Mexican-Americans had won an organized victory in the courts.

Concurrent to the activities of the "Sleepy Lagoon," was a disparaging report by Captain E. Duran Ayres, chief of "Foreign Relations Bureau" of the Los Angeles Sheriff's office. In addition to describing the social and public restrictions of foreigner's including American born Negroes and Mexicans, the differences in the manner a Caucasian and a Mexican fight, Captain Ayres concludes, incredibly, that the Indian or Latin has a inborn characteristic that has come down through the ages, the use of liquor--then the crimes of violence. In short, the chief law enforcement agency had categorically expressed that the Mexican/Latino minority possessed an inborn tendency to criminal behavior and to crimes of violence.

Roundups of Mexican youth in Los Angeles became folly. On August 10-11, 1942, the police raided Mexican neighborhoods arresting six hundred people on suspicion of robbery, suspicion of auto theft, suspicion of assault, etc. Newspapers replaced the word Mexican and devised a technique for baiting the Spanish-Speaking with the words "Zoot Suit" and "*Pachuco*." When youths were picked and photographed, they were labeled with the captions of "*Pachuco* Gangster" or "Zoot Suit hoodlum." Along with the new affluence of society during World War II, there was a revitalized ethnic pride and self awareness, a new consciousness of discrimination and prejudice. Out of this scenario arose the formation of barrio groups that commonly identified with the term *Pachuco*, probably borrowed from Pachuca, a town in Mexico. During these years, the jitterbug was in full swing and the outlandish zoot suit was in fashion. These groups adopted fashionable zoot suits as a signature of success. It could very well be that, had it not been for the much publicized "Zoot Suit Riots" of June 1943, it may have been a passing trend. Due to the existing and uneasy racial tensions a fight took place between Mexican/Chicano youths and U.S. sailors. For several nights afterwards, gangs of sailors went on a pogrom, driving through the barrios looking for and attacking Chicano youths while the police looked the other way. Acuña notes that a visible foe was the "alien" Chicano dressed in a zoot suit; moreover, sailors looking for prostitutes harassed and abused Chicanas. Sailors went on a rampage; they broke into Carmen Theater, tore Zoot suits off Chicanos and beat the youths. As a result, many Chicanos were arrested, while sailors were not charged. Word spread that *Pachucos* were fair game and that they could be attacked without fear of arrest.[34] The next night sailors returned with some 200 allies, hired twenty cabs and went on another attack of Chicano youths. None were charged with assault and the press portrayed them as heroes. On June 5, they marched four abreast down streets warning Chicanos to shed their Zoot suits or they would take them off for them. Lawlessness continued with the invasion of bars and other establishments. None was charged for the destruction of private property. On June 2, thousands of servicemen and civilians surged down main street and Broadway in search for *Pachucos*. The mob broke legs off stools to use as clubs, youths were left bleeding in the streets, a seventeen year old boy was beaten, arrested and was found by his mother in the police station naked and still bleeding. As preventive action, police arrested over 600 Chicano youths. Among the victims included Filipinos and Blacks. The major newspapers created sensational headlines praising the servicemen. Radio broadcasts contributed to the hysteria. The navy admiral D.W. Bagley washed his hands stating the sailors acted in "self defense against a rowdy element." Charges of racism were denied by city officials and were incensed when Eleanor Roosevelt commented in her column that the riots had been caused by "long-standing discrimination against Mexicans in the Southwest." A committee was appointed to investigate and make recommendations.[35] In the end little was done to implement the recommendations of the report.

Writing in the forties, George I. Sánchez underscores the origins of *Pachuquismo*, pointing to the thirties as a time when the seed was sown by "unintelligent educational measures, by discriminatory social and economic practices, by provincial smugness and self assigned 'racial'... Today we reap the whirlwind in youth whose greatest crime was to be born into an environment which, through various kinds and degrees of social ostracism and prejudicial economic subjugation, made them a caste apart, fair prey to the cancer of gangsterism".[36]

McWilliams echoes a similar explanation. "Discovering that his status approximates the second-rate school has the effect of instilling in the Mexican boy a resentment directed against the school and all it stands for. At the same time, it robs him of a desire to turn back to his home...All the attitudes he has learned in school now poison his attitude toward home, turning away from home and school, the Mexican boy has only one place where he can find security and status. This is the gang made up of boys exactly like himself who live in the same neighborhood, and who are going through precisely the same distressing process at precisely the same time"[37] The question of origin with respect to the *Pachuco* has various interpretations. Some say that the expression came from Mexico denoting resemblance to the gaily costumed people living in the town of this name; others apply it to border bandits in the vicinity of El Paso. Ricardo Sánchez, Chicano poet and activist (and former Pachuco from *"El Chuco"*) speaks of the dandies that came in from Las Vegas dressed in the fashion of Zoot suits in the forties which dramatically impacted the local Chicano population in the barrio. Chicano youths never used the term zoot suit; rather, they preferred "drapes." It is a costume that is perfect for dancing the jitterbug; it has peg topped pants with pleats, high waists up under the armpits, long loose-back coat, thick-soled bluchers and a ducktail haircut. Apart from being functional, they are sartorial, often a badge of defiance by the rejected against the outside world and most important a symbol of belonging to the inner group.[38] While McWilliams sees the *Pachuco* as more as a spontaneous development, its stereotype born in Los Angeles, others see Mexico's fascination with the Pachuco as portrayed by *Tin Tan*. In reality *Tin Tan* was closer to the *pocho* since there was always an intent to use expressions in English, a cool Mexican knowledgeable of the American mainstream. It was, in fact, the assimilation inference that became an affront to Mexican audiences and this led to the demise of the character of *Tin Tan*. Pachucos, in the U.S. were more than pocho; they had their own argot in caló, they rebelled against American institutions while still retaining many of the Mexican cultural markers (e.g. the virgin of Guadalupe tattooed to the back). In Los Angeles there were different types of *Pachuco* zoot suiters; those that highlighted coiffure, garb and select membership (dandies smelling pretty *macho*) and those that were *macho* using serious weapons chains, knives and sometimes guns.[39]

In terms of the zoot suit, allusions have already been made to the dandies in El Paso, its common use in Harlem, its various uses in Los Angeles, but Mauricio Mazón in his study thinks it may have been invented by a Saville Row tailor named E.P. Scholte towards the end of the XIX Century, adapting it from the officer's greatcoats.[40] It's popularity was national; Clark Gable, Frank Sinatra and Danny Kaye were to have work versions of the zoot suit. The zoot suit was both evocative and provocative. According to noted child psychologist Faitz Redd, the zoot suit provided "youth with a symbolic anticipation of being adult...through emphasis on adult hoarded pleasures and licenses, transgressions against taboos and supervision, rejection of adult values and behavior standards."[41]

The dress mode was neither pathological nor was it political; it was a social phenomenon that went a long with the music and affluence of the forties. Mazón in his study of *Pachuco* zoot suiters penetrates into the psychology and psychodynamics of the Spanish-Speaking youths of Los Angeles. He attests that zoot suiters were nonsensical because among other things, they took pride in their ambiguity...Zoot suiters transgressed the patriotic ideals of commitment incoherence and defiance...They seemed to be simply marking time while the rest of the country intensified the war effort...as to past and future, they had few opinions. However, irksome to adults, "the zoot suiters' flair for marking time--a characteristic richly conveyed through their animated contrariness-- was a healthy and appropriate phase in the process of maturation."[42] The world of the *Pachuco* zoot suiter was in direct opposition to the world of the defense worker and servicemen. Not only are lifestyle, culture and social ethic opposite but perhaps, as Mazón suggests, it is more of a question of understanding adolescence. He notes the connection between the adolescent moratorium, negative identity and ritual ordeals is inseparable from the processes of adolescent maturation.[43] Mazón, further, sees the symbolic annihilation of zoot-suiters as "a passive demonstration against the authority of the military, in which servicemen restored disparate feelings of depersonalization through identification with aggressor, role reversal, and projecting and displacing their anxieties. The immediate result was illusion of having renewed bonds of intimacy and camaraderie with civilians and a rekindling of group solidarity."[44] The tragedy in the end was that it "confirmed" the "criminality" of Mexican/Chicano youth promoting a stigma that was to be institutionalized by youth authorities and law enforcement officials. The injurious indictment was the projection of delinquency, deviance and marginality, a perception that was to affect succeeding generations. Studies on the Mexican and the Mexican/Chicano (Paz, Ramos, Servín) have unfortunately emphasized marginality, inferiority and hopelessness. Part of the problem was the inability to associate themselves into barrio psycho-socio-political realities. These were different forms of the existing theme of annihilation, i.e. cultural, historical political. While McWilliams ardently defends the Mexican/Chicano youth and places him within the context of social history, he lapsed into hyperbole with a one dimensional approach. Octavio Romano and Luis Valdez give credence to the concept of resistance to assimilation in relation to political consciousness.[45] In summation, Mazón contends that "the romance of victimization was a group defense mechanism that reiterated the historically recognized vulnerability of the community to racist, xenophobic and nativist attack."[46]

In attempting to globally understand the Mexican/Chicano Pachucos and the zoot suit riots, one must not try to perceive the phenomena through one focus representative of one discipline. The various historical, political, sociological, anthropological and psychological studies are all valid. One needs to integrate and synthesize the various approaches observing the roots and origins of the current situation and understanding that there is a reason for the marginal existence of thousands of deprived Spanish-Speaking citizens struggling in *colonias* and *barrios*[47] with minimal opportunity to advance within a system that caters to many interests and profit. Ultimately, one must question moreover, the ingrained colonial prejudices regarding color, race, religion and culture that persist into the 21st century in the U.S. Perhaps then, we can see Mexican/Chicano youths reacting to an environment that is not fit for self realization but rather one that narrowly defines the boundaries of survival.

PUBLIC EDUCATION AND POLITICAL ORGANIZATION

As previously stated, after World War II, Anglo-American society experienced profound technological and social changes and similarly, so did the Mexican/Chicano community. Now Chicanos understood they were entitled to the full protection under the law. They wanted fuller participation in the governance process as grievances against unfair employment, unequal education and unequal access to public facilities continued. Their numbers increased visibly as their organizations became more aggressive in suing for the civil rights of the Spanish-Speaking.

Exclusion of Mexican/Chicanos from public facilities, schools, trade unions, juries and voting remained in many parts of the country. Alonso S. Perales brings the central issues to the public in his study of discrimination against Mexican-Americans in over a hundred fifty towns in Texas.[48] In the fair employment practices act hearing, subcommittee of the committee on Education and Labor of the Seventy Ninth Congress of the U.S. Senate, Alonso S. Perales Chairman of the Committee of One Hundred , presents testimony of the unfair labor practices in Texas, particularly San Antonio, Kelly Filed, and Shell Oil Company; also, racial discrimination in restaurants where in a case from Fredricksburg, three Spanish-Speaking servicemen in uniform were refused service in the downtown cafe; likewise, the case of Private Tomás Garza, native born citizen of Ozona, Texas who was refused the purchase of Coca Cola because Mexicans were not allowed to buy refreshments. When Private Garza objected, the sheriff arrived with pistol in hand and ordered him out. When Private Garza tried to report the incident to his captain by telephone, the local operator refused to make the connection. Four months later the incident was repeated, this time for Private Arturo Ramirez and his wife; as before, they were refused refreshments because they were of Mexican descent. Private Ramirez was killed in action in France, July 10, 1944.[49]

Segregation in schools in the forties was challenged in 1946 in southern California where Judge Paul J. McCormick of the U.S. District Court heard the Méndez v. Westminister School District Case, declaring the segregation of Mexican children unconstitutional. By April 14, 1947, the Ninth U.S. Circuit Court of Appeals declared further that Mexicans and other children were entitled to "the equal protection of the laws" and that neither language nor race could be used as a reason for segregation. A year later (June 15, 1948) Judge Bon H. Rice Jr. U.S. District Court, Western District of Texas concluded (Delgado v. the Bishop Independent School District) that Mexican childrens' rights under the fourteenth amendment had been violated.[50]

In retrospect, during the mid nineties of the XIX Century when Mexican-Americans began to lose lands and socio-political rights, Anglo-American leaders sought to extend their dominance in the cultural domain. This was seen in the legislation mandating the speaking of English in public schools and the restriction of the use of Spanish in public affairs during the rest of the century. There was a disparaging attitude by Anglo-Americans toward Spanish that still exists in Texas today. In Austin in 1995, television and radio announcers still echo colonial "gringo" mispronunciations of Spanish words, e.g. "Manshak" for Manchaca, "Guadaloop" for Guadalupe and refuse to correct them even after University professors point out their ignorance.[51]

Although Mexican/Tejanos were relegated to a subordinate position in the new social and economic order, they showed great resilience in adapting to their circumstances. They continued, as could be expected, to practice their own traditions, maintain their Spanish language and sponsor their own social activities. It was a position that was forced upon them by the segregated oriented Anglo-American who relegated them to their own "reservations" in dilapidated Mexican towns across the tracks. From this sprang cultural patterns, linguistic forms and social organizations that reflected the biculturalism.[52]

Despite innumerable obstacles, Spanish-Speaking parents enrolled their children wherever they could, i.e. religious schools, public schools, private schools. Catholic schools were a natural course given the religion of most Mexican/Tejanos, although some attended Presbyterian schools. Private Mexican schools could be formed throughout the state. My father still recalls attending a "Mexican school" near Riviera, Texas. Unfortunately, Mexican Tejano children in rural areas were discouraged from attending school by landowners, "They were subjected to *rancho* schools, deplorable and unsightly thatched huts with dirt floors (*jacales*). In the XX century, increased Mexican immigration into Texas had a significant impact not only on the existing communities but on the educational institutions as well. This provided a new problem of governance, curriculum and administration. There were the special problems of overcrowded conditions, overage of students, irregular attendance, late enrollment in the fall and early withdrawal in the spring. Children, moreover, could not relate to the instructional methods or the language of the instruction. By 1920, the rapid growth and distribution of the Mexican/Tejano school age population, forced educators and policymakers to consider, what was know as the "Mexican problem," in the schools. An early study by Prof. H.T. Manuel of the University of Texas revealed (1) Mexican/Tejano school age children were increasing at a faster rate than the Anglo-American or African-American population, (2) the majority of these children knew little English and in general they did not know how to read Spanish; thus, having a dual language deficiency.[53], (3) most of these students came from poor working class families, (4) Mexican/Tejano children were not provided with equal opportunities because of racial prejudice and were either systematically denied school facilities or else provided with limited

Public School drinking facilities for Mexican-American children in the thirties.

and inferior educational provisions. and (5) Mexican/Tejano children did not do well in school where low attendance and high "push out rates" were common and many did not make it beyond the fourth grade.

Out of this surfaced the explanation of underachievement due to racial and/or cultural inferiority by prejudiced educators.[54] The other interpretation focused on poverty, migratory labor patterns, inferior educational opportunities, inappropriate curriculum and prejudice by Anglo-American school officials.[55] In the coming years this debate would resurface with race arguments predominating. Segregation of Mexican/Tejano children was not based on constitutional or statutory grounds but on school board actions and administrative regulations reflecting the desires of the dominant group population i.e. they did not want Mexican/Tejano students attending school with Anglo children regardless of their standing, economic status, language capabilities or place of residence. Guadalupe San Miguel Jr. contends that on the one hand state school officials supported and developed the English only program for purposes of assimilation in the cultural norm, and on the other hand, the exclusionist behavior of public school officials through segregated facilities, discrimination and unequal treatment; this contradictory scenario discouraged the Mexican/Tejano children from learning the language and customs educators were trying to teach them and by consequence, promoted poor school performance.[56]

In addition to economic deprivation, political manipulation and loss of social status, Mexicans/Tejanos were accused of being disloyal to the United States. Also they became the recipients of increasing violence directed at all Mexicans/Tejanos and as targets were denied continually justice in the courts with heightened contempt shown toward them by the Anglo-American population. Mexicans, for example, were brutally murdered and lynched by vigilante groups or by law enforcement agencies themselves. This contempt was echoed even in the Texas legislature where Attorney J.T.. Canales, as the only Mexican/Tejano state representative was referred to as the "greaser from Brownsville." In an investigation of the Texas Rangers triggered by J.T.. Canales, witnesses testified that the Texas Rangers, local peace officers and citizens had killed (during a decade (1910-1920)) Mexicans ranging from 200 to 5,000. Canales' outspoken defense elicited a member of the much despised Texas Rangers to threaten his life.[57] Mexican/Tejano leaders began to conduct legal challenges, or journalistic exposé by judicial, administrative and educational agencies. Boycotts, strikes and the new social and civic organizations throughout the states became the method of defense against acts of physical and cultural violence by the Anglo-American establishment.

While organizing efforts beginning in 1910 continued through the twenties, it was not until a unified state-wide organization was founded, that an effective attack on social and political inequality was possible. As cited before, the concept of the current LULAC organization was the invention of Alonso S. Perales. Essentially there are two phases: (1) the initial unification and coalition of existing social civic groups of Mexican/Tejanos in Harlingen, Texas (1927-*The League of Latin Americans*) and (2) the continuance of the first phase in a new organized format, adding the words "United" and "citizens" to the existing *League of Latin Americans*.

The latter was accomplished in 1929 in Corpus Christi, Texas under the leadership of Ben Garza. The members of LULAC were either born in the U.S. or were naturalized; they constituted printers, lawyers, business-persons and college trained individuals. Middle class in thrust, it called for the learning of English and the training to be good citizens, "To develop within the members of our race, the best, the purest, and more perfect type of true and loyal citizen of the United States of America."[58] San Miguel Jr. argues, however, that the making of citizens was not the major concern of LULAC since over half were already citizens; "Rather they were more concerned with the making of active citizens who would practice their citizenship by participating in the dominant political, economic and social institutions of the land."[59]

By the forties, Mexican-Americans were appointed to leadership positions on several federal and state committees e.g. Carlos E. Castañeda, professor in Latin-American history (University of Texas-Austin) and George I. Sánchez, a former president of LULAC in 1941, were aware of the need for curricular reform, particularly as it reflected the increase awareness of Spanish-Speaking children of Texas; Sánchez encouraged the development of curricular materials that projected linguistic, cultural and socio-economic backgrounds. This led to a series of Inter-American Relations Conferences or Forums. Moreover, Sánchez was in favor of a general campaign to educate the English-speaking and to inform them of the need to eliminate discriminatory practices against the Spanish-speaking people. Within state-wide committees, strong measures like litigation against local school districts were opposed by H.T. Manuel, Thomas Sutherland and Pauline R. Kibbe whereas George I. Sánchez, Carlos Castañeda and Alonso S. Perales favored anti-discrimination legislation and litigation.

Even the Catholic Church organized conferences regionally to discuss the problems of the Spanish-Speaking, an example of the latter was the National Catholic Welfare Conference of San Antonio on July 20, 1943. The old definition of the "Mexican problem" in the public schools was being redefined. The old definition looked at Mexican-Americans as a non-achieving homogenous group located in restricted urban areas or isolated rural areas. The poor performance was believed to be the result of limited intellectual capabilities or cultural attributes not conducive to achievement. It was believed that the solution was segregation where they would be taught English and American customs. The new definition saw them as a diverse group of people i.e. settled rural, migratory, settled urban and scattered through predominantly Anglo-American areas. Another observation was the cultural, linguistic and geographic diversity. Interest in teaching Spanish not only to Anglo-Americans but also to the Spanish-Speaking was voiced by one Austin school teacher who stated: "The time has come when we should decide that our Hispano-Texans not be a people without language, speaking neither English nor Spanish well, but that they shall be bilingual people having a good, useful knowledge of both languages."[60]

Another social and civic organization that contributed to the struggle for equal rights for the Spanish-Speaking was the American G.I. Forum. Organized on March 26, 1948 by Hector P. García, a medical doctor in Corpus Christi, Texas, its purpose was not so much in obtaining benefits for the veteran but one that directed its efforts to the family of the veteran as well i.e. to "strive for the procurement of all veterans and their families, regardless of race, color or creed, the equal privileges to which they are entitled under the laws of our country."[61] Fighting discriminatory practices in all public institutions as well as the struggle for educational equality became a primary concern for the G.I. Forum under the leadership of Dr. García. As with LULAC, the G.I. Forum considered education as "the principle weapon to fight the many evils affecting our people;" their motto became: "Education is Our Freedom and Freedom Should be Everybody's Business." Mexican-Americans were compelled to litigate against segregationist practices between 1946-1957. During the first seven years of the 1950's, there were approximately fifteen cases of discrimination in the public schools filed. Still, the mid and late 50's, called an "era of subterfuge" by San Miguel Jr., continued to react with a multitude of evasive practices which included freedom of choice plans, selected student transfer, transportation plans, classification systems based on language or scholastic ability--all these were utilized by school districts to maintain segregated schools.[62]

The restlessness of the sixties fueled by the growing black civil rights movement, the federal government's war on poverty and the anti-war sentiment, also affected the Mexican-American population whose moral outrage at governmental insensitivity toward all Mexican-Americans had been expressed by LULAC and the G.I Forum. For the first time in history Mexican Americans had played an important role in presidential and statewide elections. New organizations independent of regular political parties sprang e.g. PASO, the Political Association of Spanish-speaking Organizations; its purpose was to assist the Raza in gaining political influence. It's demands were noted and supported by a number of legislators. It also contributed to the political take over of the Crystal City elections in 1963.

At the federal level, Mexican Americans were ignored as a minority since the majority of federal programs were directed at the African-American community. As the Johnson administration neglected Mexican Americans in federal programs and appointments, when Cabinet hearings were held in El Paso instead of a White House Conference on Mexican American problems, the list of speakers excluded the more important voices of the time; César Chávez (California), Reies Tijerina (New Mexico), Rudolfo (Corky) González (Colorado).[63] At the hearings, a group of invited

Mexican American/Chicano leaders decided to walk out of the conference and hold an alternative conference in the *barrios* of El Paso; this was called *La Raza Unida*. While Mexican American leaders called for increased opportunities in all areas of American life in the hearings, the *Raza Unida*, while similar in goals, was militant in its approach. They looked towards César Chávez and Reies López Tijerina for inspiration; they were exemplary of a new mood that proclaimed that "the time of subjugation, exploitation, and abuse of human rights of *La Raza* in the United States is hereby ended forever...we commit ourselves to *La Raza*, at whatever costs."[64] Student and community militancy began to view LULAC and G.I. Forum as relatively ineffective since now confrontation was the most effective means to gain access for the excluded Chicano. High school "blow outs" or walkouts and college demonstrations for the development of Chicano studies programs took place in the late sixties and early seventies. The new actors in the socio-political arena in addition to the increase in militant organizations led to the intensification in the struggle for civil rights. Newer and more specialized professional organizations appeared to fill the needs of the times. One such organization was MALDEF.

MALDEF's creation is attributed to Pete Tijerina, a San Antonio attorney who was disenchanted with the lack of representation of Mexican Americans on Texas juries. Realizing the lack of financial resources available for jury discrimination suits, he contacted Jack Greenberg of the NAACP who advised he consult with Bill Poncus of the Ford Foundation about funds for establishing a Mexican American legal defense fund. After organizing committees to represent five southwestern states, the Ford Foundation awarded MALDEF 2.2 million dollars over five years to be spent on civil rights legal work, 250,000 of which to be channeled for scholarships to Chicano law students.

Unlike LULAC and G.I. Forum, as San Miguel observes, MALDEF did not use litigation only after all other remedies had failed; rather, it used the courts as the primary instrument to effect change.[65] In the early years, MALDEF's litigation strategy was reactive; it engaged in litigation haphazardly, without much formal planning. In the later years, it initiated internal administrative changes and became more selective in its court cases. Of its many litigation efforts, in the end the Supreme Court was forced to decide whether Mexican Americans were part of the white population, or pair them with the Black population or define Mexican Americans as an identifiable minority and pair them with Anglo-American students. The latter assumed that Mexican Americans had been subjected to pervasive official discrimination. The Court, in the end, decided that Mexican Americans for desegregation purposes were constitutionally entitled to recognition as an identifiable minority. Once the legal status of Mexican Americans was established, MALDEF began to concentrate on bilingual/bicultural education in desegregated settings as a solution to the special needs of Mexican American school children. Two strategies were formulated: (1) initiated by MALDEF was the introduction to bilingual programs as part of the comprehensive desegregation remedies in communities with large numbers of Mexican American children and (2) the use of legislation, initiated by two Mexican American legislators State Senator Joe Bernal and State Representative Carlos Truán. After much political maneuvering on both sides, the Mexican American legislative caucus and some members of the Texas Association for Bilingual Education failed to convince the task force to include bilingual education for all grades; still, "they had persuaded the task force to recommend the expansion of bilingual education through the sixth grade, to incorporate the philosophy of bilingual education in the introduction of its report and to recommend special language programs for LEP students in all grades."[66] In retrospect, Mexican Americans in their challenge to the discriminatory and assimilationist character of public education were able to produce notable accomplishments. Yet much like the existing cycles of conservatism/liberalism wavering between decades, subtle segregation and assimilative practices likewise, make their appearance from time to time. On the positive side, Mexican Americans made strides by eliminating most of the exclusionary practices in education and increased their access to all levels of the educational system particularly to secondary and postsecondary institutions. They eliminated the no-Spanish rule, verbal racist remarks by school personnel, rigid cultural dress codes, and exclusion of Mexican American cultural heritage within the curriculum and finally, the effects of the leadership established the illegality and unconstitutionality of discriminatory practices e.g. segregation based on national origin. On the negative side, the conservative decade of the Republican eighties saw Mexican Americans placed in segregated schools, in vocational programs and in remedial programs. In some places, they were denied access to Special Education programs i.e. the gifted, advanced classes in English, mathematics and computers. The curriculum in most schools continued to be assimiliationist in theory and fact. English became primary in bilingual education programs and Mexican American culture/history classes declined at the secondary and post secondary levels. San Miguel Jr. attests to four fundamental errors in the strategies of the Mexican American leadership: (1) they concentrated on influencing educational policies rather than on replacing their actions (2) their challenges to discrimination focused almost exclusively on administrative practices while finance and governance were inadequately challenged, (3) they failed to identify and eliminate the root cause of educational inequality i.e. the opposition by local school officials who circumvented anti-discrimination mandates, and (4) the most important reason for the failure to eliminate education inequality was the continuing impotence of the Mexican American community. Political power as well as important policy-making or executive positions for Mexican Americans were missing for basic reforms in schools. The dual system of instruction continues as language minority children are placed in segregated school facilities. The assimilationist character of the curriculum continues as immersion and other forms of English Only language instruction for Mexican American children are established at the local school level.[67] There are several variables to consider as we close the XX century. Much like the immigration boom in the early part of the century which created a critical mass and a "Mexican problem" for dominant society, the current population explosion of the Spanish-Speaking will become a critical factor in the political process. With the power of the vote, the Spanish-Speaking will be able to elect school officials and legislators that are responsive to the socio/cultural/political and economic needs of the Spanish-Speaking Chicanos/ Latinos i.e. Mestizo-Americans of the United States.

ENDNOTES

[1] Carey McWilliams, *North*...p. 168.

[2] Acuña cites Jorge Bustamante, "Mexican Immigration and the Social Relations of Capitalism," (Notre Dame: Dissertation, 1975) p. 50.

[3] See Edward Everette Davis, *The White Scourge*, 1940.

[4]The Imperial Valley growers began recruitment of truckloads of Mexicans in units of 1,500 and 2,000; from 1924 to 1930, an average of 58,000 Mexicans came into the San Joaquin Valley.

[5] David Montejano, *Anglos and Mexicans in the Making of Texas, 1836-1986* (Austin: University of Texas Press, 1987), p. 103.

[6] Ibid., p. 115. See also Jovita González "America Invades the Border Towns" in *Our Racial and National Minorities*, ed. Francies J. Brown and Joseph S. Roucck, pp. 472-473.

[7] Emilio C. Forto "Actual Situation on the River Rio Grande," *Pan American Labor Press*, (September 11, 1918).

[8] David Montejano, *Anglos and Mexicans*.. p. 119; citing Frank C. Pierce, *A Brief History of the Lower Rio Grande Valley*, p. 114.

[9] Webb, *Texas Rangers*, p. 478.

[10] Cited by Montejano, p. 127. Originally the words of Spanish Sheriff Emilio Forto, "Actual Situation on the River Rio Grande."

[11] Ibid. See also Emma Tenayuca, Homer Brooks, "The Mexican Question in the Southwest," *Political Affairs* (March, 1939): 259.

[12] Carey McWilliams, *North*...p. 181.

[13] Rodolfo Acuña...*Occupied*, p. 305. See also the outstanding Mexican originator of the labor movement Ricardo Flores Magón who created *Regeneración*, a mouthpiece for economic and political activity from the U.S. See the issues of February 4 and February 18, 1911.

[14] Ibid., p. 131.

[15] Ibid. See also Mark Reiesler, *By the Sweat of Their Brows: Mexican Immigration in the United States, 1900-1940* (Connecticut: Greenwood, 1976), pp. 50-51, 53.

[16] David Montejano, *Anglos and Mexicans*... p. 160. Montejano cites Seguin, Texas in central Texas as the first Mexican school.

[17] David Montejano, *Anglos and Mexicans*..., p. 195.

[18] Adela Sloss-Vento. *Alonso S. Perales: His Struggles for the Rights of Mexican Americans* (San Antonio: Artes Gráficas, 1977), p. 77.

[19] Ibid., p. 111.

[20] Ibid., p. 21.

[21] Ibid., p. 24.

[22] Ibid., p. 27. For a detailed description of the formation of LULAC see Perales' *En defensa de mi Raza*, (San Antonio: Artes Gráficas, 1936-7).
[23] Ibid.
[24] Rodolfo Acuña, *Occupied*...p. 310.
[25] Moquín, Van Doren, Rivera, *A Documentary History*, pp. 280-281.
[26] Ibid., p. 281.
[27] David Montejano, *Anglos and Mexicans.*. pp. 162-163.
[28] Ibid., p. 168. Originally from the Taylor Collection No. 101-69.
[29] This opinion reflects responses to agricultural economist Paul Taylor's interviews of Anglo-American farmers. See P.S. Taylor Mexican labor, p. 433, 436, also Taylor Collection No. 20-192.
[30] Ibid., pp. 432, 446, 449.
[31] David Montejano, *Anglos and Mexicans in the Making of Texas, 1836-1986* (Austin: University of Texas Press, 1987), p. 227. See also the Paul Taylor, "Mexican Worker," p. 441. See also Doug Foley, *From Peones to Politicos: Ethnic Relations in a South Texas Town, 1900-1977.*(Austin: CMAS Monographs, 1977).
[32] Carey McWilliams, *North*...pp. 217-226. See chapter entitled "The Mexican Problem," and section five, "The Colonia Complex."
[33] Mario T. García, "La Familia: The Mexican Immigrant Family, 1900-1930" in *Work, Family, Sex Roles, Language* (Berleley:Tonatiuh-Quinto Sol, 1980) pp.120-122.
[34] Rodolfo Acuña, *Occupied*...p. 327, cites McWilliams, pp. 244-54.
[35] See *The Los Angeles Times*, July 10, 1943.
[36] Moquin, Van Doren, Rivera eds., *A Documentary History*...p. 316.
[37] Carey McWilliams, *North*...p. 240.
[38] McWilliams cites the comments of Albert Deutsch, *Pan* June 14, 1943; also *Racial Digest*, July, 1943, pp. 3-7; *New York Times*, June 11, 1943.
[39] Joan W. Moore et al., *Homeboys, Gangs, Drugs and Prison in the Barrios of Los Angeles*, pp. 71, 64-65. Exemplary of each are the antimacho gang called "Los Polviados" ("The Powdered Ones") and the macho type by The White Fence gang.
[40] Mauricio Mazón, *The Zoot-Suit Riots: The Psychology of Symbolic Annihilation* (Austin: University of Texas Press, 1984), p. 7. See also Alan Jenkins, *The Forties*, p. 103
[41] Mauricio Mazón citing Fritz Redd, "Zoot Suits: An Interpretation," *Survey Monthly* 79, No. 10 (October, 1943), p. 260.
[42] Ibid., p. 9
[43] Ibid.
[44] Ibid.

[45] Octavio Romano, "The Historical and Intellectual Presence of Mexican Americans," *El Grito* (Winter, 1969), pp. 39-40. Also Luis Valdez "Once Again, Meet the Zoot Suits," *Los Angeles Times*,(August 13, 1978), part 3, p. 3.

[46] Mauricio Mazón, The Zoot Suit...p. 121.

[47] See the holistic approach of James Diego Vigil, *Barrio Gangs: Street Life and Identity in Southern California* (Austin: University of Texas Press, 1988), p. 1. In his introduction he states: "The lives of the street youths who comprise the barrio gang reflect multiple stresses and pressures, which result in a multiple marginality. This multiple marginality derives from various interwoven situations and conditions that tend to act and react upon one another. Although interrelated, the unfolding and interpretation of these ecological, economic, social, cultural and psychological features of the street gang suggest a developmental sequence."

[48] Alonso S. Perales, *En defensa de mi Raza*, (San Antonio: Artes Gráficas, 1936) 2 vols.

[49] Alonso S. Perales, *Are We Good Neighbors?* (San Antonio: Artes Gráficas, 1948), pp. 122-123.

[50] Guadalupe San Miguel, Jr., *Mexican-American and the Campaign for Educational Equality in Texas, 1910-1981* (Austin: University of Texas Press, 1987), pp. 119-120.

[51] Originally published in the *Austin American Statesman* with the heading of "It's Burn it, Durn it, can't ya learn it?" Professor Arnoldo Carlos Vento had the most poignant remarks on the subject: " The evolution of language is one thing, Vento adds, but purposeful mispronunciation of foreign words, especially Spanish ones, isn't part of a linguistic evolution. Instead, Vento says, it's a colonial leftover that resists giving respect and legitimacy to the Spanish language. The situation is another argument for multicultural education."

[52] Guadalupe San Miguel, Jr., *Mexican-American and the Campaign...*, p. 7. See also Arnoldo de Leon, *The Tejano Community, 1836-1900* (Albuquerque: University of New Mexico Press, 198S2). Mario Garcia, *Desert Immigrants: The Mexicans of El Paso, 1880-1920* (New Haven: Yale University Press, 1981), pp. 197-232.

[53]H.T. Manuel and C.E. Wright "Language Difficulty of Mexican Children," *Pedagogical Seminary and Journal of Genetic Psychology* 36 (September, 1929), p. 468.

[54]See the studies of O.K. Garretson, "Study of the Causes of Retardation Among Mexican Children in a Small Public School in Arizona," *Journal of Educational Psychology* 19 (January, 1928), pp. 31-40.

[55]See George I. Sánchez, "Bilingualism and Mental Measures: A Word of Caution," *Journal of Applied Psychology* 8 (December, 1934), pp. 765-772.
[56] Guadalupe San Miguel, Jr., *Mexican-American and the Campaign...* p. 58.
[57]Ibid., p. 68; see also Lee J. Stambaugh and Lillian J. Stambaugh, *The Lower Rio Grande Valley of Texas* (San Antonio: Naylor and Co., 1954), pp. 204-230; *La crónica*, (March 2, 1911, p. 89) from José Limón, "El Primer Congreso Mexicanista de 1911: A Precursor to Contemporary Chicanismo," *Aztlan* 5 (Spring, 1974), pp. 85-117.
[58]Guadalupe San Miguel, Jr., *Mexican-American and the Campaign ..* p. 69. San Miguel cites Perales' "Unification" Part I, pp. 1-2.
[59]Guadalupe San Miguel, Jr., *Mexican-American and the Campaign..*p. 69.
[60] The Austin school teacher was K. Roque Welbourne, "Spanish for Children of Hispano Descent," *Texas Outlook*, 25 (December, 1941): pp. 33-34.
[61]Guadalupe San Miguel, Jr., *Mexican-American and the Campaign....*p. 116. The quote belongs to Ed Idar Jr., executive secretary, American G.I. Forum; from a letter written to H.T. Manuel (University of Texas at Austin) dated November 21, 1959.
[62]Ibid., p. 134.
[63] Philip Ortego, "The Minority on the Border--Cabinet Meeting in El Paso," *Nation*, (December 12, 1969), pp. 624-27.
[64]Alfred Cuellar, "Perspective in Politics," in *Mexican Americans* (Juan Moore, Alfredo Cuellar) (N.J.: Prentice Hall, 1970), pp. 137-168
[65]Guadalupe San Miguel, Jr., *Mexican-American and the Campaign...*p. 172.
[66] Ibid., p. 207.
[67] Ibid., p. 218.

CHAPTER VI

CHICANO MOBILIZATION AND ORGANIZATION

As a result of a century of struggle in the civic, social, economic and political areas, notwithstanding a national consciousness that is sweeping the nation, a number of cultural/political resistance movements begin to surface within the Mexican/Chicano/Latino community during the sixties in the United States. Among the more important and visible fronts are (1) the farm workers rights movement led by César Chávez, (2) the Spanish land grant question in New Mexico headed by Reies López Tijerina, and (3) the Chicano/Latino student movement in colleges and universities as well as Chicano communities throughout the United States.

CÉSAR CHÁVEZ AND THE FARMWORKER

With regard to the farm worker's rights, Acuña, without taking credit away from César Chávez and the UFW (United Farm Workers), justifiably points to the struggles and sacrifices and confrontations of the minority ethnic and racial groups dating back to the XIX century.[1] The farm workers rights movement was one of confrontation between the exploited workers without rights and/or protection and the growers, owners of large farm operations. The battleground that was most visible, dramatic and most documented was in California, specifically in the Delano Area located in the San Joaquín Valley. In the Spring of 1965 in the Cuachella Valley, domestic pickers, largely Filipinos and Mexicans, were being paid $0.20 to $0.30 an hour less than contracted *bracero* labor. After a ten day walkout, workers were guaranteed an equivalent pay with contracted *bracero* labor. When the same was requested by the Filipino AWOC in the San Joaquín Valley, the National Farm Workers Association (NFWA) voted to join the strike. Emerging as a central figure and leader was the son of a migrant worker, César Chávez. Experienced in labor union activity (member of NFLU) and tutored in the *Rerum Novarum* supporting labor unions and social justice, César Chávez became a grass roots organizer rising to the position of general director of the National Community Service Organization. (CSO).[2] Chávez concentrated in the *barrios* where farm workers worked and lived year around. Supported by a cadre of experienced organizers (Dolores Huerta, Gil Padilla) the membership of the NFWA had risen to approximately 1,700, with ever increasing support coming from civil rights activists, Catholic priests and Chicano workers living in the U.S. Anglo-American labor after years of neglect, also joined the coattails of the movement. The Thunderbird symbol and the banner of the Virgen of Guadalupe and a red flag gave the movement the impetus and identity needed to confront the "Green Giants" like the DiGiorgio Corporation, one of the largest grape growers. The spirit of the movement was expressed later in the Boycott Day Proclamation issued by the grape growers on May 10, 1969:

> We are pilgrims on this land, and we are pioneers who blaze a trail out of the wilderness of hunger and deprivation that we have suffered even as our ancestors did. We are conscious today of the significance of our present quest. If this road we chart leads to the rights and reforms we demand, if it leads to just wages, humane working conditions, protection from the misuse of pesticides, and to the fundamental right of collective bargaining, if it changes the social order that relegates us to the bottom reaches of society, then in our wake, will follow thousands of American farm workers...we are in the midst of a great social movement, and we will not stop struggling 'til we die or win!...We mean to have our peace and to it without violence for it is violence we would overcome the subtle spiritual and mental violence of oppression, the violence subhuman toil does to the human body...the grapes grow sweet and heavy on the vines, but they will have to wait while we reach out first for our freedom. The time is ripe for our liberation.[3]

The early farm workers struggles in California soon became one of the growers and the teamsters and the farm workers and the NFWA. Fraudulent elections and underhanded tactics by the opposition created much strife and conflict for workers. Drained of financial resources, Chávez reluctantly merged the NFWA and the AWOC in the United Farmer Workers Organizing Committee (UFWOC) and after a difficult campaigning the UFWOC won the election over the teamsters and subsequently with the DiGiorgio Corporation.

By the summer of 1970 the strike approached its fifth year; the price of victory in the San Joaquín Valley had come at a high price; it had cost 95 percent of the farm workers their homes and cars. The lettuce fields of the Salina Valley was representative of sweetheart contracts with the teamsters; taking advantage of largely *bracero* labor, they provided no job security, no seniority rights, no hiring hall, and no protection against pesticides. After workers walked off the lettuce fields, the growers intensified their campaigns of violence. Chávez was jailed in the Monterey County jail for refusing to obey an injunction and was held without bail. Teamsters' violence intensified as workers were beaten, stabbed and killed in different confrontations. By 1965, membership of the UFW had diminished considerably. Chávez' strategy shifted to legislation, knowing that laws could be enforced which would protect the rights of farm workers. Working behind the scenes to get a bill to the legislature, he received support of Governor Edmund G. Brown Jr. The bill was passed outlining the guidelines for elections and bargaining. It pitted the minuscule UFW with the 2.2 million member teamster. Still, the UFW won more elections than teamsters; however, political maneuvering against the farm workers movement was still in the hands of the legislatures ergo the need to initiate Proposition 14 by Chávez and insure consistent application of the law. The UFW attempted to read the people, but the courts supported the growers and limited the right of UFW supporters to leaflet shopping centers.[4] The power oil companies (Getty, Standard, Superior) became involved in defeating Proposition 14. Arguments for the growers rested on property rights; the fact was that only ten percent of California growers employed seventy five percent of the state farm workers. The goal of Proposition 14 was to protect the farm workers by taking it our of the "arena of political blackmail", which elicited Acuña to conclude that property rights for the rich were more important to Californians than human rights.[5]

After the defeat, Chávez struggled with contracts but managed nonetheless, to win elections as growers pressed for a renewal of *bracero* programs. By April, 1977, wages had been standardized and farm workers in California earned $3.53 an hour with fringe benefits.[6] By February, 1978, Chávez had decided to call off the boycott on grapes and lettuce, concentrating his efforts on winning elections and extending his organizing efforts to Texas and Florida. Knowing that the growers, both in California as well as the Southwest and Midwest, would never grant the farm worker decent wages and work conditions, notwithstanding permit him self-respect and self-determination, it was necessary to seek protection through the union. One important objective was providing the farm laborer a share in the benefits that accrue to management with the advance of technology and science.[7]

It was César Chávez' inspiration, and influence through his *campesino* organizing effort that inspired and formulated farm worker activism in the Southwest and Midwest. In Michigan Jesús Salas organized a farm workers union called *Obreros Unidos*. In Ohio, Baldemar Velásquez and his father led the farmer worker struggle with their newspaper *Nuestra Lucha*, a weekly radio program and were part of the formation of the Farm Labor Organizing Committee, which eventually was instrumental in signing twenty two contracts in 1968. FLOC extended its protection to grievances of police brutality, better education for Chicanos and the undocumented worker. Religious backing came first by many Protestant churches, with the Catholic church joining in much later. By the 1970's the labor pool of Chicanos was relegated largely to a life of unemployment or "poverty program migrancy."[8] The disparity in incomes vis a vis Anglo-Americans was due to a "social caste" system that accentuated class differences between the two groups.[9] Still, Chicanos living in the Midwest, while lagging behind the majority society in median income, was generally higher than other regions, particularly the depressed areas of the Southwest.

The Texas farm worker movement was more difficult given its racist cultural and political background. The organizing efforts have

Campesino March led by César Chávez, Summer of 1965. (photo by George Ballis)

its roots in the early strikes of 1966-1967 influenced and inspired by the César Chávez *Campesino* movement in California. Early efforts by Margil Sánchez and Lucio Galván to found the Independent Workers Association resulted in a series of strikes calling for decent hourly wages. The per capita income of farm workers was $1,568 and earned less than a $1.00 an hour. The Independent Workers Association voted to affiliate with the National Farmworkers Association but it soon became apparent that the Texas farm workers needed autonomy from the California association. Consequently, it voted subsequently to affiliate with the AFL-CIO becoming the United Farm Workers Organizing Committee. This gave them the impetus and power to create the historic march from the lower Rio Grande Valley to Austin, welcomed by Mayors, Bishops and Legislators. The strategy was to pressure Governor Connally to call a special session to pass a minimum wage bill but he refused. Still, it brought the issues to the forefront of politics and impacted other areas of Texas into awareness of the critical issues. Demonstrations continued in South Texas, largely in Hidalgo and Starr counties resulting in the abusive intervention of the Texas Rangers and the arrests of Marshall Méndez of the Bishop's Committee for the Spanish-Speaking and Antonio Orendain, national treasurer of the United Farmworkers Organizing Committee. Five years later, a three judge federal panel ruled that Texas Rangers used selective enforcement of Texas laws, criticizing this historically infamous agency for taking sides and declared that the anti-mass picketing statute, the law against secondary boycotts and the statute on breach of peace were illegalities committed by the Texas Rangers.[10]

After returning to California Chávez left Antonio Orendain in charge of member and placement services. Orendain, like previous organizers in the Midwest had a strong voice among the farm workers in Texas with his radio program and farm worker newspaper *El Cuhamil*. Orendain while in agreement with Chávez in terms of the farm worker's struggle and rights, had a different approach and style from the *campesino* movement leader. He opposed Chávez' church orientation and was not committed, as was Chávez, to non-violent means of protest. By 1975, after rumors and bad feelings had been created between the two, Orendain formally founded the Texas Farm Workers.[11] After a series of strikes against

El Texano and Miller Ranches with open confrontation with growers and local authorities, he began his drive to collect a half million signatures demanding rights for workers and his 1,500 mile drive to Washington D.C. with 800 members were important events in the struggle for farm workers' rights in Texas, which in turn, served as a catalyst for other strikes across the Southwest. Strikes in northern Utah and northern Colorado for better housing as well as Glendale, Arizona helped the general cause of workers' rights and protection. These included assuring Social Security benefits, eliminating fraud by forfeiting workers pay when INS was called in time for payday, providing drinking water rather than water from a canal where they bathed.[12]

REIES LÓPEZ TIJERINA AND THE LAND GRANT QUESTION

New Mexico, like Texas and other Southwestern states, had been the recipient of numerous land grants between 1598 and 1848. After the U.S. invasion into these Mexican territories and subsequent possession after the U.S.-Mexican War, there was wholesale corruption and threats to the Mexican owners who had become citizens through the Treaty of Guadalupe Hidalgo in 1848. In New Mexico, between 1869 and 1871, there was outright destruction and loss of many records. In fact, by the end of the XIX century more than four fifths of the Old Mexican and Spanish land grants had been lost to the claimants, in particular to opportunistic speculators and lawyers including the federal government claiming land for national forests and preserves, driving many New Mexican *Hispanos/manitos* into destitution and welfare. The question of land grants would arise once again in the early sixties in the person of Reies López Tijerina. A charismatic figure known as *El Tigre*, Tijerina was the son of migrant laborers who witnessed the discrimination, poverty and the oppression of the Texas Rangers. Having attended a theological seminary and having spent his early years as a Pentecostal preacher and evangelist, he came to New Mexico from Texas via Mexico in the early 1960's well prepared with documentation regarding 100 million acres of property lost in the Land Grant land-grab of 1848. By 1960 Anglo ranchers (many Texas Anglos), were forcing Mexican-American *manitos* into smaller pockets of subsistence land. In 1963, he incorporated La

Alianza Federal de Mercedes, appealing to the poor and dispossessed. The *Alianza* declared:

> ...These grants were not given adequate protection by the officials of the state of New Mexico, who were either incompetent or did not care if justice was done or not to their neighbors...New Mexico has sunk into a morass of fraud, forgery and perjury...Here on the Rio Grande, the Royal Laws of the Indies existed and still exists as the local law...And when the United States of America invaded and occupied New Mexico, the Royal Laws of the Indies remained in force except as changed by legislation; but such charges apply only to newly initiated rights and do not disturb prior vested rights...The U:S. Government had no valid reason to deny any inchoate title to lands in New Mexico, and any such denial constitutes a breach of contract and a denial of justice...[13]

The *Alianza* contended moreover that the pueblos have rights guaranteed to them by the 1848 Treaty of Guadalupe Hidalgo, and by Article II, Section 5, Article XXII, Section 4 of the Constitution of the State of New Mexico:

> The rights, privileges and immunities, civil, political and religious, guaranteed to the people of New Mexico by the Treaty of Guadalupe Hidalgo, shall be preserved inviolate.... All the laws of the Territory of New Mexico in force at the time of its admission into the union as a state, not inconsistent with this constitution, shall be and remain in force as the laws of the state until they expire by their limitation, or are latered or repealed; and all rights, actions, claims, contracts, liabilities and obligations, shall continue and remain unaffected by the change in the form of government.[14]

On October 15, 1966, Tijerina and three hundred fifty *Alianza* members occupied the campground of Kit Carson National Forest asserting *ejido* rights of the *Pueblo de San Joaquin de Chama.* State police, sheriff's deputies and Rangers were taken into custody by *Alianza* members. They were tried for trespassing, fined and handed a suspended sentence of eleven months and twenty one days in jail. However, Tijerina was convicted on two counts of assault and sentenced to two years in the state penitentiary with five years probation. While appealing and released on bond, he appeared in numerous protest rallies and even attempted to make a citizen's arrest of Tierra Amarilla's District Attorney Alfonso Sánchez. There was a gun battle and Tijerina was pursued and arrested. This occurred on June 5, 1967 when Reies López Tijerina and six carloads of armed followers descended on the courthouse in Tierra Amarilla. The ensuing gun battle in which two deputies were wounded and a third abducted elicited the callout of the National Guard and the wholesale round-up of Mexican-Americans in the area. All agencies from federal to local mounted a three year campaign of criminal charges and trials leading to the imprisonment of Tijerina and the neutralizing of his militancy. According to Tony Castro his populist movement comprised mostly middle aged conservative *manitos* who had a deep obsession with land and a naive faith in justice.[15] Still, Tijerina was the foremost leader of militants even though outside of the Southwest his cause went largely unnoticed due to his image as a romantic revolutionary.[16] In 1968, Tijerina had founded a third party called *Partido Constitucional del Pueblo* which openly placed the land grant issue in the political arena. In early 1969, he called for increased social services to the poor, higher wages to city workers and made numerous appearances and speeches on college campuses. He opposed, moreover, the nomination of Warren E. Burger as chief justice to the Supreme Court. In his state, his enemies shot and burned his offices, cultural centers and clinics. One Bernalillo County deputy sheriff lost an arm trying to bomb Tijerina's office when he fell on the dynamite. On June 5, 1969, Tijerina once again attempted to occupy the Kit Carson National Forest campsite. His wife and a few other participants burned a few signs. Two days later the arrests came and Tijerina was charged with aiding and abetting the destruction of U.S. Forest Service signs and assaulting and threatening a federal agent. The court sentenced him to three years in the federal penitentiary. Chief Justice Burger, whom he had opposed previously, refused to hear his appeal, causing him to serve two prison terms concurrently. Tijerina at this point became a symbol in view that he had been convicted for political crimes as opposed to social crimes.[17] After serving over two years in prison and released on parole, Tijerina's health was poor and his outlook towards militancy had taken a change:

> I have outgrown militancy. I can see beyond it. There is more than one way to change the rich and powerful.... In my 775 days in prison, I found justice in my heart...the future of the Southwest has greater racial perspective and consequences than the Blacks and Whites in the South...As the Indo-Hispano gains his frozen spirit, he will become a greater and greater threat unless his spirit is channeled in the right direction.[18]

Along with the term *"Indo-Hispano,"* he used the descriptive term *"Mexicano"* adding to the diversity of names and group identity within the movement. What is interesting is the affirmation now of the Native-American side of the *mestizo*, which previously had been missing with the traditional label of *Hispano* in New Mexico. Tijerina now spoke of brotherhood awareness and a calling for "bilingual people to bring harmony and brotherhood between North America and South America and between the Blacks and Whites."[19] His early militancy had sprung largely because of the complacency of bilingual population of New Mexico which contributed in his eyes to the exploitation of the Indo-Hispanos. He felt that the Chicano movement, unlike the Black Civil Rights movement had failed to arouse widespread guilt and sympathy around the country. While in jail, he angrily resigned as president of the *Alianza* due to the issue of seceding the Southwest from the U.S., a resolution passed by the *Alianza* convention. It called for the Southwest to be turned over to the Chicanos who would create the nation of *Aztlan* as declared by the Chicano Youth Liberation Conference. He stated: "I am not for separatism from the U.S. My motto is justice but not independence from or revolution against the United States."[20] The new militant Chicano leadership took control of the meeting passed resolutions naming the party the official spokesman of the convention. Tijerina stormed out of the convention blaming *La Raza Unida* and Corky Gonzáles, who did not attend for usurping his own roles and the purpose of the convention. By the mid 1970's Tijerina's civil freedom had been suppressed to a great degree by his parole. He found himself in a prison outside the penitentiary as he had to confront parole officers, legal battles seeking justice from both within the law and within the Chicano movement[21]

THE CHICANO MOVEMENT: SOCIO-POLITICAL AND ACADEMIC IMPACT

Chicano activism of the sixties and seventies must be seen, not as a spontaneous development but as a long outgrowth of socio-political struggles dating back to the XIX century. Mexican-Americans had been participating, where possible, in state and local politics, in labor organizations and in forming groups for mutual protection and well-being. The latter too often was difficult in view that they had to simultaneously accommodate dominant culture and its institutions. As has been seen, Mexican-Americans as well as other minorities, faced a lack of social mobility, institutions that fostered discrimination and racism and an economic system that provided inequities to the ethnic poor. In a society characterized by hegemony to people of color and distinct ethnicity, the period for development of an assertive stance and mobilization towards a new social, economic, political and artistic resurgence took place at the end of the fifties.

There was, across continents, a new consciousness for independence, a serious questioning of imperialism and human rights. The music reflected the change of mood, from the soft tones of the early fifties to the more aggressive and blatant tones of Rock and Roll. Cultural traditions and norms were being challenged by counter-cultural movements and the New Left. The complacent society was coming apart, particularly after the country realized its waste of lives in the Vietnam War. The time was ripe to take up old grievances and to question standard policies widening the gap between the white monied classes and the color/ethnic poor. The time was ripe for a Civil Rights movement, the rise of Black Power, an Anti-War Movement, the development of the New Left, the rise of an International Student Movement and struggles of Liberation of the Third World populations. This outgrouth of consciousness developed a series of socio-cultural political movements addressing the rights of Chicanos, Native-Americans, Women, etc. It was a time of new images, youth and a new vision for America and that image was fulfilled in the person of John F. Kennedy. John F. Kennedy ushers in the sixties with new vigor and vision for a different

America addressing, in particular, the rights of the underdog and the poor. His wife, Jacqueline, likewise, represents a model that is atypical of standard America: she is polyglot, i.e. she is fluent in various languages including Spanish and French. For once, Chicanos/Latinos have a candidate that understands their plight. By 1960, Chicanos in the Southwest will be actively and emotionally involved in Kennedy's campaign organizing Viva Kennedy Clubs that ultimately provided the balance of power in Texas and swung the state's large block of electoral votes to Kennedy necessary for his victory.

ACTIVISM AND THE *CANTOS* IN THE SIXTIES AND SEVENTIES

The beginnings of Chicano activism during this period occurs in Delano, California, September 1965. This marked the beginnings of the most important unionizing effort among farm workers led by César Chávez. It is about this time that Reies López Tijerina similarly begins activism in New Mexico with the land grant rights question. A year later in Denver, Colorado, the city administration's harassment of Chicano involvement in the anti-poverty program and subsequent demonstrations called for a "Crusade for Justice" giving birth to a new Chicano nationalism several years later in 1969. The Chicano Student Youth Movement will organize in Denver via the Chicano Youth Liberation Conference. It is during this year that Chicano Studies will be enacted in colleges throughout California. This is a period of intense mobilization and nationalism and it is not surprising that it would be followed by the creation of a political party entitled *La Raza Unida* in 1972. Similarly in the arts and literature, Chicano literature is unleashed in what Philip Ortego called the Chicano Renaissance with the publication of *Y no se lo tragó la tierra* by Tomás Rivera. With the advent of small Chicano Presses, Chicanos develop, as a compliment to the socio-political movement, a literary and artistic movement through a proliferation of journals, books, murals and conferences. A year after *La Raza Unida* is born, *Flor y Canto*, a national gathering of artists, writers, poets and musicians is born in the Fall, 1973. It will be extended by the *Canto al Pueblo* (Milwaukee, 1977). Their contribution is significant in the development of art and letters giving rise to the current wave of Chicano/Latino literature in the U.S.[22]

Brown Beret Protest Against Police Brutality--Austin, Texas, October 11, 1974 (Photo by Allan Pogue)

When John F. Kennedy assumes the Presidency of the United States, the census reports an undercounted three and a half million Spanish-surnamed persons living in the Southwest. Their per capita income was $968. Compared to 2,047 for Anglo-American and $1,044 for other non-whites; 29.7 percent of the Spanish-surnamed population lived in deteriorated housing as opposed to 7.5 percent of the Anglo-Americans, while unemployment was considerably higher among Chicanos than among Anglo-Americans. [23] Educationally, Chicanos were at the bottom with Spanish-surnamed persons over 14 years of age with a grade median of 8.1 as opposed to 12.0 for Anglo-Americans. Most significant was the grade median for the Spanish-surnamed in Texas which was 4.8 years of schooling, as a result of segregated schools. Moreover, a majority of Mexicans remained functionally illiterate as they were packed into non-academic classrooms ill-equipped to take on academic courses. Too often, this was sufficient to kill any motivation on the part of the student. Acuña cites the relevance of economic exploitation to the socio-educational problems. He notes that in one congressional district during 1966, the poor received 244,000 in food assistance from the U.S. Department of Agriculture while rich farmers (0.01 percent of the population) received 5,318,892 in benefits. [24]

The inequities and disparities in education and income had become intolerable to the Spanish-speaking populace. In California and the Southwest, activists were able to end the exploitative *bracero* program in 1964. A year later, César Chávez' small union and organizing efforts with "*la causa*" ignited activism among Chicanos/Latinos throughout the U.S. Civic groups addressed the educational, linguistic and economic barriers as well as housing unemployment, police brutality, etc. via petitions and the courts as well as sit-ins and/or demonstrations.

Rendón points to the Delano/Chávez beginning as an extraordinary event that could have ended in disaster:

> what could have been just another abortive attempt, among hundreds, to organize farm workers, but unlike other strikes, the Delano *huelga* (which climaxed on July 30, 1970, with the signing of a contract with Giumarra, the largest holdout against the table grape boycott) has gained extraordinary importance. In

September, 1965, however, only a few Chicanos thought it would last...a strike and international boycott of fresh table grape produces ensued. *Huelga* was to become a national issue and to project Chávez into national recognition as a Mexican-American leader.[25]

Activism will continue as a natural course of the times despite failed political promises at the national level. The short-lived Presidency of John F. Kennedy produced only a small amount of Spanish-surnamed appointments. It is difficult to assess his tenure as President in view of the short amount of time in that office. It would appear that the Vietnam War was of considerable concern to him and the question of civil rights was foremost in his mind. However, it was the African-Americans that first awakened the conscience of America with their protests and riots. And when President Johnson pushed proposed legislation left over from the Kennedy administration, it was aimed primarily at alleviating the plight of African-Americans. Out-maneuvered for the federal dollar by African-Americans, Chicanos turned their backs on Johnson's programs. The gap widened between what Chicanos wanted and what they received. The conditions were ripe for revolution but according to Castro, it was an era when revolutionary movements were not likely to succeed: " If the violence of the 1960's taught future revolutionaries anything, it was that violent revolution cannot succeed in urbanized America, where sophisticated communications and transportation systems can deliver national guard troops quickly and efficiently to take care of any disruption." [26] In retrospect, it is interesting to note that while Black or Chicano activists' deaths drew lines of division between White dominant society and minorities, the deaths of white students in the Kent State demonstrations certainly brought attention to the insensitivity and brutality of the establishment. With respect to Castro's statement on the failure of revolutionary movements during the sixties, one can see some positive benefits, i.e. the emerging body of Chicano literature, Chicano Studies, increasing research and publications and a steady penetration into the political positions of power. Still, there remains many problems in education and employment. Ultimately, it is the economic system which is responsible for the socio-educational and economic disparities in the United States. One can readily see today that it is money that controls Congress via the Special Interest Lobbies. It was that economic base that controlled in a Hegemonic process, minorities since the inception of the U.S. For Chicanos, it was another plutocracy that was to control their economic well being since 1848.

After Chávez and Tijerina awakened the Chicano/Latino consciousness, Rodolfo Corky Gonzáles began preaching a Chicano nationalism theme that echoed the old Black Power and Black nationalism of the sixties. After the Chicano Youth Liberation Conferences in 1969 and 1970, the Chicano movement is in full blossom. The Chicano movement took its confrontational tactics and politics into the streets, and into the classrooms. Students, poets and professors become actively involved in the movement. In poetry, Ricardo Sánchez becomes the central figure of protest in his classical *Canto y grito mi liberación* at the beginning of the seventies; Rodolfo Acuña leads the struggle to departmentalize Chicano Studies at California State--Northridge; Rivera, Anaya and Hinojosa Smith launch the early phase of the development of the contemporary Chicano novel, soon followed by Arias et. al. In Texas, Américo Paredes is named director of Mexican American Studies while in the Midwest, Arnoldo Carlos Vento develops the first Chicano Studies program in the State of Michigan.

CHICANO NATIONALISM AND THE CRUSADE FOR JUSTICE:
RODOLFO CORKY GONZÁLEZ

While Chicano nationalism was espoused in various fronts, its organized roots in the contemporary seventies setting can be seen in the sixties with Rodolfo Corky Gonzáles, a former boxer and bail bondsman, who founded *Los voluntarios*, a Chicano group who effectively protested police brutality against Chicanos. The Crusade for Justice which began in April 1966, published *El Gallo*, one of the first Chicano newspapers. By 1967, Gonzáles was one of the few Chicanos protesting the Vietnam War. It was the Crusade for Justice that sponsored the Youth Liberation Conferences, the first of which was held March 27-31, 1969.[27] From this conference grew the key ideas from which the Chicano movement was to develop. The symbol of the *Mestizo* was drawn by Chicano muralist Manuel Martínez, a three-headed profile depicting the amerigenous, hispanic, and the fusion of the two, the *Mestizo*. Chicano nationalism was viewed by Gonzáles as "the key or common denominator for mass mobilization and organization." He wanted commitment to the concept of *Raza* and the Plan of *Aztlan* as a commitment to social, economic, cultural and political independence. The struggle implied control of Chicano *barrios*, pueblo lands, economy, culture and political strife. He called for a move to *Raza* values and away from Anglo-Saxon assimilation for the survival of the Spanish-speaking people living in a fragmented and insane environment.[28] Rodolfo Corky Gonzáles became a major figure in the movement when his Crusade for Justice sponsored the Youth Liberation Conference. Here he christened the young Mexican Americans as "*Chicanos*" a term that belonged to the barrio, resurrected from the days of the Pachucos in the 1940's. *Pachucos* became the symbol of protest against Anglo-America's social ostracism, and prejudicial educational and economic practices. It was an affirmation of individuality which had been previously demonstrated in the "zoot suit riots" of June 1943 in Los Angeles, California. Thus they became to be revered as folk heroes. Other terms used included *carnales, tío tacos, vendidos, Aztlan* making reference to themselves as *mestizos* in a bronze continent.[29]

ETYMOLOGY OF "CHICANO" AND EL PLAN ESPIRITUAL DE AZTLAN

The etymology of the word Chicano was thought to be from the colonial pronunciation of *Mexica* i.e. the x pronounced with a *sh* sound. And then adding the hispanicized ending to denote "citizen of" (*Me-shicano*). While popular then and even now, it is an impressionistic and simplistic theory. The only verity is that it came from the *Aztekah Náhuatl*. In the first place, it is *Metzikah* singular, and *Metzitzin* plural. The *Aztekah Náhuatl* word *Çikanni* actually existed then and was pronounced "*Chicani*" and it referred to a person with great strength, both physical and spiritual. One only has to look at a map to discover the archeological ruins of "*Chicanna*" in southern Mexico to verify its pre-Columbian origin. No doubt, it was preserved by the native *campesinos* of the interior of Mexico and was subsequently brought into the southwest by any of the many migrations of workers since colonial times.

At the Youth Liberation Conference the newly named Chicanos adopted a moving declaration entitled *"El plan espiritual de Aztlan"* which stated in part:

> In the spirit of a new people that is conscious not only of its proud historical heritage but also of the brutal *Gringo* invasion of our territories, we the Chicano inhabitants and civilizers of the northern land of *Aztlan* whence came our forefathers, reclaiming the land of their birth and consecrating the determination of our people of the sun, declare that the call of our blood is over power, our responsibility and our inevitable destiny. We are free and sovereign to determine those tasks...we do not recognize capricious frontiers on the Bronze Continent. Brotherhood unites us...with our heart in our hands and our hands in the soil, we declare the independence of our *mestizo* nation. We are a bronze people with a bronze culture...we are a union of free pueblos. We are *Aztlan. " Por la raza todo, fuera de la raza nada.* (All for the people, nothing outside of this). [30]

The "epic" poem "I am Joaquín" attributed to Gonzáles by all historians today has been challenged by Ricardo Sánchez, who was present at these historic meetings. Before his death, Sánchez, who spoke and wrote fearlessly as a Chicano rebel and poet, cites the poem to be the work of the Jewish wife of Jesse Sauceda, a Denver based attorney. It was, according to Sánchez, delivered to Abelardo Delgado for translation. Since Gonzáles was the *jefe*, it was natural to allow him to take credit as the leader of the Youth Conference. [31]

Nonetheless, the work itself served as an inspiring piece of *movimiento* literature, such that Luis Valdez, originator of the *Teatro Campesino* will convert it into a film.. According to Castro, "Gonzáles saw nationalism flowing naturally from the family, developing into tribalism and finally transforming itself into alliances that brought about changes within political, economic, educational and social systems of the United States." [32] The movement moreover, would have to be politicized and the idea of *Aztlan* with its own people and language was carefully calculated to stir Chicanos to embrace nationalism. [33] His rhetoric of self-determination, nationalism, machismo and the need to use more forceful methods provided a challenge and a new mood to the movement of the seventies. In addition to adopting a name, a homeland, and a language, delegates at the Youth Liberation Conference under the leadership of Gonzáles, agreed to create an independent Chicano political party, thus achieving an independent power base for the movement. He suggested that the party be named *Congreso de Aztlan* (*Aztlan* Congress). The creation of a Chicano party, however, had already taken place on the local level in Crystal City, Texas by José Angel Gutiérrez under the name of *La Raza Unida* in 1970. The confrontation of two strong personalities was inevitable; each had a different ideological stand, a different style. In the El Paso Convention, Gonzáles suffered several setbacks including the nomination of the party's national chairmen. In another meeting in Albuquerque they confronted each other at the *Congreso de Aztlan*. Essentially Gonzáles took a hard line isolationist stance while Gutiérrez, who unlike Gonzáles' was polished and as a former member of MAYO, preferred political diplomacy and inclusion of middle class Mexican Americans, liberals, students, blacks and poor whites. Chicanos faced a dilemma and a split over their two Chicano leaders.

JOSÉ ANGEL GUTIÉRREZ AND MAYO

José Angel Gutiérrez has been labeled by some as a Chicano prodigy, a new breed of Chicano professional, college educated but still a Chicano with the old dream of revolution. There are sharp contrasts between Gutiérrez and the other leaders: "Chávez is cautious, Gutiérrez is self-confident; Tijerina is aggressive, Gutiérrez cunning; Gonzáles is uncompromising, Gutiérrez fluid." [34] Very early, Gutiérrez was accusing the *Gringo* of racism and cultural genocide against the Mexican-American by stripping him of his language and culture. For Gutiérrez, *Gringo* described a certain breed of Anglo; it was an attitude of a foreigner:

> If you ask a Chicano what a *Gringo* is, he knows, especially if he lives in South Texas. If you live across the tracks...he's the guy who puts the shaft to you when you go to the employment office, the one that makes you feel like you're getting a handout when you're on welfare, the sheriff who kicks your ass, then sticks you in jail without any regard for family or friends...they simply want to stay in power and keep building the same kind of political leaders. [35]

Gutiérrez' leadership begins with MAYO, the Mexican-American Youth Organization, which he and Mario Compeán, Willie Velásquez, Juan Patlán and Ignacio Pérez organized in 1967. A year later the Ford Foundation reported that Mexican-Americans were the most disorganized and fragmented minority in American life and that they needed a national organization to promote their social, economic and political needs. Funds were subsequently channeled through the Southwest Council for La Raza and the Mexican-American Legal Defense and Education Fund (MALDEF). The latter was patterned after the NAACP Legal Defense Fund. Through the leadership of Albert Peña Jr., unity councils and agencies were set up to end racial stereotypes, wage, job and educational discrimination, obtain better housing programs and stimulate political activity. Subsidiary organizations in *barrios* put pressure on groups and gave Chicanos/Chicanas a voice, created productive rallies and marches. Schools were targets as MAYO recruited the young; their tactics were confrontational in the streets, but their militancy never extended beyond their rhetoric. Conflict arose with a highly respected Mexican-American Congressman, Henry B. González. Essentially it was a confrontation between the older liberal and the new style militant. Gutiérrez' rhetoric was inflammatory and statements like "eliminate the *Gringo*" to González promoted racial hatred, "drawing fire from the deepest wellsprings of hate." [36] Henry B. González wanted to work within the system while MAYO militants wanted to change the system. González saw Gutiérrez and others stirring up tension promoting chauvinism, seeking opportunities for self aggrandizement; he saw the Chicanos imitating the protest tactics of Blacks, wasting money from the Ford Foundation. In the end Henry B. González did not think that protest was bad against age old grievances; rather he felt that a decent cause demands a just and decent program of action. He saw it was a just cause but he did not see a decent program of action. It was the classic case of not only a generation gap but of conservative versus activist approach to a problem. [37] González' public protest extended, moreover, to the Ford Foundation officials ending the funding it enjoyed in the past. Still, MAYO chapters were being organized throughout Texas and other states as activism in

Texas was highlighted by a protest of 2,000 Chicanos at Del Rio, Texas. The VISTA Program had been canceled by Governor Preston Smith because VISTA workers had participated in a protest rally against the police's beating of Uvalde resident Natividad Fuentes and his wife. With Gutiérrez and MAYO at the forefront, the Chicano leader delivered a Chicano manifesto and taped it to the county courthouse plate glass front door:

> La Raza is the affirmation of the most basic ingredient of our personality, the brownhood of our Indian ancestors wedded to all the other skin colors of mankind. Brown is the common denominator of the largest number among us--a glorious reminder of our Aztec and Mayan heritage. But in a color mad society, the sin of our coloration can be expiated only by exceptional achievement and successful imitation of the white man who controls every institution of our society. La Raza condemns such a system as racist, pagan and self-destructive. As children of La Raza, we are heirs of a spiritual and biological miracle where in one family blood ties unite the darkest and the fairest...On this day, we serve notice on Del Rio and the nation that for their sake and ours we are willing to lay down our lives to preserve the culture and language of our ancestors, to blend them with that which is best in these United States of America, our beloved country...we shall escalate the defense of...freedoms here at home to honor those who fell for them yesterday...we are committed to non-violence even while living in the midst of officially tolerated violence. We are prepared, however, to be aggressive as it may be necessary, until every one of our Mexican-American brothers enjoys liberty of shaping his own future.[38]

CRYSTAL CITY AND *LA RAZA UNIDA*

Gutiérrez' highpoint was his return to his hometown, Crystal City for the purpose of organizing politically. Crystal City was 85 percent Mexican American, with segregated neighborhoods where Anglo Americans held the political and economic power. It was a test case and the plan was for Chicanos to take over the school board, the city council, the county government and several businesses in two years. It began with a three week student boycott crippling the school system ending with the granting of most of the student demands. The boycott had been effective because it involved students from the first grade through high school; it had the approval and participation of most of the Chicano parents. It attracted national attention and established negotiation between students and the school board trustees.[39] This had been a city, like many in Texas that punished children for speaking Spanish, a city with school without provisions for bilingual education, an area where Mexican Americans twenty-five or older had a median education of only three years. According to Acuña, the Texas Rangers patrolled the area terrorizing Mexicans in general. Anglo authorities protected their privilege through fraud and intimidation at the polls and the use of the Texas Rangers. They controlled the ballot box by holding its primary elections shortly after most Chicanos left as migrants to the northern areas of the U.S. When Chicanos returned, they had a choice between an Anglo Republican or an Anglo Democrat. The introduction of *La Raza Unida* Party was inevitable and a natural course of action in the Spring of 1970. In the first election, *La Raza Unida* won control of the school boards in Crystal City, nearby Carrizo Springs and Cotulla. In four years, they had filled twenty three of twenty-four administrative positions with Mexican-Americans, had increased the school budget from one million to three million and had changed the faculty from sixty five percent Anglo to seventy percent Chicano. The new officials arranged for federal home improvement and rehabilitation loans, assisting contractors on business ventures and eventually took control of the previously Anglo-run businesses in Crystal City. By 1974, Texas leaders in the El Paso convention wanted to see *La Raza Unida* become a national party despite Gutiérrez' insistence of keeping it a regional party. The *Raza Unida* Party ticket of Ramsey Muñiz in Texas was significant drawing 214,118 votes underscoring the Chicano's frustration with the standard Democratic party. Additionally, it took Chicanos into the world of American politics as independents unafraid to criticize the political establishment without fear of ostracism from the Democratic or Republican ranks. The issue of an independent voice is still relevant and, perhaps more so, in the nineties.

ENDNOTES

[1] Rodolfo Acuña, *Occupied...*p. 268. Here Acuña refers to Native Americans, Mexicans, Chinese, Japanese as well as other ethnic and racial groups

[2] Peter Matthiessen, *Sal Si Puedes: And the New American Revolution* (New York: Dell, 1973), pp. 13-14. Whereas Acuña credits Father McDonald of San José for his tutoring in the Rerum Novarum, Matthiessen points to the activism of Father Mark Day a young Franciscan priest assigned to the farm workers in 1967. See also discussion on the bracero program and Public Law 78, pp. 17-19.

[3] Moquín, Van Doren, Rivera eds., *A Documentary History...*pp. 364-365.

[4] On Proposition 14, see the following *Los Angeles Times* articles "Chávez Asks FCC to Halt Radio, TV Ads by Prop 14 Opponents" (Oct. 19, 1967); "Farm Workers Ordered Off 2 More Centers" (Oct. 15, 1976).

[5] Rodolfo Acuña, *Occupied...*p. 278. See also the *Los Angeles Times* articles of Harry Bernstein ("Arguments Obscure Prop 14's Basic Points"), Oct. 31, 1976; and Narda Zachino ("At Prop 14 Headquarters Farm Workers Cheer Chávez—Even in Defeat"), Nov. 4, 1976.

[6] In 1965 domestic laborers i.e. Mexican Americans, Filipinos etc., were being paid one dollar an hour; in Texas, braceros were exploited at the rate of one penny a pound for picking cotton!

[7] Armando Rendón, *Chicano Manifesto* (New York: MacMillan company, 1971), pp. 146-147.

[8] Rodolfo Acuña, *Occupied...*p. 282.

[9] Vernon M. Briggs, Jr., Folgel, Schmidt, *The Chicano Worker* (Austin: University of Texas Press, 1977), p. 74.

[10] Rodolfo Acuña, *Occupied...*p. 286. Originally from a newspaper report entitled "U.S. Judges Rap Ranger Acts in Valley," *San Antonio Express*, (June 27, 1972).

[11] See *The Struggle of the Texas Farm Workers Union* (Chicago: Vanguard, 1977), pp. 4, 14-15.

[12] See Tom Kuhn "Citrus Grove Field Hands Go on Strike," *Arizona Republic*, (Oct. 4, 1977).

[13] Moquín, Van Doren, Rivera, *A Documentary History...*p. 350-51.

[14] Ibid, p. 354.

[15] Tony Castro, *Chicano Power: The Emergence of Mexican America* (New York: Saturday Review Press, 1974), p. 113.

[16] Ibid, p. 112.

[17] See Richard Gardner, *Grito: Reies Tijerina and the New Mexico Land Grant War of 1967* (New York: BoBBS-Merill Company, 1970), p. 290.

[16] Ibid., p. 112.
[17] See Richard Gardner, *Grito: Reies Tijerina and the New Mexico Land Grant War of 1967* (New York: Bobbs-Merill Company, 1970), p. 290.
[18] Tony Castro, *Chicano Power...*, p. 124.
[19] Ibid., p. 125
[20] Ibid., p. 127.
[21] Ibid., p. 128.
[22] Arnoldo Carlos Vento, "Origins and Significance of *Canto al Pueblo*: Image, Symbol and Identity of an Aesthetic Movement." Paper delivered at the Western Social Science Conference in Oakland, California, Spring, 1994.
[23] Leo Grebler, Joan W. Moore, Ralph C. Guzmán, *The Mexican-American People* (New York: Free Press, 1970), pp. 106, 126, 185, 251.
[24] Rodolfo Acuña, *Occupied America*, p. 351. Acuña cites Robert Coles and Harry Huge, "Thorns on the Yellow Rose of Texas," *New Republic* (April 19, 1969): 13-17.
[25] Armando B. Rendón, *Chicano Manifesto* (New York: MacMillan and Company, 1971), pp. 122-124.
[26] Tony Castro, *Chicano Power...*, pp. 12-13.
[27] Armando B. Rendón, *Chicano Manifesto* (New York: MacMillan and Company, 1971), p. 168.
[28] Ibid.
[29] Tony Castro, , *Chicano...*, p. 132. *Carnal* here means brother; *carnalismo* being brotherhood. *Tío Taco* is an Uncle Tom while *vendidos* are sellouts. Mestizo is the fusion of hispanic and pre-Columbian stock while *Aztlan*, while known to the movement as the Southwest or homeland, is inaccurate. It does refer to the homeland of the Aztecs but this is not the mainland and it is in a remote prehistoric time frame. See my article entitled "Significado de Aztlan: De la prehistoria al presente," in *Canto al Pueblo*, (San Antonio: Artes Gráficas, 1978), pp. 75-78. This myth was created, like many myths of *Aztekah* culture by post-hispanic writers under the hand of censorship and alteration of the *Sanctum Officium* (The Inquisition) which lasted 300 years in Latin America. For a review of 15 myths of Aztecs created by the colonials see my article entitled, "Aztec Myths and Cosmology: Historical Religious Misinterpretation and Bias," *Wicazo Sa Review*, (Spring, 1995), pp. 1-22.
[30] Tony Castro, *Chicano Power...*, p. 133. See also *El Grito del Norte*, Vol. 2, No. 9 (July 6, 1969).
[31] Ricardo Sánchez, "The Clarion Sounded"in *S.A.*, Summer, 1992.
[32] Tony Castro, *Chicano...*, p. 133
[33] Ibid.

[34] Ibid., p. 148

[35] Ibid., p. 149.

[36] From the Congressional Record 91 Congress, 1 Session, (April 22, 1969).

[37] Tony Castro, *Chicano*..., pp. 156-157

[38] José Angel Gutiérrez, "Aztlan: Chicano Revolt in the Winter Garden," *La Raza* I, No. 4 (1991), pp. 34-35.

[39] Ibid.

CHAPTER VII

CHICANO ACADEMIC, ARTISTIC AND CRITICAL ACHIEVEMENTS

CHICANO STUDIES: ART, LITERATURE AND CRITICISM

CHICANO STUDIES PROGRAMS

The sixties in the United States represented a moving away from the traditions and status quo that heretofore had been taken for granted. It marks a new consciousness, a sincere probe into the politics and philosophy of the nation. There is a questioning of values, politics, the war in Vietnam, government motives and the economic system of exploitation. Traditions are challenged by counter-cultural movements; minorities, long exploited in the U.S. and awaiting their turn for recognition and justice, explode into the scene within a fragmented America. For Chicanos, the Youth Liberation Conferences held in Denver in 1969 and 1970 constitute a preamble to the structure and organization of Chicano Studies in Academia. Chicano students subsequently applied pressure to universities via demonstrations and rallies to not only institutionalize Chicano Studies but to retain Chicano students. The result was the establishment of Chicano Studies programs and departments throughout the country.

The document that best underscores the structural and organizing element leading to the creation of Chicano Studies is *El Plan de Santa Bárbara*. Meeting in Santa Barbara, California, students, faculty and community members created an 155-page document which stated the goals, aspirations and the curricular structure for Chicano Studies in Higher Education.[1] It outlined the need for control, autonomy, structure, organization, flexibility, finances, support, staffing and presented, moreover, listings of exemplary courses and B.A. degree models.[2] In California alone, over fifty programs were created by the pressure placed on university administrations by Chicano students. While there appears to be spontaneous demonstrations throughout California campuses, Merrit College in Oakland, California, may have been one of the first Chicano Studies programs under the leadership of Froben Lozada.[3] Most were programs with curricular offerings granting a bachelor's degree with varying names: Chicano Studies, *La Raza* Studies, *Mechicano* Studies. Three campuses, San José, Los Angeles and Northridge offered Master's Degrees in Chicano Studies. In many cases, the larger universities formed their programs around centers, e.g. University of California system (except Berkeley) and the University of Texas-Austin.

Outside California , Chicano Studies programs were created in Washington State University, University of Washington, the University of Colorado at Boulder, Alamosa State; in New Mexico, the University of New Mexico-Albuquerque and New Mexico Highlands University; at Texas, Chicano Studies was centered at the University of Texas-Austin and the University of Houston. In the Midwest where there was a sizable population of both Chicanos and Puerto Ricans (mostly in the larger cities), joint programs were offered in Chicano/Boricua Studies at the University of Indiana, Wayne State (Detroit) and Iowa. The University of Wisconsin-Milwaukee, likewise, through the Spanish-Speaking Outreach Institute served both the Chicano and Puerto Rican students. Programs/departments were also found in Notre Dame, University of Minnesota, Michigan State University and the University of Michigan-Flint.[4] As a former Chicano Studies Director in three universities, I can categorically state that Higher Education did not embrace these programs but rather saw them as temporary curricular programs which could be eliminated, particularly if they were not departmentalized. The solution was to respond with the funding of soft moneys usually grants that were not part of the hard moneys i.e. state funds of the university budget. In this manner, it would not be permanently institutionalized and its legitimacy could be questioned. After the seventies and with the beginning of the conservatism of the

Reagan-Bush years, Chicano Studies were dropped in most universities. Those that survived were either departmentalized or were providing a useful curricular and research function and/or were continued by the pressure of certain key players. Such was the case with the University of Texas-Austin, California State University-Northridge, and the University of Michigan-Flint. Texas because of the conservative fabric of its dominant society, usually responds much later than California. While the University of Texas-Austin had been the host of *Flor Y Canto* in 1975, there was not a permanent full-time director until 1978. It was the pressure from MECHA, the Chicano Culture Committee, some Chicano graduate students and the leadership of Americo Paredes, that the Center for Mexican American Studies was to continue and develop.[5]

California State University was one of the few places where Chicanos were to secure the institutionalization of a department in Chicano Studies. Here, the consummate leader is Professor Rudolfo Acuña. Acuña, is one of the few professors that has earned the title of activist. There were, unfortunately , too many faculty that exemplified rhetoric, political games and egotism in addition to self-aggrandizement and power seeking , particularly positions of authority with considerable compensation. One can say that many were unconsciously caught up in the *chingón* syndrome inherited by the *gachupín* side of their culture rather than conducting themselves in a communal, sharing mode from their Pre-Columbian side of culture. The rhetoric of *carnalismo* and *familia* was temporary leading often to an abusive individualism contrary to the goals and spirit of the Chicano movement. Often, separatism and extremism was reflected by students leading to useless violence to one another. Such was not the case with Prof. Acuña who participated and suffered violence at all levels. His sacrifices should not go unnoticed; his efforts led to the creation of the largest Chicano Studies Department at Northridge, with eighteen full time professors, eighty percent of whom were tenured. Through the leadership of Prof. Acuña, the curriculum developed was interdisciplinary ; the method was teaching skills by reinforcing identity and collective consciousness. The philosophy of Professor Acuña was not the creation of Super Chicanos but to prepare technicians to serve the people; this would equip students with the skills necessary to survive in other disciplines.[6] In the University of Michigan-Flint, a cadre of Chicano students, largely sons and daughters of migrant families from Texas, along with the support of María De Leary (of the Challenge Program), pressured the University to hire a faculty member with a background in Mexican Literature and the Chicano experience. This led to the creation of Me-Chicano Studies under the directorship of Arnoldo Carlos Vento who developed the first Chicano Studies program in the State of Michigan. He, moreover, sponsored a series of Chicano conferences which featured the *Teatro Campesino*, Alurista, Feliciano Rivera, Ralph Guzmán, Frobén Lozada, and Philip Ortego among others. Another feature of this program was the creation of Chicano Studies Abroad through which Chicano students improved their linguistic and academic/cultural skills in residence every summer. The program was so successful that it included parents and community members allowing for the chartering of a full flight from Detroit to Mexico City. As Feliciano Rivera can attest, the University of Michigan-Flint Chicano student and community body was one of the few, if not the only program, where there was no inter-ethnic dissent.[7]

CHICANO STUDENT ORGANIZATIONS

In the universities, colleges and high schools, students organized groups to represent their concerns both of a cultural and political nature. This led to the creation of MECHA (*El movimiento estudiantil Chicano de Aztlan*), UMAS (United Mexican American Students), MAYO (Mexican American Youth Organization) and MASA (Mexican American Student Association). In all cases, students spoke of Chicano power which could mean either empowerment separatism or revolution. Most understood that the basic objective of the schools was the indoctrination of the dominant materialist values and the maintenance of a curricula that sustained the interests and power of the ruling class. Each organization created their own Chicano newsletters, and spoke through activist newspapers and publications such as *El Grito del Norte, El Gallo, El Papel, El Grito, Con Safos, El Chicano* and *El Degüello*. Tomás Ibarra-Frausto asserts that "if the student movement did not sustain a politics of qualitative social change, it did contribute to the raising of Chicano political consciousness which served as an impetus to a flowing of artistic experimentation.[8] Plastic artists form their own organizations e.g. *Mala Efe* Group from Oakland, California, the *Con Safos* group from San Antonio, Texas and the *Artesanos Guadalupanos* from Albuquerque, New Mexico. The artistic tendencies flourishing varied but what was most applied was a direction towards graphic art and muralism. Community cultural centers sprang across the country like the *Toltecas* in *Aztlan* in San Diego, California, The Royal Chicano Air Force in Sacramento, California and the Guadalupe Cultural Arts Center in San Antonio, Texas. These provided new and fresh means for expressive forms as seen by the Chicano community. It was a rare and exciting period when creative expression was seen within the context of historical consciousness; it was a renewal and affirmation of a cultural legacy, a type of cultural renaissance.

JOURNALS AND SMALL PRESSES

Among the early important Chicano journals of this renaissance are *El Grito*: A Journal of Contemporary Mexican American Thought, *Con Safos* , *El Pocho Che*, and *De Colores*. The first is the creation of *Quinto Sol* Press, the first Chicano press founded by Octavio Romano. Characteristic of this journal was its diversity , publishing almost all of the significant Chicano poets and authors from distinct geographical locations. In addition to poetry, the short story, it promoted the latest critical essays on the topic of *Chicanismo* in both the liberal arts as well as the social sciences. In its comprehensive scope it reflected the pluralistic nature of Chicano reality. It accomplished the goal of eliminating blatant stereotypes and literary clichés among Mexican Americans. *Quinto Sol* Press has the distinction of publishing the first comprehensive anthology of contemporary Chicano literature with its issue entitled *El Espejo*. Similarly, *Pajarito* Publications Press from Albuquerque, New Mexico had the distinction of publishing the first Chicana anthology under the editorship and inspiration of Linda Morales Armas. While *El Grito* was academic oriented, *Con Safos* reflected the urban *barrios* of East L.A. It's aim was to capture the soul of the *barrio*, its language, history and lifestyle. It promoted the language and style of the *Pachuco* and the *vato loco*; it was a gesture of defiance and the total and indifferent rejection of *Gabacho* society. It carried a positive vision of *barrio* life. Most issues had a glossary of *barrio caló* as it attempted to validate the *barrio*'s own distinct vitality and dynamics. Poems in *Con Safos* expressed *carnalismo, la palomilla, la ganga, la vida loca* with warmth, humor and irony. While *Con Safos* reflected the East L.A. Chicano *cholo* experience, *El Poche Che* reflected a Third World militant perspective of *Raza* artists, poets and writers of the Northern California area. It was the inspiration and the result of the Third World student strike in 1969. Their scope was international, thus moving beyond the regional nationalism of Chicanos. Parallels of *Raza* struggles between the U.S. minority and those in Cuba, Nicaragua and Third World countries were underscored. The ethnic international composition of the Bay Area was natural for this approach; thus the poetry, music and literature reflected a diverse group of *Raza* who maintained a Third World political orientation in their bilingual-bicultural aesthetic expression.[9]

Often missed is the contribution of *Pajarito* Publications; the creation of José Armas and wife Linda Morales Armas. Like *Quinto Sol* Press, it published a literary journal i.e. *De Colores* which featured a diversity of poetry, articles and short pieces of fiction. As previously stated, it has the distinction of being the first Chicano Press to focus attention on the Chicana, thanks to the efforts of Linda Morales. As part of the *De Colores* series, a special anthology entitled *La Cosecha: Literatura y la mujer Chicana* was dedicated to the "mujer Chicana." Linda Morales Armas expresses the need in the introduction:

> There is a clear void of documentation and of journals to present the case for the mujer Chicana...A need to critically analyze ourselves to determine who we are, what we want and where we are going...Chicanas hold a distinctive perspective of the world around them...we are culturally different from other women in the U.S. We are also different from the white women in that we are the recipients of racist attitudes which have oppressed our culturally different Mestizo pueblo in this country...but we also have the added burden of living in a world geared for men. We find ourselves at the very bottom of the social ladder and the way up and out of this restrictive condition must be made ultimately by our own initiative.[10]

Another major journal developed through the auspices of Chicano Studies at UCLA was *Aztlan*, a journal focusing particularly on socio-political questions within the Chicano movements. While many journals have ceased to publish, *Aztlan* continues to flourish today in part due to its association with a strong institutionalized program within the UCLA system. Other journals and/or newsletters that fitted the informational need included *Caracol, Rayas* and *La Raza*. Some successful poets went on to create their own journals; such was the case with Alurista with *Maize: Cuadernos de Arte I Literatura Xicana* and Lorna Dee Cervantes with *Mango*.

THE *FLOR Y CANTO* AND *CANTO AL PUEBLO* FESTIVALS: POETRY AND ART

Concomitant to the development of new creative Chicano expression is the creation of national art and literature festivals entitled *Flor Y Canto* an *Canto Al Pueblo*.[11] The organizational beginnings take place at USC, under the auspices of the Chicano Studies Center during the Fall, 1973. Here a small cadre of Chicano writers plan and organize what will later be a broader more purposeful national festival. Still from this beginning, the first *Flor Y Canto* anthology of Chicano literature was published. The objectives were established in the first meeting: (1) to provide a national forum for all Chicano writers, affording equal time to all participants, (2) to create an atmosphere conducive to creative exchange as well as a critical environment for growth and development and (3) to promote the appreciation of Chicano literature extending it to the people of the community.[12] It was with these objectives that the *Festival Floricanto* II was organized in Austin, Texas under the auspices of the Center for Mexican American Studies in 1975. Here, a number of important questions were raised regarding Chicano literature, the movement and the publishers. Since 1975 a third festival was organized in San Antonio, a fourth in New Mexico and a fifth in Arizona. The continuation of these cultural-literary festivals is seen in the birth of *Canto Al Pueblo* in Milwaukee, Wisconsin in 1977.

The creation of the new label, *Canto Al Pueblo*, has political and organizational implications. *Canto Al Pueblo* was both the continuation and the beginning of a new cultural-literary festival. It promoted dialogue and creativity as experienced with *Flor Y Canto*

Canto al Pueblo I. Upper top left:*Canto Mural*, Arnoldo Carlos Vento.Left Center Alurista. Top right: Tino Villanueva, *Teatro Pinto* Lower right: Zarco Guerrero.

with the old constituency gaining new membership nationally. It retained the concept of *Canto* denoting creative expression and connoting the search for truth regarding the Chicano condition. The inclusion of the word Pueblo meaning "people" has political implications. It is an attempt to bring back the focus on the socio-political arena as opposed to purely aesthetic art for art's sake orientation. This concept and name properly belongs to Ricardo Sánchez who clearly saw the *Flor Y Canto* falling away from political consciousness. Originally, the idea of creating a national festival was discussed and planned on January 5, 1977 in the first meeting between Ricardo Sánchez and then Director of the Spanish-Speaking Outreach Institute of the University of Wisconsin-Milwaukee, Arnoldo Carlos Vento. At a later date a third figure, Reimundo Tigre Pérez will figure in the organizing of the *Canto Al Pueblo*.[13] The central focus was to be at the level of the worker and the community, to become the *pueblo*:

> No nos creemos capataces o dioses o sacerdotes. Somos gente que trabajamos con la cultura con el arte, para desarrollar pensamientos y presentárselos a la gente. Si lo quieren aceptar, bueno y si no, es cosa del pueblo.[14]

Canto Al Pueblo was not exclusively for Chicanos; its scope was pluralistic; the first *Canto Al Pueblo* included Puerto Rican artists and poets, Black, White and Native American representatives. Beyond poetry, and critical literature, it featured muralism, theater and musical groups, all with socio-political messages.

As a result of the first *Canto Al Pueblo*, held in Milwaukee April 29-May 8, 1977, a special issue of *Grito del Sol* was issued featuring the artists and writers of *Canto* and before the first national festival was over, the second *Canto Al Pueblo* was destined for Corpus Christi, Texas.[15] *Canto* III originally scheduled for Pueblo, Colorado, was unfortunately canceled due to unforeseen conflicts;[16] however, a Midwest *Canto Al Pueblo* was created in St. Paul, Minnesota, bringing new life to its forgotten Chicano/Latino *barrio*. Documentation of this event was covered by *Nosotros* and a Minneapolis/St. Paul television station.[17] The fourth and final *Canto* (and perhaps the most integrated with Native Americans) was *Canto Al Pueblo* IV (1980) in Tempe, Arizona. While the Native-American element had been a part of all the *Cantos*, it is not until *Canto* IV that we have Native American representation in full force. Tribal representation was national: the Mohawk Nation (Mad Bear); the Lakota Nation (Crow Dog), the Pima Nation (Walking Beaver), Hopi, Navajo, Apache (Philip Cassadore). Moreover, Mexico (*Tlakaelel*), Central America and El Salvador (María E. Castro) are further represented. Here, the Chicano and brothers from the South shared in the sacred Native American rituals at the Fort McDowell Reservation. As noted in former *Cantos*, an anthology is published and coverage of the *Canto* IV extended to Europe as German visiting lecturer (U.T.-Austin) Frank Geerk published an anthology entitled, *Poesie Zeitzschrift für Literatur* and an article in *Basler Magazin*[18]

1980 marks the end of the *Canto Al Pueblo* but it is also a marker for the beginning of a decade of conservatism in the United States with the Reagan-Bush administrations. As a consequence, Chicano Studies programs throughout the nation suffered from funding cutbacks if not total elimination. Funding sources for minority aesthetic festivals are to be severely reduced but the spirit and work of cultural artists continue in the respective Chicano/Latino populations in the United States. It marks the end of an era of great aesthetic productivity in the arts and literature; it provided a forum by which young writers and artists could develop. Moreover, it not only continued and contributed to the Chicano/Latino Movement, but created future literary, artistic and academic leaders: Dr. Ricardo Sánchez, Dr. Arnoldo Carlos Vento, Dr. Alberto Urista, Dr. Tino Villanueva, Dr. Juan Bruce Novoa, José Burciaga, Lorna Dee Cervantes, Zarco Guerrero, Nephtalí Deleón, Tigre Pérez, Mario Acevedo Torero and Carlos Rosas, among others. We note, moreover, in the early *Flor Y Cantos*, the collaboration of Tomás Rivera, Rolando Hinojosa-Smith, Ron Arias, Luis Valdéz, Américo Paredes, Juan Gómez Quiñones, Bernice Zamora, José Flores Peregrino, Carmen Tafolla, Sergio Elizondo, Francisco Lomelí, Frank Pino, Raul Salinas, Luis Omar Salinas, Miguel Méndez and Gustavo Segade.

In the end, the *Canto*'s philosophical objectives went beyond artistic and literary productivity; it was a movement away from Western philosophy and dominant United States culture. Poetry in

Canto al Pueblo I. Top left Center: Torero. Left Center: José Montoya, Ricardo Sánchez, Nephtalí de León. Lower Left: Ablelardo Delgado. Center: Las Cucarachas. Bottom Center: Lorna Dee Cervantes.

the seventies was represented by the powerful protest verse of Ricardo Sánchez, the Pre-Columbian image and concept of Alurista, the peoples poetry of Abelardo, the *cholo* poetry of José Montoya and the *barrio* experience of Raul Salinas. Others instrumental in the movement were Reimundo Tigre Pérez, Tino Villanueva, Lorna Dee Cervantes, Evangelina Vigil, José Burciaga, Angela de Hoyos and Bernice Zamora. In the eighties Pat Mora and Alma Villanueva voice the Chicana's soul while Gary Soto moves the political protest poetry to a more academic form while Jim Sagel retains the folkways of the small town *manito* of northern New Mexico. Of all the movimiento poets, Ricardo Sánchez stands out as the forerunner of Chicano protest poetry of the late XX century. His *Canto y Grito mi liberación* set the tone for the Chicano poetic movement in the beginning of the seventies.

RICARDO SÁNCHEZ : LIBERATIONIST AND HUMANIST POET

Ricardo Sánchez has been characterized as creative, as dynamic, as a sharing individual, dogmatic, a maverick, a *barrio* rebel, a threat, a bato loco, a universal man and a Chicano Walt Whitman. In one interview in the late 70's, he characterized himself, not as a bilingual or bicultural person but rather one with a tertiary approach to life and writing, a triune pyramidal person that had created the third form of his person i.e. the *Mestizo*.

Canto y Grito mi liberación established him as a major artistic voice in the Chicano movement. For Sánchez the *Canto* metaphorically was the song of the breaking of dawn, the gentle song of flowers opening up to the *Padre Sol:* it was the *Canto* of life. His *Grito* was the outcry, the affirmation that one is born to be free, to be oneself in terms of how one is. Together it is the festival of *Chicanismo* and at once liberational. Ricardo Sánchez did not care to change his cultural reality for anyone. What motivated him was a lifetime/struggle pain and confrontation. He knew who he was and thus, he respected himself. He said, "The first obligation is to respect oneself, to arrive at a personal truth [that] one wants to share with one's progeny..."[19] He felt that his worth was determined by himself and not by outsiders. Chicano, then becomes

A definition of action, of realization within all that I am, not some fragmented term of genocide handed me by a system only concerned with digitizing me, amortizing my humanity by numbing me within a stereotyping/statistics driven process of dehumanization.[20]

While *Canto y Grito mi liberación* was the outcry and manifesto of liberation, *Hechizospells* was the philosophical explanation. It is the response to the human condition that is central to all of Ricardo Sánchez's poetry. When he achieves this he releases the slave within and leads him toward his realization as a worthy caring being willing to confront destructive elements i.e. elements that are anti-humanistic. He asserts his right to become himself and the responsibility to do it humanely. His poetry thus was part of the body of liberationist literature which has integrated within it a moral imperative to education. It is though the liberationist literature that we question so that "we may reflect on our humanity and make determinations that are life giving." The poet wants to create a grander sense of our humanity, hoping that in the future we can reflect and state that "we acted ethically, caringly and humanely."[21] Those poets, writers and academicians that work outside the resistance movement are but "commodities that white Amerika can trot out as new tokens...to have deliver the dulcet tones which do not truly offend those whose largesse and power have historically offended humanity..." to those critics who arrogantly postulated that *Aztlan* was an exercise in Romanticism, he responds:

> *Aztlan* is more than a mythical notion, more than a moth dream in some cowering poet's trip; it is a land that was stripped from our ancestors, it is our *tierra* in all senses of the word and our *mestizo-Indigena corazones* yearn to recapture a heritage patrimony and destiny brutally taken from us...[22]

The outcry of Ricardo Sánchez is the anger that still is locked within, "it is the fomentation of outrage in an outcry to liberation". To many, this can be offensive, particularly those who are comfortable or those who want to be allowed to survive; it is unsettling to those from Latin America that come here to be citizens, and to "Mexicans who crave acceptability like some of their ancestors did when they embraced Maximiliano and became mariachis for the *franceses* who were colonizing them."

Ricardo Sánchez, while crying out with dissatisfaction at society, is a poet that is enamored with life itself. Life is a celebration; he breathes and lives each moment to the fullest. His eyes capture the details one normally takes for granted. This celebration is mirrored further by *Canto Al Pueblo* where artists and writers celebrate and build new bridges, for art belongs to the people and through it "we can know our feelings and our real past." Art and literature are mirrors of our mindsouls. As *mestizos* by history, we can live in multiple worlds as gente íntegra that we can be." He sees mediocrity throughout society, a humanity that has had plastic surgery, an America that does not change, mass producing the same shapes and types of human beings.[23]

But Ricardo Sánchez sees beyond national borders for he realizes that the destiny of *La Raza* is tied to the destinies of all the people of the earth

> ...that our struggle is but another face of universal quest for freedom---that male/female relations must become egalitarian...
> that we must learn to see beyond the confines and barriers of our *barrios*, states [and] country to a world that is multi-hued and polylinguistic.[24]

He calls for taking all the meaning of our existentiality to the world, without losing our identity so that we can broaden our experiences enriching our commitment to liberation, and the total transformation of human society.

The last phase of Ricardo Sánchez is characterized by a mature historically reflective and philosophical voice as evidenced by *Border Bones: Sketches from the Pass*. Sánchez's new voice is not so much a *grito* as it is a new voice which is incisive and flowing projecting a mature confident professional synthesis that is both historically and socially based; it is a macroscopic view of *La Raza* from Pre-Columbian times to the present. It is analytical, honest and engageé. Thus, Ricardo Sánchez saw through the process of humanization, the bridging of peoples in a true *carnalismo* or brotherhood. Towards the twilight of his year, he remained positive amidst a world trapped in violence and decadence: "Maybe I no longer have a people or home or *Causa* to look toward because I

Ricardo Sánchez: Liberationist Poet and Activist.

simply yearn to arrive at freedom and not a limited notion of humanity." To Ricardo Sánchez, the universe was his world if only there was more time for each of us "There is so little life time for each of us, maybe 70 or so years or even a hundred, and I want to pack the universe into my being, perhaps to give a grander sense of being, to my limited self."[25]

The poet in serious reflection humbled himself as he thought of the moments or years left to him:

> And I mean to make what moments or years remain for me to live, count, conquering my fears and sharing *lo poquito que sé*, for the world is big, beautiful, loving, hurting and in a turbulent process of change–*quiero ser un granito de arena en la playa humana.*[26]

In his last years each day became a struggle, an encounter with survival; here the poet reflects on one's modification in health as well as literature: "I stumble each day trying to make sense and somehow surviving until the next moment, never truly knowing if I shall survive one bout with diabetes to another encounter with diverticulitis. My large intestine is decreased by 18 inches, yet I survive and I wonder about how we modify ourselves as I cut out nouns, adjectives, adverbs and even verbs from my poems and articles."[27]

Where will Chicano poetics be placed in the future? What is the destiny of our efforts? Ricardo Sánchez in his ironic wit reflects on its disinterment in some distant future: "Will the future disinter our bones and sing praises to Chicanosaurian poetics in some distant mausoleum of diversity? Whatever our destiny it will be something that we will have created through the pain of daring to be ourselves at whatever cost."[28]

In the end, Ricardo Sánchez will have a secure place in Chicano history as a forerunner of the late XX century Chicano protest poetry. He will be remembered for many things but his most salient characteristic will be his uncompromising position to be truthful, to be oneself, to have integrity so that we also can be whole, integrated and humanized beings.[29]

LUIS VALDEZ AND THE *TEATRO CAMPESINO*

In the theater the pioneer and father of Chicano theater is Luis Valdez. Originator of the *Teatro Campesino* in 1965, his theater was adjunct to the Farmworkers struggle of César Chávez. The theater was mobile, creative and political. It improvised, using Farmworkers and their campesino vernacular and focused on social issues through a series of actos (acts) whose aim was to inspire the audience of Farmworkers, students etc. into action by illuminating specific social problems and suggesting possible solutions.[30] In 1967, the *Teatro Campesino* left Delano and established *El Centro Campesino Cultural* in Del Rey, California. Instead of using *campesinos* with no theatrical training, Valdez began employing students using a *rasquachi* style expressing diverse themes ranging from the *huelga* and Farmworkers rights to Vietnam and racial discrimination. By 1969, the *Teatro Campesino* had received critical acclaim in a festival at *Theater des Nations* in Paris, France. The group settles in Fresno, California continuing to experiment and evolve. It used the *corrido* as a dramatic form and published its ideas in its own journal of Chicano drama. By 1970, Valdez begins to visualize a shift in perspective as seen later in his *"Pensamiento Serpentino"* published in 1973.[31] Ybarra-Frausto points to two phases of his theater (1) the popular theater focused on class struggle based on economic values and (2) a theater with "secular spirituality...which probes the psychic memory and sub-conscious myth structure of Chicanos." Some saw it as a universal orientation; others saw it as a move away from the theater of the people.[32] Whatever assessment is made, Luis Valdez's *Teatro Campesino* was the most important and original dramatic expression of the Chicano movement. It represented and explored the Chicano vernacular speech, it brought social issues to the forefront of the people and brought new and fresh visual dramatic art to a high spontaneous and artistic level. Luis Valdez will, in the eighties and nineties, move up to the silver screen as a playwright, director and producer in a number of films reflecting Chicano reality. His *Zoot Suit* won critical acclaim as a play in Los Angeles before it was made into a movie. Following Luis Valdez in theater is Carlos Morton. Of his works, *Johnny Tenorio and Other Plays* is his most representative of his theater.

Early *Actos* Phase of Luis Valdez' *El Teatro Campesino*

PROSE FICTION: THE NOVEL AND SHORT STORY

Of the genres that receive the most attention is the novel. The contemporary Chicano novel while written before the seventies, properly begins with the literary work of Tomás Rivera (*Y no se lo tragó la tierra*, 1971), Rudolfo Anaya (Bless Me Ultima, 1972), both winners of the *Quinto Sol* prize for literature. These are followed by Oscar "Zeta" Acosta's *The Revolt of the Cockroach People* (1973), Miguel Mendez's *Peregrinos de Aztlan* (1974), Ron Arias' *The Road to Tamazunchale*, Alejandro Morales' *Caras viejas y vino nuevo* (1975), Estela Portillo Trambley's *Rain of Scorpions* (1975), Aristeo Brito's *El diablo en Texas* (1976) and Rolando Hinojosa-Smith's *Klail City y sus alrededores* (1976).

As a by-product of the seventies, the novels written are by Chicanos that are trained and schooled in literature via academia. These novelists were cognizant of structure, style and form as they documented a people and a culture. The techniques vary but the verisimilitude of the culture of the Chicano/Mexicano, *Tejano* or *manito* is reflected in autobiographical events encased within a literary framework. In almost every case, there is a boy protagonist, the theme of oppression, the search for identity and man's inhumanity to man. But also there is a warm and caring people who, despite incredible odds, are resilient to survival.

Tomás Rivera's *Y no se lo tragó la tierra* documents the migrant experience which he experienced as early as 1935 through 1956 when he was in junior college.[33] Within the migrants he saw a spiritual strength. As a writer he had no distinct political purpose when he wrote that he merely wanted to be "creative and totally human." However, he did feel that if the Chicano did have a distinct perspective it would be looking at the world through the eyes of the oppressed. His novel is a short work structured through fourteen short stories and thirteen vignettes with a prologue and epilogue. His style is concise, his narrative impressionistic. It's value lies in its verisimilitude of characters, themes, conditions and language of the Chicano migrant stream. It conveys not resignation amidst oppressive conditions, but a will to succeed and an optimism for a better tomorrow. The young boy protagonist in the end conquers his fears and overcomes obstacles, myths and unproductive traditional thought in the search for his identity. Rivera's novel like Hinojosa-

Smith and Anaya's novel properly belong to the first phase of the contemporary Chicano novel i.e. the regional socio-cultural historical narrative. Similarly, Rolando Hinojosa-Smith attempts to document his past experiences and in this case, south Texas in the Rio Grande Valley. Born and raised in Mercedes, Texas, he creates in his work a mythical county called Belkan with various other fictitious names representing Valley towns i.e. Jonesville on the river--Brownsville; Klail City--Mercedes; Edgerton--Edinburg etc.

Like Faulkner's Yoknapatawpha, the counties of Willacy, Cameron and Hidalgo become Belkan County which in turn represents a macrocosm of Valley Chicano society. Hinojosa-Smith's technique is different from Rivera's. Rather than the concise, compact structure and cast of characters of Rivera, we see instead the construction of a myriad of characters through sketches depicting their customs, habits and speech; each colorful and unique in their respective areas. Hinojosa-Smith draws directly from his academic training in Peninsular literature, particularly XIX *costumbrista* narrative as well as familiarity with the literature of the middle ages. His first work *Estampas del valle y otras obras*, winner of the *Quinto Sol* prize in 1972, reminds us of the *Cuadros de costumbres* in their depiction of customs, traditions, celebrations, speech and social types; it goes beyond the physical description of the external aspects of reality.[34] Tone, humor and foreground of special effect phrases remind us of Mexican novelist Juan Rulfo. Indeed, in *Generaciones y semblanzas* (a reprint and translation of *Klail City y sus alrededores)*, he titles a short narrative section *"Los perros que ladran"* borrowed from the Rulfo short narrative *"No oyes ladrar los perros?"*[35] His use of hundreds of characters in his novels is reminiscent of Camilo José Cela's *La Colmena;* hundreds of characters are presented in a series of monologues, dialogues seemingly fragmented to present a mosaic of Spanish-Speaking in their respective linguistic and cultural milieu. Dominant Anglo-Saxon society is external to the development of the Chicano world in Belkan County. Any cultural resistance here is not posed as an ideological issue but as an independent structure existing apart from the Anglo world. By using biographical sketches, he is able to portray characters through anecdotes or a series of episodes. This anecdotal or episodic approach becomes a testimony, much like the

Spanish chronicles. Some would argue that it diminishes the potential for the internal development of character's minds. Given the use of testimony as a device in the Spanish-American Novel, this would not be true. His best work is probably his *Klail City y sus alrededores*, winner of the *Casa de las Americas* prize for the best novel in Spanish from the U.S. Like *Estampas*, there is a lack of an omniscient narrator; there is instead a number of characters that collaborate as narrators through a series of monologues, dialogues, written documents, letters and radio announcers. The subsequent reprint and translation in the U.S. of *Generaciones y semblanzas* uses a title borrowed directly from Fernán Pérez de Guzman's *Generaciones y semblanzas* written c. 1650.[36] The first part of *Generaciones* appears stylistically more formal and rigid than the second and third parts. It is in the third part, however, that we see the author experimenting with new dialogue techniques such as multiple simultaneous dialogues and dual perspectives within a written document. What seems to be absent is a well defined or developed character or plot. Hinojosa, however, is not concerned with a delineated progressive plot line; he contends that this can be seen only after you read the complete Klail City Death Trip series. In Hinojosa-Smith's work, there is no one central hero because there are no heroes in the world he creates. His characters are everyday people who do everyday things. By presenting a number of themes through his anecdotal/ collage technique, the world of Belkan County becomes his stage in the theater of South Texas Valley Chicano culture.

Representative of the traditional form is *Bless Me Ultima* (1972) by Rudolfo Anaya. Like Rivera's novel it questions the static religion of the Catholic church but unlike Rivera's work it suggests an alternative way of looking at the cosmos. Through Tony, the boy protagonist, the rich naturistic beliefs of Ultima, the healer woman (*curandera*) is transmitted. It is an ancient Native-American perception of the cosmos that is credible and understandable to the protagonist. Like Rivera, he captures the folkways, customs, and speech patterns of the Spanish-Speaking, albeit in English but of the rural plains ambiance of New Mexico. It's inclusion of mythology in *Manito* society ranging from Pre-Columbian to current times is rich and varied.[37]   In Anaya's *Bless Me Ultima*, there is conflict within the cultural milieu but rarely is there external Anglo conflict or political questions raised within society. However, as in Agustín Yáñez's *Al filo de Agua,* it raises many questions regarding the validity of the Catholic Church in *Manito* society.

The second phase of the contemporary Chicano novel takes place in the mid-seventies with the publication of *The Road to Tamazunchale* by Ron Arias in 1975. Ron Arias takes the Chicano novel out of the context of oppression and deals with a deeply personal and individual theme: death. While he is able to bring in a low rider as a character, a "wetback" theme, an East L.A. setting and an occasional sprinkling of Spanish, his concerns for death are universal via the protagonist Fausto. As in works previously mentioned, humor abounds and language is skillfully woven. In this work, characterization is achieved and there is a definite and defining plot with varying themes related to Chicanos. What makes this work different is the development of the psychological framework of the protagonist through post-expressionist dream-fantasy transitions making reality appear unreal. Some critics have labeled the work Magical Realism. Eliud describes it as representative of the new novel of current modernism.[38] While it does attempt to confuse objective and subjective reality, I do not believe it achieves a magical reality; rather it probes more into the mind, the psychological aspects of the protagonist Fausto. In this respect, it falls more into the psychological/modernist novel.[39] One must, however, commend Arias for his ability to explore interior reality and states of consciousness. The "new breed" of character that he develops carries unlimited plot possibilities. Some of the techniques employed are reminiscent of Cervantes' *Quijote* and his influence of Goethe's Faust, Michelangelos' David and Gabriel García Márquez is evident. When it appeared in 1975, *The Road to Tamazunchale* was controversial in some circles because it departed from the point of view of visible reality. Critics who advocated political and social realism saw it as irrelevant, reactionary and commercial while aestheticians welcomed it with the highest regard[40] Also important during the seventies were the first time novels of Aristeo Brito's *El diablo en Texas* (1976), Miguel Méndez' *Peregrinos de Aztlan* (1974) and Jim Sagel's *Tu nomás honey* (1981). Aristeo Brito's novel captured Chicano oppression and discrimination in West Texas, in the hottest area of Texas, Presidio. It is skillfully written, decidedly literary with influence from the Mexican writers. Structurally, it is comprised of three parts, the last being too short and underdeveloped. Still, it showed great promise from a literary standpoint. Miguel Méndez's entry novel depicts the connection of *Raza* between Mexico and the U.S., projecting pride in the Pre-Columbian roots. While it shows flashes of stylistic brilliance, it suffers from a unified structure. His recent novel, *The Dream of Santa María de la Piedras*, however, is without fault and very literary. In the case of Jim Sagel, his collection of short stories is worthy of mention in view that it was the recipient of the *Casa de las America's* prize for literature for writers from the U.S. in 1981. Sagel, as a writer acculturated into *Manito* society accurately depicts the small urban, northern New Mexico *Manito*. He introduces the new themes of the handicap, dying with dignity and the woman as an active and important character. Unlike Anaya who captured the rural plains traditional setting, Sagel captures the contemporary small town folkways of northern New Mexico.

In the eighties, the Chicano novel experiences new directions as well as new writers. Of the writers of the seventies, Hinojosa-Smith is the most prolific as he continues his genealogy of Belkan County. Similarly, Anaya, continues to develop myth as a response to dehumanization while Arias and Brito are noticeably absent in their literary creations. Rivera, because of his untimely death, left us with one key work; Jim Sagel continues to write poetry and short stories of the people he knows best. One direction, with few exceptions, that is apparent is the shift from Spanish to English. After *Klail City y sus alrededores*, Hinojosa-Smith begins his transition to English in an effort to reach the U.S. audience. Only two Chicanos published in Spanish during the eighties: Miguel Méndez and Arnoldo Carlos Vento. The problems of publishing in Spanish are many: (1) a restricted U.S. audience, (2) restricted publishing outlets and (3) when publishing in Latin America in mainstream presses, the competition is intense in view of the excellent writers being recognized internationally from Latin America. The second novel of Méndez, published in Guadalajara is perhaps his best literary effort. Like Brito's *El diablo en Texas*, it displays a decided Mexican literary influence; it's style is flowing and metaphorically visual and its structure more unified than his first work. Published by Bilingual Press as a bilingual edition, the English translation is less than perfect in view of the many mistranslations (or lack thereof) of dialectal Chicano speech. Arnoldo Carlos Vento's *La cueva de Naltzatlan* (1987) is a work that was published under the Series of Mexican Writers for *Fondo de Cultura Económica* in Mexico City. Distributed in Latin America, it is virtually unknown in the U.S. Still, it is appropriate to consider it since part of the time-space of the co-protagonist Santos Aguila de la Paz, occurs in South Texas in the Rio Grande Valley. Like Hinojosa-Smith's *Klail City y sus alrededores,* it takes place in the small town setting circa the late 40's, in this case Santa Maria, Texas (San Juan, Texas). It is different in that it's style is Magical Realism, and it is not limited to a specific region. It's displacement of time and space links three time/space realities with triplicate parallel characters. It's language, like Méndez, links the *Raza* between Mexico and the U.S. Here, however, there is great detail on Aztec culture and history as it attempts to provide a type of Roots for the Chicano/Mexicano co-protagonist. One of its main objectives is to present an autocthonos perspective of Aztec culture and history which to date has been distorted largely through a reiteration of clerical European post-Hispanic interpretations. One of the new features in terms of characterization is the projection of the female as a primary activist character in the personality of Jesusita Candelaria. *La cueva de Naltzátlan,* now out of print, represents the first of a trilogy of novels by the author; the second novel, completed, is entitled *En el nombre del Padre y del Hijo* and is currently in press in Mexico. The eighties is characterized, also by the proliferation of Chicana writers.

The eighties and nineties are indeed the decades of the woman. While Rolando Hinojosa-Smith, Alejandro Morales and Miguel Méndez continue to write in the eighties, the new Chicano novelists are Floyd Salas (*Buffalo Nickel*) and Victor Villaseñor (*Rain of Gold*) while the Chicana novelists are represented by Sandra Cisneros (*Woman Hollering Creek*), Lucha Corpi (*Eulogy for a Brown Angel*), Roberta Fernández (*Intaglio*) and Irene Beltrán Hernández (*Heartbeat/Drumbeat*), among many others.[41]

ENDNOTES

[1] *El Plan de Santa Barbara: A Chicano Plan for Higher Education* (Oakland: La Causa Publications, 1969).
[2] Ibid., pp. 16-18, 94-128.
[3] See the *Berkeley Daily Gazette*, April 7, 1969. Feature Page; "Ethnic Militancy, Peralta JCD and Lozada Having a Good Time," states that President Norvel Smith of Merrit College will appoint Frobén Lozada to head a department of Latin and Mexican American Studies.
[4] It should be noted that the first Chicano Studies program in Michigan was created in 1972 under the name of Me-Chicano Studies by Professor Arnoldo Carlos Vento. The name is a *double-entendre* meaning both Mexican and Chicano Studies and phonetically a metaphor for *Mexica*, thus laying the pre-Columbian foundation to Chicano studies via Mexican roots.
[5] With the leadership of Professor Vento and the harmonious cooperation of Maria de Leary and the Challenge Program supportive services and the philosophy of *comunidad, carnalismo* and *familia*, the University programs worked hand in hand with the Chicano community playing an integrated role in their social/cultural activities. Among the early faculty included Professor David Berlanga, and Andy Montes and Visiting Professor Feliciano Rivera.
[6] Tomás Ibarra-Frausto, "The Chicano Movement and the Emergence of a Chicano Poetic Consciousness" in *New Directions in Chicano Scholarship* ,Romo, Paredes ed. (San Diego: Chicano Monograph Series, 1978), p. 96.
[7] The first permanent Director for the Center for Mexican American Studies was Professor Arnoldo Carlos Vento. During his tenure (1978-1981), he doubled the curricular offerings and was responsible, as liason to President Flawn, for the recruitment of Ricardo Romo, José Limón, Rolando Hinojosa-Smith, Rudy de la Garza, and Manuel Ramírez III. Most important was the creation of an autonomous publications unit made possible by leasing and using its own typesetter thus obviating expenses and responsibility to the University of Texas Press.
[8] Rodolfo Acuña, *Occupied...*p. 393. See also Ronald W. López and Darryl D. Enos, *Chicanos and Public Higher Education in California* (Sacramento: Joint Committee on the Master Plan for Higher Education, California Legislature, December, 1972).
[9] Ibid., pp. 98-102.

[10] Linda Morales Armas, ed. *La Cosecha: Literatura y La Mujer Chicana* (A special issue of *De Colores: Journal of Emerging Raza Philosophers*, vol. 3, no. 3) (Albuquerque: Pajarito Publications, 1977), p. 3.

[11] Flor y Canto is the translation of the Aztekah festival call *In Xochitl, In Kuikatl* meaning literally *la flor, el canto* (flower and song). Originally it consisted of a gathering of artists, poets, philosophers from various nations comprising the Confederation of Anauak, their purpose was to seek truth beyond, in the deeper dimensions of consciousness. Thus, unlike the contemplation of the Greeks, it was a profound search into *Neltiliztli* or the root and foundation of things.

[12] See the introduction of Professor Segade to *Festival de Flor y Canto: An Anthology of Chicano Literature* (Los Angeles: UCLA Press, 1976).

[13] For a comprehensive history and analysis see Arnoldo Carlos Vento, "Origins and Significance of *Canto al Pueblo*: Image, Symbol and Identity of an Aesthetic Movement." Presented to the Western Social Science Conference in Oakland, California, April, 1994. To be published in a Ricardo Sánchez Anthology from the proceedings of *Border Voices* (El Paso, Sept. 1995).

[14] (Trans.) "We do not believe to be overseers, Gods or priests. We are people who work with the culture, the art to develop thought, to present to the people. If they want to accept, fine; if not it is the decision of the people..." See Ricardo Sánchez "Interview" in *Caracol*, April, 1978, p. 7.

[15] *Canto al Pueblo: An Anthology of Experiences*. Leonardo Carrillo (eds.), Corpus Christi: Penca, 1978.

[16] The *Canto al Pueblo III* was to be organized by Joaquín Lefebre of Pueblo Colorado but unforeseen conflicts among leaders forced cancellation of the *Canto*.

[17] Betsy Lee, *"Canto al Pueblo," Nosotros*, vol. 4, no. 3, may 1980, p. 62.

[18] Frank Geerk, *Poesie Zeitschrift für Literatur* (Switzerland: 1980); See also "Ein roter Mann im Weissen Haus?", *Basler Magazin*, no.29(July 19,1980), pp.1-3, 15.

[19] Luis Leal and Arnoldo Carlos Vento, "Ricardo Sánchez: An Interview By Luis Leal", in *The Ricardo Sánchez Reader: Critical Essays and Anthology*, P. 19. (Under Editorial Review).

[20] Ibid. p. 20.

[21] Ibid. p.26.

[22] Ibid. p. 34.

[23] Ricardo Sánchez, "Some Thoughts on Writing", *Hechizospells* (Los Angeles: CSC Publications, 1976), pp.x-xx.

[24] Ricardo Sánchez, "P-78 One World Festival", *Rayas*, no.6, (November-December, 1978), p.4.

[25] Luis Leal and Arnoldo Carlos Vento, *The Ricardo Sánchez Reader...*, p33.

[26] Ricardo Sánchez, "P-78 One World Poetry Festival," p.10.

[27] Luis Leal and Arnoldo Carlos Vento, *The Ricardo Sánchez Reader*, p.25.

[28] Ibid. p.37.

[29] Arnoldo Carlos Vento, "Ricardo Sánchez: His Life, Work and Contribution," *Border Voices Conference*, El Paso, Texas (September 29, 1995).

[30] Tomás Ibarra Frausto, "The Chicano Movement...", p.87. See also *Luis Valdez y el Teatro Campesino: Actos* (San Juan Bautista, California: Cucaracha Publications, 1973.

[31] Luis Valdez, *Pensamiento Serpentino, a Chicano approach to the Theater of Reality* (San Juan Bautista, California: Cucaracha Publications, 1973).

[32] Tomás Ibarra Frausto, "The Chicano Movement...," p. 88.

[33] Juan Bruce Novoa, *Chicano Authors: Inquiry by Interview* (Austin: University of Texas Press, 1980), p. 140.

[34] Charles M. Tatum, "Contemporary Prose Fiction: Its Ties to Mexican Literature," *The Identification and Analysis of Chicano Literature*, ed. Francisco Jiménez (New York: Bilingual Press, 1979), p. 55.

[35] See Juan Rulfo's collection of short stories in *El llano en llamas*

[36] Hector Calderón, "On the uses of Chronicle, Biography and Sketch in Rolando Hinojosa's *Generaciones y Semblanzas*," *The Rolando Hinojosa Reader*, ed. José David Saldívar (Houston Arte Público Press), 1986, p. 136. Another title borrowed from medieval literature reflected in Hinojosa's *Claros Varones de Belkan* is from Fernando de Pulgar's *Claros Varones de Castilla*.

[37] Arnoldo Carlos Vento, "Mito y símbolo prehispánico en la literatura Chicana y Mexicana: *Bless Me Ultima*." Paper presented at the *MLA* convention in San Francisco, 1979.

[38] Eliud Martínez, "Ron Arias' *The Road to Tamanzunchale*: A Chicano Novel of the New Reality," *Latin American Literary Review* 8, 10 (1977): pp. 55-61.

[39] In the early sixties, Seymour Menton, Luis Leal and other wrote about Magical Realism without concretely defining it. The following is a working definition from my unpublished book length manuscript on Magical Realism: "The point where the objective and subjective meet, the synthesis of Appollonian and Dionysian realities which form a whole, utilizing irony and myth, recreating itself in an eternal time-space cyclical sequence of events."

[40] Juan Bruce Novoa, Chicano Authorship...p. 237.

[41] Additional works by Chicano novelists mentioned include: Rolando Hinojosa-*Smith Rites and Witnesses* (1982), *The Useless Servants* (1984), *Dear Rafe* (1985), *Partners in Crime* (1985), *Claros Varones de Belkan/Fair Gentlemen of Belkan* (1986), *Becky and Her Friends* (1990); Rudolfo Anaya *Heart of Aztlan* (1976), *Tortuga* (1979), *The Legend of La Llorona* (1984), *The Adventures of Juan Chicaspatas* (1985); Miguel Méndez *El Sueño de Santa María de las Piedras* (1989), *Que no mueran los sueños* (1991); Sandra Cisneros *House on Mango Street* (1983), *Woman Hollering Creek* (1992); Floyd Salas *Tattoo the Wicked Cross* (1969), *Lay My Body on the Line: A Novel* (1978), *What Now My Love* (1994); Lucha Corpi *Delia's Story* (1989), *Variations on a Storm* (1990), *Cactus Blood: A Mystery Novel* (1995); and Victor Villaseñor *Jury: The People vs. Juan Corona* (1977), *Macho* (1991).

CHAPTER VIII

CHICANO CULTURAL INHERITANCE, IDENTITY & AWARENESS

CULTURE, FOLKLORE AND LANGUAGE

SOUTHWESTERN CHICANO DIALECTS

When Queen Isabela of Spain asked for a justification of the creation of a Spanish grammar by Antonio de Nebrija, she was told "your majesty, language is the instrument of empires." This quote reveals not only the political motives of Spain but it also reveals Isabela's dominance of her Castille over Aragón. Thus, language is also the instrument of culture; it reveals attitudes, folkways, dialectal preferences, and worldviews. Chicano dialects as a phenomena of interaction between various cultures is first studied by Aurelio M. Espinosa in New Mexico.[1] Particularly unique in New Mexican Spanish are the archaic Spanish expressions. While many New Mexicans, proud of their Spanish heritage (ergo, their insider term of *Hispano*), would like to link their *Southwest*ern brand of Spanish to Spaniards, it is more a case of isolationism that permitted the maintenance of archaic Spanish expressions in the geographically detached northern New Mexico. The rural *campesino* and syncretic Native- American south of the border also has retained many archaic expressions. In this case, social and racial discrimination forced the isolation of these poor socio-economic groups in Mexico over a period of 300 years of colonialism. Examples of archaic expressions include *mesmo, onde, trujo and asina*. This type of lexicon can be found in the classic Spanish works of *Don Quijote de la Mancha, La Celestina* and *El poema del Mio Cid*. Ironically, when Anglo-American Spanish teachers castigated and humiliated Chicano students for using *onde* and *asina*, they did not know, in their ignorance, that these were true Castillian words from classical works of the past.[2] Some expressions evolved between the archaic level and the contemporary level e.g. *asina* (from *ansi mesmo* to *ansina mesmo* to *asina mismo* to *así mismo*) while others developed during colonial times e.g. *muncho*, as used by Friar Juan de Pineda.[3] Unique to the speech of South Texas is the use of accenting the first syllable of the first person subjunctive e.g. *háyamos, póngamos* etc. and the use of *semos* for *somos*. Both are expressions that were in use of the XV and XVI centuries.[4] Other archaic terms in current use are *vide* for *ví, estilla* for *astilla, culeco* for *clueco, vagamundo* for *vagabundo* and *rede* for *red*.[5]

Another language system that plays a significant role in the development of chicano dialects is *Aztekah Náhuatl*. The impact of this language is certainly understood from a historical and geographical standpoint. There are literally thousands of words in current usage in the language of all Spanish- speakers from Mexican ancestry. Even the Spanish criollos after one generation were using different vocabulary, much of which was "mexicanized" i.e. from an *Aztekah Náhuatl* derivative. Of the many lexical terms used growing up as a Chicano in South Texas included *esquite* for popcorn (from *esquitl*); *zoquete* for mud (from *zóquitl*); *zacate* for grass (from *zákatl*); *pisca* for cotton picking (from *pixka*); *cuates* for buddies (from *kóatl*); *mayate* for black person (from *máyatl* or black bug) and *calcos* for shoes (from *kactli*). Other words derived from *Aztekah Náhuatl* include *escuincle; tacuache piocha, nel* and *yanqui*.[6]

Among the *barrios*, and in particular to street youths is the use of *Caló*. Essentially, it is the argot introduced by the gypsies into the Americas. It is found in Spain and in every Spanish speaking country in the Americas. In Mexico it sometimes is referred to as *Caliche* while in Spain it is called *germanía*.[7] Because of its esoteric qualities and its intention to not be understood by the authorities, it is seen as an underground language. It is very much alive and well in the federal penal institutions. It is plastic and metaphoric and often inventive in expression. It may borrow from *Aztekah Náhuatl,* Haitian or other foreign sources and adapt that vocabulary to its own argot. Pure *Caló* words include the following *baisa* (hands), *jura* (cops), *chavalo* (boy), *pápira* (money), from *Aztekah Náhuatl* we derive *calcos* or *cacles* for shoes; its Aztec word is *kactli* (shoes). In the same manner, *shante* (house) comes from *shantli,* also house in *Aztekah Náhuatl.* From the Portuguese word *pipiripao,* modern *Caló* derives *pipirín* (snack). Its expression may be exemplary of rhyme and alliteration e.g. *"ontablas que no te había vidrios"* from the Spanish *Dónde estabas que no te había visto* (where were you that I didn't see you?); *Está uno iguanas, ranas, tu sábanas* from the Spanish *"Está uno igual, tu sabes* (it is the same, you know); and *"oranas las otrofas"* from the Spanish *"ahora las otras copas* (and now the rest of the drinks). During the *Chicano Movement* of the late sixties and seventies, the *Pachuco* argot of *Caló* became well accepted: the *Pachuco* was looked at as the anti-hero of the movement for his historic role in the Zoot Suit riots of the 40's in Los Angeles i.e. having stood his ground to the violent confrontation with Anglo-American sailors. From Mexican literature and/or cinema he is the *Periquillo* of Lizardi, the *Pito Pérez* of Romero or the *Tin Tan* of the Mexican cinema but in the Chicano sense, one that is activist and rebellious. Thus, the *Pachuco* was seen as a heroic model and his street speech was used not only by university students but by professors in their lectures during the Chicano movement of the sixties and seventies.[8] The language system most readily seen as impacting the Chicano dialect is English. It has been referred to as Tex-Mex but this stereotype is not only inaccurate but is derisive in characterization. It connotes a bastardization of the Spanish language. While many English words do function as loans, as can be seen, the language of the Chicano/a is rich and varied and actually was four language sources to form its dialects i.e. archaic Spanish, English, *Aztekah Náhuatl* and Caló or Romany.[9] With respect to English, it should be noted that since the Chicano/a is educated formally in English and is constantly bombarded with English by the media, it is only natural that he think and speak with English words. The impact of English, moreover, has been felt for sometime worldwide. In Mestizo-America it is so abundant that there is a dictionary of Americanisms. With the introduction of North American television programs, technical terms and North American companies into Mestizo-America, there is a veritable invasion of English vocabulary into Spanish speech. At one point smog was known as *neblumo* i.e. the combination of smoke and fog translated into Spanish. Now it is simply the same word with a slight Spanish pronunciation in Mexico. Instead of the diminutive *Pedrito* the phonetic representation of Pete is used i.e. *Pit* in Spanish. In the U.S., most interesting is the ability of the Chicano/a to code switch i.e. move from one language to another within a sentence. This is a natural process for bilingual/bicultural people as witnessed in the French speaking Canada, and some parts of Cajun country in Louisiana. While some expressions are direct translations (*ay te wacho*: I'll see you there) others are not e.g. *cuelgo los guantes* (to hang it up) when changed slightly to *cuelgo los tenis* means to die. The influence of English can be seen in *chispa* (meaning spark) for spark plug; *daime* for dime; *mama grande* for grandmother, but sometimes an authentic word in Spanish is used with a variant meaning e.g. *mecha* (wick in Spanish) but now meaning matches since it is similar phonetically. In some cases, there is simply no Spanish equivalent e.g. there is no position of sheriff in Spanish; thus, it is merely reproduced phonetically in Spanish i.e. *cherife*. Sometimes the Chicano will be creative and invent a word like *yuta* from u-turn. Without realizing he/she may use archaic Spanish expressions that English likewise has borrowed form Latin e.g. *ofertar* (to offer), *augosto* (August) and *liberarte* (liberate). It should be noted, however, that the Chicano's knowledge of Spanish may often be passive i.e. he knows or has heard the word before but was able to recall the English quicker since this was in the more active linguistic phase.

Finally, we can conclude that language can be a tool not only for communication but also for social and racial discrimination by dominant hegemonic groups. It should never be seen in a static purist state but rather as a dynamic, ever changing and evolving form of communication, representative of its historical relationship. The Chicano dialect in its richness and diversity must be seen as a natural phenomenon of a bilingual/bicultural person, one that projects itself in a multi-lingual and universal plane.

RAZA HUMOR

Among *Mestizos* and particularly bilingual/bicultural Chicanos and/or "Latinos," humor is a significant element in the culture and daily existence. In South Texas, joke sessions in Spanish, English or both are held in all types of occasions, either in a social setting on a work break.

José R. Reyna categorizes the different types of jokes: (1) jokes based on misunderstandings of language, numskull jokes; cleverness; lies and exaggerations; blasón populaire; *Perico* jokes; jokes about men; jokes about women.[10] Because Chicanos/as are bilingual/bicultural, several meanings can be derived from phrases that have been extrapolated from either language e.g. *coger* (to take; to copulate); *venirse* (to return; to ejaculate); *chile* (chili pepper; penis); *huevos* (eggs; testicles). Some times words have different meanings in Mexico and the U.S. e.g. *alto* (stop; tall). Sometimes Chicanos play on the phonetics of a Spanish verb that may sound similar to a noun in English e.g. *puse*. Misunderstandings of Spanish by Anglo-Americans serve likewise, as a basis for jokes, e.g. the social worker that wanted to greet the Spanish speaking clients that did not know the Spanish for "greet;" ergo she hispanicized the word and said "*Estoy aqui para greetar a Uds!*" In Spanish *gritar* means to shout thus she actually said, "I am here to shout at you."

One of the differences between African-Americans as a minority and Chicanos and/or Latinos is that the former generally operates monolingually in English while the latter is flexible in various languages. This poses a problem for comedians since their audience becomes limited, particularly in the national U.S. media. Because of the formal aspects of Spanish/Mexican culture, there are some jokes that are not meant for mixed company. Still, Reyna attests that women have their own sessions e.g. hospital workers, nurses, etc. Jokes about Anglos are not always portrayed in pejorative terms; sometimes, especially when the Anglo accepts Spanish or a Spanish cultural trait, it is often taken in a very positive light by the Chicano, e.g. "me too Lupe jokes." Recent immigrants or undocumented Mexican arrivals are the source of many jokes by Chicanos. Some seen as *mojaditos* or *alambristas* (undocumented Mexican) become the basis for ridicule because of their unfamiliarity with modern artifacts. Using subtle social discrimination against

Native Americans from Mexico *(Indito)*, the American born Chicano can make a normal setting into a ridiculous one by a play with words, e.g. an undocumented Mexican *campesino* has just traversed the desert and is coming into Indio, California (literally Indian, California). When the new arrival asks a Chicano *¿Cuanto me falta pa Indio?* The Chicano takes advantage if the potential double entendre and responds, *"¡Nomás te faltan las plumas desgraciado!"* Here the question can be interpreted two ways (a) the way it was meant, i.e. how far do I have to go to get to Indio? or (b) how far do I have to go to be Indian? The whimsical Chicano answer is "All you need is feathers, dammit!" Chicanos/as can also play and invent words from Spanish to English: from *chingadera* it can become *"la chingadaire;"* from *no seas soflamero*, we get "Don't be *soflamis;"* from high society we get "high *sociégate."* Women in the traditional jokes were more passive, but some jokes indicate that they can take the lead and be aggressive, e.g. the joke where Pancho Villa separates all the ladies from their husbands, to which one husband objected; the wife retorts who's in charge here, you or Pancho Villa?

African-Americans can also be a target of jokes by the Chicano. Reyna cites the story about a Chicano ordering a beer from an African-American. Here the Chicano says, "Give me a beer nigger!" The bartender insulted asks the Chicano how he would like it if it were reversed. Thus, they trade places with the African-American now demanding "Give me a beer, Mexican!" The Chicano quickly answers, "Sorry, we don't serve niggers." In the forties, African-Americans were referred to as *parnas* by the Chicanos (from partners) probably because this was a term used by them when addressing Chicanos since both shared the lower socio-economic scale of society in the *Southwest*. However, there is a color discrimination in the Hispanic culture since to be *hüero* is always better than to be *moreno* (better to be fairer than dark-skinned) and the existence of the pejorative word of *mayate* for (Blacks) is proof of this racial European origined bias.[11]

CURANDERISMO

Curanderismo is the art of healing within the folk culture of the *Spanish-Speaking*. Within the Mexican tradition, it combines both European and Native-American methods that include Moorish humor theory, gypsy prognostic practices, spiritualism, Aztec botanical knowledge and psychic energy manipulation.[12] *Curanderos* or healers have been greatly misunderstood and consequently maligned by the middle and upper class social groups and the medical establishment. Too often it is easy to point the accusatory, Inquisitional finger at *Curanderos*/as that are providing an excellent health service to the community of the poor. The charge by the middle class is usually derisive often one of witchcraft. While it cannot be denied that there are those who are into witchcraft (in every culture), the vast majority of the *Curanderos* are hardworking individuals who sacrifice their time and families to assist those in need of help. A *Curandero* or a *Curandera* may specialize in one of several area (a) *partera* (midwifery), *huesero* (chiropractic type of care), *sobador* (therapeutic massage), and *espiritista* (spiritualist). But in every case each has medicinal herbal knowledge that has been passed on for centuries regarding a wide variety of ailments. Trotter and Chavira divide the healing of *Curanderos* into the following basic categories: (1) the material level, (2) the spiritualist level and (3) the psychic level.[13] Most *Curanderos*/as operate in the first level. The second group are largely followers, although not exclusively, of the *Niño Fidencio,* a boy healer whose miraculous healings are called for through his intercession in the spiritualist world. These followers are known as *Fidencistas.* The third category is the most difficult to document since science today does not have the theory or knowledge, much less the understanding of how it works. There are a few, however, who have been able to explain a theoretical framework via neo-physics. Essentially, it involves a manipulation of the molecular structure of matter which defies the standard understanding of the body. Of this latter category the most famous are the psychic surgeons of the Philippines. Some quantum physicists believe that consciousness is at the root of the material universe. The theories of Bohr, Hisenberg, Einstein and Wheeler have expressed a multi-dimensional universe where the influence of the observer is unavoidable in co-existing superspace. The idea of consciousness controlling and organizing the biogravitational field provides the plausible scenario of the mind healing almost all diseases since diseases can be traced to disruptions in the space-time organization of living matter. One physicist conjectured that since healers are a link between the patient and the cosmos, the knowledge of self organization that is contained in superspace is somehow transmitted through the healer to the patient.[14]

Of the positive effects of *Curanderismo* is the healing by synergy (only recently verified by Bernie Segal), the contribution toward balanced mental health through positive counseling and therapies, the availability of health care otherwise not available to millions who do not have health insurance, the relating to a person who understands your language, and culture. The corresponding *Curandero* can, therefore, make culturally and healthy recommendations to each patient. Standard general practitioners unfortunately separate themselves from their patients for objectivity not realizing that it presents a distance and possible barrier for synergetic response and healing. The common complaint is that MD's today are more concerned about money and its accumulation than the healing and welfare of their patients. Often they call in efficiency experts to see how the office can make more money each succeeding year. Another more serious problem admitted by some MD's is the dependence and questionable relationship with the pharmaceutical industry who underwrites much of the activity of medical practitioners including incentives for paid vacations. The problem is obvious: a clear dependence on drugs as the primary solution and the inability to prescribe alternative non-drug oriented holistic remedies or therapies.

One of the most prevalent medical problems of our times is *iatrogenic* illness. It means literally "doctor caused." This results from surgical complications, wrong medications, side effects of drugs or other treatments and the debilitating effects of hospitalization. [15]

Another major problem is the symptomatic approach which deals with the effect and not the cause. Thus, medicine is seen from an allopathic level rather than a body/mind process where prevention is synonymous with wholeness. There is a close relationship between thoughts, emotions and health; yet the medical establishment would rather deal with placebos and drugs. *Curanderos/as* understand synergy and the relationship between thoughts, emotions, health and the spiritual needs of each person. In many ways, they are the real precursors of the Holistic Health movement. Another distinction is that they are not materialists for a true *Curandero/a* cannot fix a charge in view that healing is not relegated to him/her but comes from higher sources. Thus, he cannot exploit, as often happens in the medical profession. When I used to teach pre-medical students, I would ask in the form of a questionnaire a series of questions related to their goals including why they were going into the medical profession. The majority invariably answered "because of the money." Is this not one of the major problems? Fortunately, decadence is not eternal and evolution and cycles within society move forward. As we approach the 21st century, more young medical students are demanding change within the structure of the medical profession. Doctors must go into the profession because they want to help the unfortunate and the poor with or without remuneration. They must establish a link on par with the patient (like the *Curandero*) and establish a co-operative healing approach without being co-opted by the big money industries. Research must be less myopic and focus less exclusively on the bio-plasmic body; it needs a marriage of disciplines, i. e.. physics, chemistry, biology, psychology, and anthropology so that it can better understand the workings of pathology and the healing process of different groups. The future is bright with advanced non-invasive procedures, as evidenced by psychoneuroimmunology, laser, light and sound. It must not be locked in into a mechanistic Newtonian and Cartesian world where the universe is mechanically fixed; rather, it needs to have as Einstein said "Imagination (because it) is greater than knowledge." Only then can there be vision beyond our outmoded form of existence.

CHICANO MUSIC

Chicano music encompasses traditional forms of Mexican music i.e. *Ranchera, Cumbia, Corrido, Vals* but it also has its own home grown music in the form of *Conjunto* Tejano and modern Tejano pops. Manuel Peña in his excellent work on *Conjunto* music of Texas, cites secondary sources that shed light to the beginnings of musical groups in Texas.[16] These point to Monterrey, Mexico as an important source of both material goods and culture for Mexicans living in Texas particularly around 1860. During this period, European culture and the role of Maximilian maintain the status quo and the elite. The latter attend opera while the popular classes cater to salon music and dances i.e. Polka, Schottische, Waltz, Minuet,

Quadrille and *Danza Habanera*. While the semi erudite *criollo* caters to imported salon music, the *Mestizo* dances to a mixture of rhythms, including *tropical*. Monterrey was not only a major industrial center but a cultural one as well; it possessed organized orchestras, military bands, arts center, theaters and public concerts featuring *Pasodobles, Polkas, Marchas, Contradanzas, Chotís, Mazurcas,* etc. Because there was an abundance of *maestros* of music, its influence extended to San Antonio, Corpus Christi and Laredo and did not diminish until the twenties when the border was closed due to North American economic expansionism. It was the filtering down of the music from the upper classes to the working class that created in simplified fashion makeshift ensembles. It took on different styles: (1) rudimentary accordion ensemble, (2) string/wind ensemble and (3) solo or duet with guitar accompaniment. By the thirties, orchestras had added to the violins, guitars, contrabass and mandolins the saxophones, trumpets and piano, largely used by society organizations. In terms of stylistic break-throughs, this came in the form of solo performance in both vocal and instrumental music i.e. accordion and the violin; the guitar or *bajo sexto* with violin plus the *tambora de rancho*. The accordion became a favorite instrument because it was inexpensive and was readily available from duty free border towns; moreover, the cost of hiring one musician was relatively low. By the golden years of the twenties, there were a number of groups that created a new market for the record companies: Los Hermanos Bañuelos (1920), Pedro Rocha (1928), Lupe Martínez (1928), etc with the first accordion recording by Bruno Villarreal (1928). As was the case with African-American musicians, Mexican/Chicano musicians were exploited with verbal contracts and flat fees of $15-$30 per record. The early accordion musicians were seen with dubious reputations by society. Such were the negative perceptions by the Spanish-Speaking middle class and wealthy elements of society who disassociated themselves from the activities of the masses. It was not until after the post-war years that lyrics came into play at dances.

Of the forerunners of the Chicano *Conjunto* style was Narciso Martínez who de-emphasized bass and chord elements for the more articulated melody lines at the tribal end giving a snappier and lively quality unforeseen in the twenties. Narciso Martínez known as

Tejano Conjunto Poster, San Antonio, Texas (by Diana Edwards)

El huracán del valle, played mostly instrumental music, anywhere he could muster some coins; often, he had to work as a stoop laborer to make ends meet. The first generation of Chicano *Conjunto* musicians (thirties and forties) also featured Santiago Jiménez, known as *El flaco de San Antonio*. His style was softer, a legato mode of articulation as opposed to the marcato style of Martínez. He is credited to have introduced the *tololoche* or contrabass into *Conjunto* music. Others from this generation include Lolo Cavazos and Pedro Ayala. It was Ayala that crystallized new stylistic trends in the late forties, inspiring younger musicians like Valerio Longoria and Tony de la Rosa. His style was snappy using 16th note fingerings with a more pronounced marcato technique. This brought forth the second generation (1950's-1960's) of *Conjunto* musicians which included Tony de la Rosa, Mingo Saldívar, Ruben Vela, Rubén Naranjo, and Valerio Longoria. The third generation (1970's-1990) includes the *Conjunto* as a national folk form, internationally recognized from Germany to Japan. Among the many artists include Santiago Jiménez Jr., Flaco Jiménez, Los dos Gilbertos, Roberto Pulido, David Lee Garza, Emilio Navaira, Estéban Jordan, La Tropa F and Los Aguilares.

Beyond this original folk music, Chicano artists gain national prominence with the performance of Sonny Ozuna during the rock and roll era. It was his big band sound in *Sonny Ozuna and the Sunliners* that gave rise to national recognition and broke new ground in mainstream record companies. Such was the case with *Little Joe y la Familia* whose song *Nubes* became the anthem for the Farmworkers Movement. The seventies and eighties saw a revolution in sound as new Chicano/ Latino artists and composers began to blend the synthesizers and electric guitar with the accordion and traditional rhythms. The music was lively, contemporary and danceable. The lyrics contained a wide range of themes from the humorous to the tragic, from family to love. As audiences and markets expanded, the new and younger generations of listeners increased. Tejano/ Latino artists became known internationally in the Spanish-speaking markets; some, like Selena and Emilio Navaira were able to establish "crossovers" into the mainstream audiences and music. The new Tejano sounds produced a large number of new groups with sounds and styles changing from year to year. Some of the more successful Tejano bands include *Mazz*, La *Mafia*, La *Tropa F*, La *Diferenzia* and *Ternura*. Other bands popular with the Spanish-speaking of Mexican descent include *The Home Town Boys*, *Los Palominos*, *Los Musicales*, *Los Desperados* and *Río*. Among the male vocalists, outstanding headliners included Ram Herrera, Robert and Bobby Pulido, Gary Hobbs, David Lee Garza, Michael Salgado, David Mares, Joe López, Jay Pérez, and Emilio Naviara. Among the female singers, Lydia Mendoza stands out in the thirties while in more modern times, Laura Canales begins a trend of female vocalists that have continued to the present international heights of Selena.

It was Selena Quintanilla Pérez that opened the door for other aspiring young artists. Her premature and tragic death brought about great emotion and attention to her life, to her ebullient personality and ethical/moral character. The result was a new Hollywood release entitled simply *Selena*. As she became an icon in the Tejano music arena, numerous young girls aspired to follow her as a role model, bringing , further, a new pool of talent to the Tejano music scene. According to Abraham Quintanilla, his daughter Selena, "was the youngest female artist to win the Tejano Music Award of Entertainer of the Year at the age of fifteen.[17] When asked if there is another artist of her stature in the making, Mr. Quintanilla pointed to Jennifer Peña, who at the age of thirteen, won the honor of Entertainer of the Year in Texas. Her CD entitled *Pura Dulzura*, moreover, is reaching the heights of platinum.[18] Other young female vocalists include Shelly Lares, Elsa García, Stefani, Becky Mesa. among many others coming into the music scene. Women also are playing the accordeon (Chavela , Eva Ibarra and Priscila). In the folk area, Tish Hinojosa has distinguished herself in both Spanish and English as vocalist and performer in a wide section of audiences. Currently, there is a plethora of creativity among Chicano/Latino artists; new styles and forms are being created both in Spanish and English reaching not just a national television audience but an international one via Johnny Canales and *Univisión*. *Conjunto* is so popular in Japan that several Japanese groups have created their own *Conjunto* bands; one such group made its American debut at the internationally known *Tejano Conjunto Festival* in San Antonio, Texas.[19] There are currently artists that are ready to make the cross-over and move Chicano music into mainstream America.

CHICANO CINEMA

Mexican/Chicano stereotyping can be traced back to the XIX century dime novels which in turn give rise to a number of Hollywood films portraying negative Chicano/hispanic stereotypes. Charles Ramirez Berg explores films that portray the aforementioned; he cites six Hollywood stereotypes of the Hispanic (1) the Bandido, a shifty, dishonest, dirty, violent, treacherous type; a villain that dates back to the silent greaser films (*Broncho Billy and the Greaser* [1914]), (2) the Half-breed Harlot, a lusty hot tempered harlot type who is a slave to her passions (Doc Holiday's woman *Chihuahua* in *My Darling Clementine*), (3) the Male Buffoon, a second banana comic relief, a target of ridicule (Pancho in the *Cisco Kid,* Ricky Ricardo in *I Love Lucy*), (4) the Female Clown, the male buffoon's female counterpart, a dingbat with base instincts (Lupe Vélez in *Palooka*, Carmen Miranda in *The Gang's All Here*, (5) the Latin Lover, (Valentino in *The Sheik*) and (6) the Dark Lady, circumspect and aloof, opaque (Dolores del Río in *Flying Down to Rio*).[20]

Films depicting verisimilitude of Chicano characters date to 1954 with *Salt of the Earth* in which Mexican American zinc miners reenact their strike won against racist employers. Similarly, Rick Tejeda Flores' *Si Se Puede* is a portrait of César Chávez during a 24 hour fast to protest proposed legislation against strikes and boycotts in Arizona,and Crystal City. Severo Pérez's study of the rise of *La Raza Unida* in Crystal City, Texas. In the vein of Chicano history, Hector Galan's *Los mineros* and Beverly Sánchez Padilla's *El corrido de Juan Chacón* demonstrate the enduring prestige of *Salt of the Earth* by Herbert Biberman. *I am Joaquín* produced by Luis Valdez and the *Teatro Campesino* dates to 1969 while Jorge Luis Ruiz's *Los Vendidos* written by Luis Valdez is another early landmark. In 1979, Sylvia Morales adds to the early feminist responses to patriarchal versions of Chicano culture in her film entitled *Chicana*.[21] The period that negates derogatory characterizations is called the period of counterimaging cinema; this is best seen in the eighties with Luis Valdez's *Zoot Suit* (1980), *La Bamba* (1989), Cheech Marin's *Born in East L.A.* (1987), Ramón Menéndez's *Stand and Deliver* (1988) and Robert Redford and Moctesuma Esparza's *Milagro Beanfield War* (1988). Here Chicanos are creating their own images. While

Selena Quintanilla accepting a Grammy Award.

some take issue with stereotypes and heritage questions, there is no question that the cinema has progressed towards more independence as a growing Chicano/Latino film industry emerges as "*La Nueva Onda.*" This term describes a recent trend of non-Hollywood filmmakers. Forefathers of this new wave include Hector Galán, Beverly Sánchez Padilla, Lourdes Portillo, Paul Espinosa, Sylvia Morales, Susana Rocho and Jesús Treviño among others.[22] Rather than fashioning themselves after the Valdez model of Chicano filmmaking through major studio support, the *Nueva Onda* film makers have fashioned themselves after the Robert Rodriguez model of guerrilla filmmaking whose roots are found in Spike Lee's *She's Gotta Have It* example. By definition, *La Nueva Onda* is a trend towards an independently produced U.S. Chicano/Latino audience. Recent films receiving praise include the 1995 Sol Award winning Severo Pérez for directing the film adaptation of the classic Chicano novel of Tomás Rivera *...And the Earth did not Swallow Him.* Winner of the same prize a year earlier was Hector Galán for his documentary on Tejano music entitled *Songs of the Homeland.* While Hollywood may stay out of the production of Chicano/Latino films, it certainly will stay in the Chicano/Latino film distribution. There are various reasons that point to a boom in Chicano/Latino film (1) the critical mass of Chicano/Latino population is accelerating higher than any other group, (2) there is a growing number of young *Nueva Onda* filmmakers that have a growing number of prominent Latino film and video festivals to display their work and, (3) there is more access to video, filmmaking equipment via university programs. Thus, Chicano/Latino cinema is the next and most promising field to dominate as we approach the end of this century

CHICANISMO/CHICANIDAD : FROM PRE-COLUMBIAN ROOTS TO MESTIZAJICANIDAD

ORIGIN AND MEANING OF "CHICANO": PHILOSOPHICAL AND SOCIETAL IMPLICATIONS

The word Chicano became popularized during the Chicano movement and came into mainstream vocabulary via the print and visual media. Because it was a term that was used by the lower socio-economic oppressed classes within the Spanish-speaking of Mexican descent, it became the linguistic symbol for the struggle for the rights of Chicanos and Latinos during the sixties and seventies. It's linguistic roots are found in *Aztekah-Náhuatl* and *Maya-Quiché* cultures which provide not only a foundation for the *Chicano Movement* but pride as inheritors of an advanced ancestral culture and civilization. Although western writers and historians have reiterated a negative savage and sanguinary image of Aztecs , invented by medieval Spanish chroniclers, history eventually will be corrected and it will become clear, that indeed, this model adopted by the *Chicano Movement* has the basis for a new and future model of society. Its non-Western structure with its primary characteristics of communal governing models, the sharing and distribution of the wealth, the respect for all living things both in the human, plant and animal worlds, the understanding of ecological balance, the understanding and role of energy in the cosmos, its mathematical and astronomical understanding of life are but a few of the philosophical perceptions that will become part of the future world of society. While there was a type of utopic and almost mystical feeling of the glorious past, Chicanos were faced with more black and white realities that were at once brutal, violent and invasive in terms of their daily existence vis a vis dominant Anglo-American society. Rendón in "a personal manifesto" declares that he is a Chicano

> because of the fusion of bloods, history and culture...because of a rising awareness...of a fresh rebirth of self...in spite of scorn or derision, in spite of opposition even from my own people...hopeful that my acceptance and assertion of Chicanismo will mean a better life for all my people, that it will move others into making the same act of will to accept and develop a new found identity and power...and I will resist any attacks against me or anyone else who is a Chicano...Chicano encompasses a new way of looking at life, at interpreting history, of defending our social role, of rejecting an alien and degrading concept which the gringo would rather have us accept...to be a Chicano means that a person has looked deeper into his being and sought unique ties to his brothers in la *Raza*...[23]

Thus, to be a Chicano/a is to have consciousness of who you are, one's identity, as one becomes aware of the cultural/historical past and present so that the Chicano/a can, through a process of election and self determination, create his own future. The new emerging Chicano, as Romano pointed out in his essay on the historical and intellectual presence of the Mexican American, has discovered the full range of the meaning of biculturalism.

PLURALISM AND UNIVERSALITY OF VASCONCELOS' *LA RAZA CÓSMICA*

Borrowing from the essays and ideas of José Vasconcelos, Chicanos saw in their pluralism a universal man that combines all the racial strains and cultures of the world ergo *La Raza Cósmica*. But because of the medieval colonial hierarchical class structures, *la Raza* paid its price in pain, suffering and isolation.

As a people, after having suffered the hegemony of the exploitative violent and racist Spanish and *Criollos*, the hegemony of the French, the *caudillismo* of Porfirio Díaz, the destruction of the Mexican Revolution and the violent invasion of the U.S. in the Southwest, the Chicano in the sixties and seventies burst into the scene looking for vindication of the American past after four hundred years of debasement from European ethnocentric racism. Guillermo Fuenfríos, observed in the early seventies that the Chicano was becoming consciously tricultural. He noted the significance of the emergence of the consciousness of *La Nueva Raza* should come about in a moment of crisis in Western civilization, unparalleled in human history, a time that witnesses the total impotence of Western-Christian Marxist Humanism to curb the disastrous long range effects of technological development. He cites contemporary thinkers (Paz, Marcuse, Brown) that point to a new direction, one that opposes linear rational thought (Norman Brown), one that calls for the resurrection of the spirit of Orpheus and Narcissus (Marcuse), the reconciliation of the body, soul and world (Octavio Paz). The Chicano is poised to be the link between the Western and non-Western worlds. "He has access to the occidental modes of rational thought, he is heir to the lyrical and poetic tradition of the Mediterranean and he has recently discovered the dignity and wonder of the non-rational indigenous mind."[24]

The question arises with respect to the specific characteristics of the Chicano/a in the late XX century. To what degree do these represent, as a syncretic culture, European, Anglo-American or *Pre-Columbian* mindset? Rendón classified the following as exemplary of the diversified Chicano: (1) individualism, (2) tough and thorough stoicism, (3) spiritual integrity, (4) keen grasp of the sense of human dignity, (5) dependence on family structures and internal resources, (6) independence from alien social forms or services, (7) tolerance of outlandish dress and speech and (8) revulsion of elders towards younger Chicano militants.[25] What is missing are not only other key characteristics but the roots and relation to the culturefrom which it borrows such characteristics.

CHICANO CUSTOMS AND CELEBRATIONS: CHOLOS, HISPANOS, LATINOS AND MESTIZO-AMERICANS

From the Mexican brother/sister south of the border, there is a love of celebrations and rituals as can be seen in traditional holidays (*16 de Septiembre, Cinco de Mayo, Día de los Muertos*, etc.) and a resistance to break away totally from the extended family reinforced by familial gatherings, baptisms, *quinceañeras*, and *bailes*. Unlike the brother/sister south of the border, the Chicano/a is skilled in code switching with various languages and dialects; he/she is active, not passive. Depending on the socio-economic level and the relationship to Mexico, the Chicano/a will adhere more to one culture than the other, e.g. a first generation *barrio* person, isolated to a great degree from dominant Anglo-American society will be more closely aligned to the traditional, extended Mexican family. Nathan Murillo notes the following characteristics in the Mexican family: material things while a necessity are not an end; work is viewed as survival not as a value; the poet, teacher, philosopher is more revered than the financier; time and space is in the present and not in the future, the interpersonal relationships are not blunt but have a concern for the respect of other's feelings as touch, feel, taste, smell are important as it brings a closeness to the other person.[26]

There was during the *Chicano Movement* a sense of *carnalismo* or brotherhood that linked him/her to an ancient tradition; moreover he/she viewed family as the foundation from which all decisions derive with respect, love and unity as central characteristics therein; the Chicano/a has a deep love and respect for mother earth; he/she sees himself/herself as a new emerging *Mestizo/a* who recognizes not only his hispanic roots but his *Pre-Columbian* roots but concurrently adding a third culture (Anglo-Saxon) creating a multicultural self. The Chicano/a is a rebel when necessary as has been evident in the cases of Gregorio Cortez, Juan N. Cortina, Reies López Tijerina, César Chávez and the *Chicano Movement.* According to his/her socio-economic level and region his/her dialects are rich and diverse; they include Aztec origin expressions, archaic Spanish, Caló and Hispanicized English expressions. There is no one model for the Chicano/a; they range from the poor and not assimilated who speak little English to the middle and upper leveled socio-economic classes that are assimilated that speak largely English and understand little Spanish. The Chicano male is generally characterized by *Machismo*, a chauvinistic trait also found among the Anglo albeit in a distinct form. As an aspiring middle class person, the Chicano/a discriminates socially against the recent arrival, often undocumented from Mexico by using the derisive term *"mojado."* The Chicano/a has a unique sense of humor and as a consequence there exists within the cultural tradition the joke telling sessions not just among males but also females. Some Chicanos/as, particularly in *barrios* are territorial. In music he is diversified although there is usually a favorite musical type in distinct regions. He can, nonetheless, be at home with *Cumbia, Polka,* Country, Rock, *Chotis, Tacuachito* or modern *Tejano.* As a multicultural person, he may dream in Spanish or English according to the person. Finally, the Chicano/a is a hardworking person who knows how to save and build for a future.[27]

What is important is to understand the origins of these characteristics so that the Chicano/a can better understand his cultural inheritance and be in a better position to choose the more positive aspects of his/her culture and eliminate those that are counterproductive. Beginning with Rendón's listing of characteristics, individualism is a definite European and Western trait that was present similarly in the Spanish and the Moor, unfortunately, in an extreme form. The stoicism and spiritual integrity is the direct inheritance from our *Pre-Columbian* ancestors. The unity of the family, while present in both traditions, is unique among Mestizo-American nations where there are large Amerigenous populations. Here there is a more spiritual, rather than formal sense of family. The Chicano/a is proud and their integrity usually prevents them from relying on social forms or services.

Rendón's idea of tolerance towards outlandish dress and the elders revulsion toward younger Chicano militants are more offsprings of modern societal development. Here he is alluding to the *barrio* styles which are stylistic ways of creating identity and also the resistance of the elders towards change in the old traditions. The reference to celebrations and fiestas and the resistance to break away totally from the extended family are connected directly to the mother culture south of the border where patriotic events and Catholic Church rituals are integrated into the family structures. However, code switching is a characteristic only to Spanish-Speakers raised in the U.S., a trait that can be traced back to 1848 with the Treaty of Guadalupe Hidalgo, and the imposition of a new culture and language on the native Spanish-Speakers of the Southwest. Murillo's idea of materialism being a necessity and not an end needs to be qualified. This is applicable to the very poor who suffer isolation and discrimination and who are usually confined to stoop labor and/or the *barrios*. As Chicanos/as have become more integrated and have become part of the middle class, they have become more materialistic with the upper socio-economic classes generally accepting the materialistic oriented Anglo values. With regard to perceptions of teachers and philosophers as more revered than businessmen/women and time for the Chicano/a is the present as opposed to the future, the aforementioned role does not apply where there is upward socio-economic mobility and old world traditions are eliminated. Because of the "latin" oriented culture, there is in all romance language groups a different approach with touch, feel, taste and smell uniquely contributing to the closeness to the other person. One should add however, as Pedro Henriquez Ureña noted as a member of the *Ateneo de la Juventud* in Mexico, the Mexican is different from the old world Hispanics e.g. his proverbial courtesy, integrity of spirit and nobleness of character.[28] This, no doubt, are the contributions of the *Pre-Columbian* heritage. Likewise, the Mexican's sense of *carnalismo* or brotherhood, while a Christian principle from the Master himself but rarely practiced in the Christian world, was a fundamental principle within *all Pre-Columbian* cultures from Alaska to South America. This principle was expressed, for example, by the Maya with *In Lakesh* or you are my other self.[29] Thus what I do to you I do to myself, ergo a spirit of brotherhood and fraternity; a spiritual respect for all living things. This is why within the *campesino* and in the subconscious of all Chicanos there is a love for mother nature; She represents the creation of life; She sustains us and that is why in *Pre-Columbian* times, She could not be owned or fragmented or sold. It is for everyone and not for the one individual to monopolize. The rebellions by Chicanos/as are part of the historical oppression that the *Raza* had to endure through the ages; it points to a people that are not passive but are willing to fight for their rights. The Spanish language of the *Southwest* is rich and diverse, a by product of many linguistic integrations pointing to the impact of *Pre-Columbian* languages, old Spanish, gypsy expressions and English. Within the joke telling sessions, the Chicano/a is creating a variety of linguistic levels of dialects and languages leading to jokes that can only be understood and appreciated by a bilingual person. If the *barrio* person (*Pachuco/cholo*) is territorial, it is because he suffers isolation in a very oppressive environment. Thus, his code switching, graffiti and "*ganga*" slang are mere *barrio* markers for his identity and his territory. As a *Mestizo*, the Chicano/a can enjoy and appreciate many music styles of his culture; he/she is at once comfortable with *Cumbia*, Polka, *Vals* or modern *Tejano* sounds, likewise, he/she can be comfortable with Country and Rock. As the Chicano/a becomes more integrated into American society, as a person who must work hard to climb the socio-economic ladder, he/she does away with spendthrift habits, to plan and save for a better future. As we move to the end of the XX century, more Chicanos/as are moving to urban areas, becoming more educated and more integrated into dominant society. There is across the U.S. political arena, a wave of conservatism that insists on the old "colonial" model characterized by xenophobia, hispanophobia and general racism to preserve a monolingual White America. The cutbacks in funding toward minority programs of all kinds is symptomatic of the times. The imposition of the term *hispanic* by Congress to the diverse *Spanish-Speaking* groups creates a whitewashing of the diverse *Spanish-Speaking* groups (Puerto Rican, Argentinean, Mexican, Cuban, etc.). Chicanos/as as well as Latinos/as do not want labels from the outside; if they are to label their identity it must be an "insider" label. Besides Mexican migration, in the last twenty years, there has been an increase in *Spanish-Speaking* groups from various parts of Latin America (*Salvadoreños, Guatemaltecos, Nicaragüenses, Cubanos, Puertoriqueños*). Generally, when not addressing Spanish- Speakers of Mexican ancestry, the term *Latino* is used as an insider term. This is not to say there are not specific insider labels for these groups (e.g. *Neo-rican, Boricua*)[30] but generally this is an umbrella term which has been accepted. The term *hispanic*, like *Latino* regardless of its insider/outsider link is not an accurate cultural marker for the *Spanish-Speaking* groups, because it obviates, the Native American side of the *Mestizo* culture. For some years in papers and lectures, I have been advocating the term that would be all inclusive, culturally speaking. The term is *Mestizo- Americano* or Mestizo-American. All *Spanish-Speaking* groups in their cultural lineage have a mixture of many bloods and races; it is a blending of the *Pre-Columbian* spirit with the European/Arabic and African strains (and recently Anglo-Saxon integration), thus the creation of a multi-racial, multicultural product of the future. This is what Vasconcelos called *mestizaje*. Nobel laureat Octavio Paz also reiterates the observation. It is not only accurate but appropriate; rather than being exclusivist it is all inclusive, rather than being divisive, it calls for unification . That is why the Chicano/a/Latino/a of the past must affirm their rightful place as Mestizo- Americans in North American Society.

THE CHICANA/LATINA: CULTURAL INHERITANCE, STRUGGLE AND AWARENESS
ROLE OF WOMEN IN HISTORY: PRE-COLUMBIAN MODELS VS. WESTERN MODELS

The secondary role and status of women in the Western world has been a cultural pattern that continued with only superficial modifications. This secondary status originates in the Judeo-Christian tradition and implies the woman on the one hand is a marked or stained, culpable Eve and on the other hand one that must be faithful, pure and devoted to the family with the virtues of chastity, humility, loyalty, submission and sacrifice. Different cultures have seen the *mujer* in distinct manners; for example, the Arabic and Dutch cultures see the plump, obese female as beautiful.[31] Virginia Woolfe sees in the Western model a type of enchanted female of the home characterized by her enchanting, alluring qualities, a lack of egotism, understanding, sacrificing, home-bound, passive, pure and inactive mental thought. Much of how the women is viewed depends often on cultural history. Data is impermanent and modified due to historical reasons. Thus, the existence of the feminine condition is not due to biological reasons but rather to historical ones[32] To try to understand the woman in the traditional manner i.e. as an appendix to the history of man, is without question, an error. As one reviews the various epochs via the literature, each historical period has its *raison d'être*. The German historian Ranke saw all of the epochs "within the same distance to God;" each with its internal logic and historical reasons. But literature often deforms reality; it captures rather the extraordinary, that which is worthy of remembering, that is strange, marvelous, infrequent or strange. The female of the Middle Ages (before the courtly love period) was crude and often drank with the men. Masculinity was the only model for them at that time.[33] When courtly love was injected culturally, it's primary origin and impetus was related to wars and knighthood. The woman, while an object of idealization was still an object that needed to be pure, submissive, weak and a channel to be conquered. This negative Western legacy is to be felt immediately by the first victim of the European invasion of the Americas i.e. the Native-American woman. She will be raped, used and abused by the Spanish. She will be a concubine and because of the European color/race prejudice, will be treated like an animal during the colonization of Spanish America.[34] The English and the Americans do not practice miscegenation with the Native-American population; rather, the natives are segregated , seen as heathens, primitive and thus not worthy of being Christians, such that a Minister organizes an army of Christian pilgrims and wipes out a whole village of Iroquois women, children and men. [35] This racist attitude toward Native-Americans will be reflected throughout the expansionist American period particularly in the XIX century pilgrims, historians and dime novels. Raymond Paredes cites Spanish miscegenation with the natives as the most objectionable practice to Americans in the XIX century.[36] They saw the offspring as stained by the primitive, regressive and savage native ergo their biased and racist attitude that will be continued throughout the XX century.

THE CONTEMPORARY CHICANA/LATINA: THE NEW MESTIZA-AMERICAN

As a *Mestiza*, the Chicana and Latina must live with her heritage but she must also realize that she has inherited largely through a hegemonic process, a European/Western model which is negative and counterproductive to the integrity of the female. It is hegemony that not only exploits but also distorts. I refer to the distortion of fact and reality of the culture that is exploited. I have mentioned that the first victim in the Americas was the Native female but along with that victimization was the distortion of her culture and civilization by a culture that was intent on erasing all native thought and practice. This was accomplished efficiently by the *Sanctum Officium* or the Inquisition in charge of censorship and the altering of historical documents.[37] Thus, to date we have not only a biased view of *Pre-Columbian* culture but a misrepresentation based on misinterpretation. This was due largely to politics and religion, notwithstanding, a diametrically distinct culture. Even if the Spanish had not had an Inquisition, one doubts they would have understood the highly advanced scientific and metaphysical view of the Pre-Columbian world.[38] It is important that the *post hispanic* sources written under the supervision and censorship of the Church, be scrutinized and challenged as invalid, biased and false. The perpetuation of colonial myths by the Spanish regarding *Pre-Columbian* cultures clearly represents a hegemonic revisionism. As women increase in numbers in Academia, they must be careful not to fall into the colonial trap which portrays a chauvinistic Judeo-Christian view of the Native American/*Pre-Columbian* female. Iris Blanco, in her article on the cultural conditioning of the female in the Pre-Hispanic world relies, on the post-hispanic codex written by *Mestizo* and Christian Don Fernando Alva Ixlilxóchitl.[39] While recognizing it as a source, it has, nonetheless, received many negative reviews by scholars. Here, the author uses it as a base for understanding the *Pre-Columbian* world of the female. References to concubines, slaves, oaths of Christianity, penitent lashing, drinking, rape, suicide, idleness and general decadence are socio-cultural characteristics that are found in European medieval society

26.

La Mujer: Images of the early seventies.

and not *Pre-Columbian* society, ergo these intercalations or insertions of European reality by the *Sanctum Officium* into the documents of Fernando de Alva Ixtlilxóchitl. The *Pre-Columbian* Aztec world is one that is guided by the laws of nature and the universe. Their view of reality is not religious but rather scientific. The highly advanced knowledge in mathematics and astronomy are the basis for their understanding of the universe. Their high culture as exemplified in their complex art, architecture and poetry is one that follows mutual respect for each other's spirit. The Mayan saying of *In Lakesh* illustrates the interrelationship of all humanity since it means "you are my other self" thus, what is good for me is good for you; what is bad for me is bad for you. This high principle produces fraternity and respect for one another. Since the *Pre-Columbian* world was not based on a materialistic society, one eliminated exploitation, profit and greed. Since its base is communal and not competitive, one shares the general wealth as opposed to the Western/European materialistic based model that monopolizes and profits individuals. Thus, the female, like the male, is not part of the aggressive competitive world of the materialist model. She has the highest socio-spiritual rank in Aztekah society. She represents creation and like Mother Earth, she is given the highest esteem and regard. Because, everyone is born with different talents and propensities (as seen partially through the *Tonalámatl* as well as the educational process) each person is seen *from within* and not from without as in the European/western model. All elected governing heads had to show spiritual greatness before assuming a position of authority. Native American women have always had a voice in the democratic governing process. The Council of Women, whether Algonquin, Lakota, Pima or *Metzika* of Mexico are proof of the independence of Native American women. In *Aztekah* society, women had complete administrative and economic control of the household. One notes that they did not have to consult with the husband regarding commercial transactions in the market place. Moreover, if one had the propensity and talent, one could be an artist, chemist (*Xóchitl* in Toltec times),[40] or a governing head.

This harmonious world was violently broken by the invasion of the European Spanish. As the first victim of the Invasion, the Native-American woman is relegated the lowest place in the socio-human ladder, equal to that of a beast. She is used, abused, made into a concubine, forced into prostitution and taught to paint her face, so that she could be white. This is the broken world of the *post-conquest* Native, which appears in the Spanish chronicles and post-hispanic codices, often confused for the *Pre-Columbian* world of the female.

The Chicana/Latina contemporarily is the descendant, in part, of the Native American. Thus, she is a *Mestiza*. As a Mestiza-American, she has inherited to a larger degree a European/hispanic tradition which perpetuates *Machismo*, a trait, imported from Mediterranean cultures.[41] Américo Paredes in his study of *corridos* analyzes *Machismo* stating its origin to the post-revolutionary period i.e. after 1930 to the present.[42] There is no question that the brutal realities of the Wild West and the Revolution contributed to a sense of manliness; however, the extreme and exaggerated *soberbia* of the Spaniard coupled with his low regard to Native-American women set the standard and model for *machismo* 400 years before the Mexican revolution. The *Mestiza*, despite the male oriented European cultures, has inherited positive models: in war, the *Mestiza* women fighting alongside warriors against the Spanish in *Metziko-Tenochtitlan*; the *soldadera*, likewise during the Mexican Revolution; in literature Sor Juana Inés de la Cruz, an omnisapient and extraordinary genius writing circa 1765, considered the precursor of feminism; Gabriela Mistral, poet and nobel laureat; Maria Luis Bombal, first contemporary novelist; Rosario Castellanos, Amerigenist novelist and feminist; Elena Garro, Elena Poniatowska and Isabel Allende as leading contemporary novelists and writers. In the United States, the woman of Mexican or Hispanic descent had a dual barrier with two cultures that exploited her individual worth with colonial attitudes towards women stemming from medieval thought as passed on through Mexican and/or Hispanic culture. To add insult to injury, Anglo-American attitudes reflecting hispanophobia places Mexican culture in the U.S. at the bottom of the socio-human ladder. Thus, as noted before, the Mexican woman was traditionally seen in her domestic role by her own culture, but was used by opportunistic Anglo-Americans through the institution of matrimony with the ulterior motive of acquiring land. Such was the case with Captain Mifflin Kennedy in

South Texas who married the wealthy widow Petra Vela de Vidal, "who helped him court the support of a large number of Mexicans whose vote was essential to the maintenance of his power."[43] Not all Mexican women were accepted; according to Arnoldo De Leon, only the *güeras*, the light skinned women, preferably with blue eyes, were singled out. As more Anglos moved into the area, this procedure declined and racially mixed couples became subject to social disapproval and eventually persecution.[44]

PRECURSORS OF MESTIZA FEMINISM

Historically, U.S. Mexican/Chicana/Latina women have displayed will, determination and survivability. They have been the backbone of the Chicano/Latino family. Mario T. García, in his essay on the Mexican family between 1900-1930, clearly demonstrates the flexibility and survivability of the Mexican family under extremely difficult economic circumstances and stresses. In the rural areas, harvesting the crops was a full family affair. In the urban areas, women secured jobs as domestics, laborers in garment industries and canneries. Women not only maintained and reproduced male workers though their roles as housewives and mothers, but also had to labor outside the home to supplement family income working and experiencing a "double day."[45] Even before the turn of the century, certain women rose to fame because of their heroic postures. J.T. Carnales, in his study of Texas history, dedicates a chapter to the "Angel of Goliad" whose deeds and humanism have forever been remembered by both sides of the cultural/military conflict in Texas circa 1836. Known largely as Sra. Alvarez and as *Panchita*, she was responsible for saving the lives of twenty one Texas men, who were to be shot by order of Santa Ana. Her merciful heart, unyielding courage and extraordinary exertions induced Urrea's officers to evade and disobey Santa Ana's orders to shoot all prisoners.[46] In the 1870's, Lucy Eldine González of Johnson County, Texas published newspapers, pamphlets, and books, traveled and lectured extensively leading many demonstrations. In 1905, she was a founding member of the Industrial Workers of the World; similarly, Sara Estela Ramírez (Laredo, Texas), Elisa Alemán (San Antonio, Texas) were active in labor unions and workers' rights in the first part of the XX century.[47] Outside of the labor movement and

Brown Beret Chicana Protesting Shooting of Santos Rodriguez,
Austin, Texas, 1983 (Photo by Allan Pogue)

in the political organizing of Mexican/Chicano citizen's rights was Adela Sloss from San Juan, Texas. An honors high school graduate in 1925, she was inspired by the early political ideas of Alonso S. Perales and collaborated in the formation of the prototype civic league of what is now *LULAC*. The idea and formation properly belongs to Alonso S. Perales who had conceived the unification of existing Mexican-American organizations as early as 1919. Adela Sloss not only was a founding member of *League of Latin Americans* (Harlingen, Texas, 1929) but became a staunch defender of *Raza* rights the rest of her life, writing largely in newspapers in Texas. Her book of memoirs reflecting the political activity of Alonso S Perales was written at the age of 75.[48] During the thirties, the second generation resistance was seen through the Mexican American Movement, an outgrowth of the *YMCA*. From this membership, Luisa Moreno became the principal organizer in 1938 of *El Congreso de los Pueblos de Habla Española*, a national conference whose stated purpose was "the economic and social and cultural betterment of the Mexican people, to have an understanding between Anglo-Americans and Mexicans, to promote organization of working people by aiding trade unions and to fight discrimination actively".[49] Another activist in New Mexico and Colorado during the twenties, thirties and forties was Isabel Malagram González. She led strikes and was a founding member of *La Asociación Nacional Mexico Americana*.[50] During the sixties, the farm labor struggle continued, now with the leadership of César Chávez. As an organizer of the Community Service Organization, César Chávez moved to Delano where he carefully selected a cadre of proven organizers. Among them was Dolores Huerta, a tiny, brash assistant whose efforts aided Chávez in attaining victory over the oppressive growers in California.[51]

During the seventies, the Chicanas/Latinas' role in society becomes more in focused. By 1969, the Chicano Student Movement was born in the Youth Liberation Conferences in Denver, Colorado with the Chicana as an integral part of the movement. By 1970, many Chicano organizations began women caucuses e.g. *La Comisión Feminil Mexicana* (Sacramento, 1970); *La Conferencia de Mujeres por la Raza* (Houston, 1971). Francesca Flores organized in L.A. one of the first anti-poverty agencies, while Alicia Escalante founded the Chicano National Welfare Rights.[52] Chicano/Latino activity spread to professional groups such as the Mexican American Business and the Professional Women's Club, the League of Mexican-American Women, and the Hispanic Women's Council. In Literature, Linda Morales-Arms publishes the first Chicana anthology entitled, *La Cosecha: Literatura y la Mujer Chicana* under the auspices of *De Colores* in 1977. Linda affirms in the introduction:

> This study and reflection is what will provide a road to achieving our self-identity and further the total liberation of the *pueblo Chicano*...Chicanas hold a distinctive perspective of the world around them.... We are culturally different and therefore, have different values, traditions, lifestyles and history from other women in the U.S...we are the recipients of racist attitudes which have oppressed our culturally different *Mestizo* pueblo in this country...but we also have the added burden of living in a world geared for men. We find ourselves at the very bottom of the social ladder and the way up and out of this restrictive condition must be made ultimately by our own initiative.[53]

Since the publication of this anthology, there has been a plethora of creativity among M*estiza* women in the U.S. within Chicano Literature in the seventies including Estela Portillo Trambley, Lorna Dee Cervantes, Evangelina Vigil, Bernice Zamora and Angela de Hoyos. It is in the eighties, however, that Chicano literature witnesses an explosion of women into the literary and academic scene. In literature, new entries include Alma Villanueva, Rosemary Catalcos and Pat Mora in poetry and in prose fiction include Sandra Cisneros, Lucha Corpi, Roberta Fernández and Irene Beltrán Hernández as a few of the new players. Due to the rise of women receiving college degrees, many have gone on to pursue Ph.D.'s and other professional degrees. The number of representatives are spread through the Humanities and Social Sciences and we could not do justice to its members by naming a general number of representatives. They range from the identity politics of Gloria Anzaldúa to the Pan-Indianism of Inés Hernández-Ávila. Suffice it to say that this number is increasing as witnessed by the Women's Studies Chicana/Latina hirings and proliferation of publications and materials related to Chicana/Latina feminist issues. Antonia Castañeda is a scholar studying the Chicana/Latina. She points to the neglect of research vis a vis women of color and the perpetuation of the dark-skinned stereotype of a woman not gentle but savage and non-Christian. She proposes the decolonization of history, its rewriting, going beyond present studies, looking at the intrinsic elements of societies and perhaps questioning the ideology of Western thought.[54] Elizabeth Cowley, in her treatise of Women's Liberation concludes that while the economic and gender status of women is changing, these are only the first steps toward a revolution in human relationships. The problem now is with the socio-economic ideology of the Western world. Not until there is complete change will women be really emancipated from economic exploitation and emotional restrictions of society and cease to be an expression of the property forms of a competitive society.

ENDNOTES

[1] Aurelio M. Espinosa, "Studies in New Mexican Spanish," *Revue de Dialectologie Romance*, 1909-1415.

[2] This writer can attest to the negative attitudes of Anglo Spanish teachers of the 50's in the Rio Grande Valley of South Texas, not only was the Chicano student made to feel inferior but he was punished in Physical Education for using Spanish. In 1995, similarly, Chicanos in Pflugerville, Texas were prohibited from using Spanish in High School. The students made it into Raza humor, translating their Spanish names i.e. José SantaMaría became Joe Saint Mary, Rubén Estrada became Ruben Road etc.

[3] Fray Juan de Pineda, "Agricultura Cristiana," dialogo XXII: "Munchos bastardos...florecían por los discursos de los tiempos."

[4] The original form in Latin was *sumos*, the intermediate evolved form was *semos* while the modern form currently is *somos*. This can be found in Ramón de la Cruz' *La presumida burlada* while *Háyamos* can be found in old *El Romance de Virgilios*.

[5] See Carlos Martínez Vigil, *Arcaísmos españoles usados en América*, Montevideo (no date).

[6] The early dictionaries created by Spanish friars were replete with inaccuracies. For an up to date reference work, see Santamaria's *Diccionario de Mexicanismos*. See also Juan Luna Cárdenas, *Tratado de etimologias de la lengua Aztékatl*, Mexico, 1950.

[7] Other countries have the following labels: Portugal--*caláo*; Chile--*coa*; Brazil--*ciria*; Argentina--*lunfardo*; Perú--*replana*.

[8] Arnoldo Carlos Vento, "Estudio etimológico: una perspectiva socio-linguística e histórica del habla Chicano," *Work, Family, Sex Roles, Language* (Berkeley, Quinto Sol/Tonatiuh, 1980), pp. 196-207.

[9] Arnoldo Carlos Vento, "Estudio etimológico...p. 197.

[10] José R. Reyna, *Raza humor* (San Antonio: Penca, no date), p. 17.

[11] The term mayate is actually Aztekah Náhuatl; it refers to a black bug. The Aztecs did not have color discrimination; here the Mexican/Chicano takes an insignificant black bug and projects a pejorative sense to the African American equivalent of "nigger." See Arnoldo Carlos Vento, "Estudio etimológico: una perspectiva socio-linguística e histórica del habla Chicano", *Work, Family, Sex Roles, Language* (Berkeley: Quinto Sol/ tonatiuh, 1986), p.199.

[12] Robert T. Trotter, Juan Antonio Chavira, *Curanderismo* (Athens: University of Georgia Press, 1981)..

[13]Ibid.

[14]Bob Toben, Sarfetti, Wolf, *Space, Time and Beyond* (New York: E.P. Dutton and Co., 1975), p. 157.

[15]Marilyn Ferguson, *The Aquarian Conspiracy* (New York: St. Martin's Press, 1976), p. 245.

[16]Manuel Peña "Origins: Texas-Mexican Music prior to 1930", The Texas-Mexican Conjunto: A History of Working Class People (Austin: UT Press, 1985),pp. 19-45.

[17] Telephone conversation with Abraham Quintanilla, June, 1997.

[18] Ibid.

[19] The group referred here is called *Los Gatos*; their debut was a total success. Their pronunciation was flawless and their selection of *corridos* was excellent.

[20]Charles Ramirez-Berg, "Stereotyping in Films in General and of the Hispanic in Particular," *The Howard Journal of Communications*, vol. 2, no. 3 (Summer, 1990), pp. 286-300.

[21]Steven G. Kellman, "Splendors of Chicano Cinema," *Texas Observer*, July 12, 1994, pp. 19-20.

[22]Alex Avila, "The Growing Independent Latino Film Industry in Texas and the Emergence of 'La Nueva Onda'," *Arriba*, Sept. 1995, p. 19. See also Charles Ramirez-Berg, "Images and Counterimages of the Hispanic in Hollywood," *Tonantzin*, vol. 6, no. 1, 12-13, Nov. 1988; Chon A. Noriega, *Chicanos and Film: Representation and Resistance* (University of Minnesota Press), 1992.

[23]Armand Rendón, Chicano Manifesto (N.Y.: MacMillan Co.,1971), pp. 319-20.

[24]Guillermo Fuenfríos in *Aztlan: The Anthology of Mexican American Literature* (New York: Random House, 1972), pp. 283-288.

[25]Armando Rendón, *Chicano Manifesto*, pp. 17-41.

[26]Nathan Murillo, "The Mexican American Family" in *Chicanos: Social and Psychological Perspectives* (St. Louis: Mosby Company, 1971), pp. 97-108.

[27]Arnoldo Carlos Vento, "Imagenes y esencia del Mexicano y Chicano: Mestizaje y Mexicanidad," paper presented at *UNAM*, Mexico City, 1993.

[28]Antonio Castro Leal, *Juan Ruiz de Alarcon, su vida , su obra*.(Mexico: 1943),pp. 205-207. Study originally presented as member of the *Ateneo de la Juventud* in Mexico City circa 1907.

[29]See Domingo Martinez Paredes, *El Popol Vuh tiene razón*.(Mexico: Orion, 1968).See introduction.

[30]See *Borinquen: An Anthology of Puerto Rican Literature*. eds., María Teresa Babín, Stan Steiner (New York: Random House, 1974), p. 2.

[31]Rosario Castellanos, *Mujer que sabe latín* (Mexico: SEP, 1973), p. 10.

[32]Julian Marías, *La mujer en el siglo XX* (Madrid: Alianza Editorial, 1980), pp. 14-15.

[33]Middle Ages reference to crude women

[34]Rosario Castellanos, *Mujer que sabe latín* (Mexico: SEP, 1973), p. 26.

[35]Shirley Hill Witt, Stan Steiner ed., *The Way: An Anthology of American Indian Literature* (Toronto: Vintage Books, 1972), pp. 4-5.

[36]Raymond Paredes, "The Origins of the Anti-Mexican Sentiment in the United States," in *New Direction in Chicano Scholarship* (San Diego: University of California Press, 1977), pp. 139-165.

[37]See Arnoldo Carlos Vento, "Aztec Myths and Cosmology: Historical Religious Misinterpretation," *Wicazo Sa Review*, vol. XI, no. I, Spring, 1995, pp. 1-23.

[38]Ibid.

[39]Iris A. Blanco, "El sexo y su condicionamiento cultural en el mundo prehispánico," *Between Borders: Essays on Mexicana/Chicana History* (Encino, CA: Floricanto, 1990), pp. 363-371.

[40]Juan Luna Cárdenas, *La casa de Jade* (Mexico: Editorial Aztekatl, 1960).

[41]Machismo is clearly seen in Arabic/Spanish cultures and other Mediterranean cultures. It is the *soberbia*, or arrogant and extreme individualism of the Moor/Castellano that adds to the already demeaning attitude towards women.

[42] Americo Paredes, *Folklore and Culture on the Texas-Mexican Border* (Austin: CMAS Books, 1993), pp. 233-234.

[43]Rudolfo Acuña, *Occupied America*...p. 41.

[44]Arnoldo De Leon, "White Racial Attitudes Toward Mexicanos in Texas, 1821-120 (Texas Christian University, Ph.D. Dissertation, 1974), pp. 112-113; 115-116, 122. For aspects of persecution see E. Larry Dickens, "Mestizaje in the 19th Century Texas," *Journal of Mexican American History* 2, no. 2 (Spring, 1992), p. 63.

[45]Mario T. García, "La familia: The Mexican Immigrant Family, 1900-1930," *Work, Family, Sex Roles, Language* (Berkeley: Quinto Sol, 1979), pp. 129.

[46]Quoting Dr. J.H. Barnard's Journal (Dec. 1835-June 1836) J.T. Canales *Bits of Texas History* (San Antonio: Artes Gráficas, 1950), pp. 47-66.

[47]Rodolfo Acuña, *Occupied America*, pp. 194-195.

[48]See Adela Sloss-Vento, *Alonso S. Perales: His Struggles for the Rights of Mexican Americans* (San Antonio: Artes Gráficas).

[49]Rodolfo Acuña, p. 317.

[50]See Martha Cotera, *Profile of the Mexican American Women* (Austin: National Ed. Laboratory, 1976), pp. 93-96.

[51]Tony Castro, *Chicano Power. The Emergence of Mexican America* (N.Y.: Saturday Review Press, 1974), pp. 85-86..

[52]Rodolfo Acuña, p. 403.

[53]See *La cosecha: Literatura y la mujer Chicana* in *De Colores*, vol. III, no. 3 (Albuquerque: Pajarito Publications, 1977), p. 3.

[54]Antonio I. Castañeda, "Women of Color and the Rewriting of Western History: The Discourse, Politics, and Decolonization of History," *Pacific Historical Review*, pp. 501-533, 1992.

BIBLIOGRAPHY

Azcué y Mancera, Luis. *Códices Indígenas*. Mexico: Editorial Orión, 1966.

Acuña, Rodolfo. *Occupied America: A History of Chicanos*. New York: Harper and Row, 1981.

Angulo, Carlos Muñoz. *Historia de Mexico*. Mexico: D. F.: Editorial Tl.I. Aztékatl

Armas, Linda Morales. Ed. *La Cosecha: Literatura y la mujer Chicana*. A special issue of *De Colores: Journal of Emerging Raza Philosophies*. Vol. 3, no.3. Albuquerque: Pajarito Publications, 1977.

Arrom, Juan José. "Criollo , definición y matices de un concepto". In *Certidumbre de América*. Havana: 1959.

_____ *Esquema generacional de las letras hispanoamericanas*. Bogota: Caro y Cuervo, 1963.

Babin, María Teresa and Stan Steiner, ed. *Borinquen: An Anthology of Puerto Rican Literature*. New York: Random House, 1974.

Bancroft, Hubert Howe. *History of Arizona and New Mexico*. Albuquerque: Horn and Wallace, 1962.

Barker, George Carpenter. *An American-Spanish Argot and Its Social Function in Tucson, Arizona*. Tucson: University of Arizona Press, 1970.

Barrera, Mario, Alberto Camarillo and Francisco Hernández. eds. *Work, Family, Sex Roles, Language*. Berkeley: Quinto Sol, 1971.

Batra, Roger. *La Jaula de la melancolía: identidad y metamorfosis del mexicano*. Mexico: U.N.A.M., 1987.

Benítez, Fernando. *Los primeros mexicanos*. México: Bibioteca Era, 1962.

Berg, Charles Ramírez. *Cinema of Soliltude: A Critical Study of Mexican Film*. Austin: University of Texas Press, 1992.

Brack, Gene M. *Mexico Views Manifest Destiny, 1821-1846: An Essay on the Origins of the Mexican War*. Albuquerque: University of New Mexico Press, 1975.

Bréhier, L. *L'Egllise et l'orient au moyen age: Les croisades*. Ed. Paris, J. Gabalda et fils, 1928.

Briggs, Vernon M. Jr, Folge, and Schmidt, *The Chicano Worker*. Austin: University of Texas Press, 1977.

Bustamanate, Jorge. *Mexican Immigration and the Social Relations of Capitalism*. Notre Dame: Dissertation, 1975.

Camp, Santiago Valenti. *Las sectas de las sociedades secretas a través de la historia de México*. México: Edicion Valle de México, 1975.

Canales, J. T. *Juan N. Cortina, Bandit or Patriot?* San Antonio: Artes Gráficas, 1951.

_____*Bits of Texas History*. San Antonio: Artes Gráficas, 1950.

Cárdenas, Juan Luna. *Fuego Nuevo*. Mexico D. F.: Editorial Aztékatl, 1990.

_____ *Historia Patria*. México: Editorial Aztékatl, 1956.

_____ *Ilhuikayotl: Kosmosofia*. México: Central Kosmosófica de Anauak.

_____ *La casa de jade* México: Editorial Aztékatl, 1950.

_____*La ceremonial del Fuego Nuevo*. México: Editorial Aztékatl, 1990.

_____*La matemática de los Aztecas*. México: Editorial U.Tl.I Aztékatl.

_____*"México: estudio de su significación"*,. Paper presented to The Mexican Society of Geography and Statistics. México D.F., 1966.

_____*Si hubo sacrificios humanos y actos de antropofagia en América*. México: Editorial Aztékatl, 1993.

_____*¿Conoce Ud. la ciencia suprema?* México: Central Kosmosófica de Anahuak, N. D.

_____*Prehistoria de América*. México: Editorial Leyenda, 1944.

Casarrubias C., Vicente. *Rebeliones indígenas en la Nueva España*. México: S.E.P., 1963.

(De las) Casas, Bartolomé. *Brevísima relación de la destrucción de las Indias*. México: Metro,1974.

Caso, Alfonso. *El Pueblo del Sol*. Mexico D. F.: Fondo de Cultura Económica, 1955.

_____ *La religión de los Aztecas*. México: Enciclopedia Ilustrada Mexicana, 1945.

Caso, Antonio. *El Problema de Mexico y la Ideología Nacional*. México: Libro México, Editores S. de R.L., 1955.

Castañeda, Carlos. *Our Catholic Heritage, 1519-1933*. Vol.9 (The Church in Texas since Independence, 1836-1950). N.Y.: Arno Press, 1976.

Castellanos, Rosario. *Mujer que sabe latin*. México: SEP, 1973.

Castillo, Adelaida R. del. ed. *Between Borders: Essays on Mexicana/ Chicana History.* Encino, California: Floricanto , 1990

(del) Castillo, Cristobal. *Fragmentos sobre la obra general sobre historia de los mexicanos.* Florence: Landi, 1968.

Castro, Tony. *Chicano Power: The Emergence of Mexican America.* New York: Saturday Review Press, 1974.

Castro Leal, Antonio. *Juan Ruiz de Alarcón, su vida su obra,*.México: 1943.

Chamberlain, Samuel E. *My Confessions.* New York: Harper and Row, 1956.

Chartres, Fulberto de. *Historia Hierosolymitana.*: Ed. Haggenmeyer. Heidelberg, 1913.

Chimalpain Cuauhtlihuanitzen, Domingo. *Memorial breve.* Trans. Walter Lehmann. Stuttgart, 1958.

Clavijero, Francisco Xavier. *Historia antigua de Mexico.* México: Porrúa, 1964.

Coe, Michael. *Mexico.* New York: Thames and Hudson, 1980

Cotera, Martha. *Profile of the Mexican-American Women.* Austin: National Ed. Laboratory, 1976.

Cuellar, Alfred and Joan Moore. *Mexican Americans.* New Jersey: Prentice Hall, 1970.

Davies, Nigel. *Los mexicas: primeros pasos hacia el imperio.* México: U:N.A.M., 1973.

_____*The Toltec Heritage: From the Fall of Tula to the Rise of Tenochtitlan.* University of Oklahoma: Norman, 1980.

_____ *The Aztecs: A History.* New York: Putnam and Sons, 1974.

DeLeón, Arnoldo. *The Tejano Community, 1836-1900 .* Alberquerque: University of. New Mexico Press, 1982.

_____*White Racial Attitudes Toward Mexicans in Texas, 1821-1920.* Texas Christian University , PhD. Dissertation, 1974.

De Voto,Bernard, *The Year of the Decision.* second edition, Boston: 1961.

Díaz del Castillo, Bernal. *Historia verdadera de la Conquista de la Nueva España.* México: Ed. Robredo, 1933.

Durán, Diego. *Book of the Gods and Rites.* trans. Heyden and Horcasitas. Norman: University of Oklahoma Press, 1971.

Durán, Fray Diego. *Historia de las Indias de la Nueva España e Islas de la Tierra Firme. 2vols.* México: Porrúa, 1967.

El Plan de Santa Barbara: A Chicano Plan for Higher Education.
Oakland: La Causa Publications, 1969.

Fagan, Brian M. *The Aztecs.* New York: Freeman and Company,
1984.

Ferguson, Marilyn. *The Aquarian Conspiracy.* New York: St.
Martin's Press, 1976.

Festival de Flor y Canto: An Anthology of Chicano Literature.
Alurista, Cervantes, Gomez-Quiñones, Pacheco and Gustavo
Segade eds. Los Angeles: U.C.L.A. Press, 1976.

Foley, Doug. *From Peones to Politicos: Ethnic Relations in a South
Texas Town, 1900-1977.* Austin : CMAS Monographs, 1977.

Forto, Emilio C. *Actual Situation on the River Rio Grande.* Pan
American Labor Press, September11, 1918.

Fuenfríos, Guillermo. *Aztlan: The Anthology of Mexican American
Literature.* New York: Random House, 1972.

García, Mario. *Desert Immigrants: The Mexicans of. El Paso, 1880-
1920.* New Haven: Yale University Press, 1981.

García, Rubén. *La malinche.* México: Editorial Aztékatl.

Gardner, Richard. *Grito: Reies Tijerina and the New Mexico Land
Grant War of 1967.* New York: Bobbs-Merill Company,1970.

Garibay, Ma. Angel. *Panorama literario de los pueblos nahuas.*
México: Porrúa, 1979.

_____*Teogonía e historia de los mexicanos.* México: Porrúa,
1973.

González, Jovita Mireles. "America Invades Border Towns", in *Our
Racial and national minorities.* Frances J. Brown and Joseph S.
Roucek. Austin: PCL Library Stacks, University of Texas-Austin

_____*Jovita González Manuscripts and Works (1925-1980).*
Austin: Benson Latin American Collection, University of Texas-
Austin.

Guibert, Rita. "*The New Latin Wave: Octavio Paz*" Interview in
Intellectual Digest, December, 1973.

Gramci, Antonio. *Selections from the Prison Notebooks of Antonio
Gramci.* Ed .trans. Quintin Hoare and Geoffery Nowell Smith. New
York: International Publishers, 1989

Grebler, Leo, Joan W. Moore and Ralph C. Guzmán, *The Mexican-
American People.* New York: Free Press, 1970.

Greenwood, Robert. *The California Outlaw: Tiburcio Vásquez*: Los Gatos, California: Talisman Press, 1960.

Gurria, Jorge. Lacroix, *La caída de Tenochtitlan*. Mexico D.F.: Ediciones Conmemorativas,1974.

Hanke, Lewis. *History of Latin American Civilization*. Boston: Little, Brown and Co., 1973.

_____*The Spanish Struggle for Justice in the Conquest of America*. Boston: Little, Brown and Co., 1965.

Hassler, Peter. "Sacrificios humanos entre los Mexicas y otros pueblos Indios: ¿Realidad o Fantasía?" in *Ce Acatl*, Part 1-2, nos. 51-52, 53-54, 1993.

Hroch, Mirslav and Anna Skýbová. *Ecclesia Militans: The Inquisition*. Trans. Janet Fraser. New York: Dorsett Press, 1988.

Ibarra-Frausto, Tomás. *Luis Valdez y el Teatro Campesino: Actos*. San Juan Baustista, California: Cucaracha Publications, 1973.

Iturriaga, José. "El caracter del mexicano" in *La estructura social y cultural de México*. México: Fondo de Cultura Económica, 1951.

Ixlilxóchitl, Don Fernando de Alba. *Obras históricas*. México: Editorial Nacional, 1952.

Katz, Friedrich. *Situación social y económica de los Aztecas durante los Siglos XV y XVI*. México: U:N:A:M., 1966.

Krickeberg, Walter. *Mitos y leyendas de los Aztecas Incas, Mayas y Muiscas*. México, D. F.: Fondo de Cultura Económica, 1971.

Lamar, Howard R. *The Far Southwest, 1846-1912:A Territorial History*. New York: Norton, 1970.

Lang, Verlag Peter. *Menschenopfer bei den Azteken? Eine quellen und ideologiekritische Studie*. Bern, Switzerland: 1992.

Leonard, Pitt. *The Decline of the Californianos: A Social History of the Spanish Speaking Californians, 1846-1890.* Berkeley: University of California, 1970.

León. Portilla, Miguel. *La filosofía náhuatl*. México: U:N.A.M., 1974.

_____*Los Antiguos Mexicanos*. México: Fondo de Cultura Económica, 1973.

_____*Toltecáyotl: Aspectos de la cultura Nahuatl*. México: Fondo de Cultura Económica, 1980.

_____*Visión de los vencidos: relaciones indígenas de la Conquista*. México: U.N.A.M., 1972.

Llorent, Antonio de. *La historia crítica de la Inquisición en España*. Barcelona, 1835.

Lotts, Virgil N., Mercurio Martínez. *The Kingdom of Zapata* . San Antonio: Naylor Company, 1953.

López, Maria del Carmen Nieva. *Mexicáyotl*. Mexico D. F.: Editorial Orión, 1969.

López Austin, Alfredo. *La educación de los antiguos nahuas*. México: Ediciones El Caballito, 1985.

Marías, Julian, *La mujer en el siglo XX* . Madrid: Alianza Editorial, 1980.

Markham, Clements R. *First Part of the Royal Commentaries* .(Inca Garcilaso de la Vega). London: The Hakluyt society, lst series, nos. 41, 45, 1869-1871, no.45.

Martínez, José Luis, *El ensayo mexicano moderno*. México: Fondo de Cultura Mexicana, 1958.

Martínez Paredes, Domingo.   *El Popol Vuh tiene razón* (México: Editorial Orión, 1976..

_____*Hunab Ku: síntesis del pensamiento maya*. México: Ed. Orión, 1973.

_____*Parapsicología maya*. México: Porrúa, 1977.

Matthiessen, Peter.   *Sal Si Puedes: And the New American Revolution*. New York: Dell, 1973.

Mazón, Mauricio. *The Zoot-Suit Riots: The Psychology of Symbolic Annihilation*. Austin: University of Texas Press, 1984.

McWilliams, Carey. *North from Mexico*.   New York: Greenwood Press, 1968.

(De) Mendieta, Fray Gerónimo. *Historia eclesiastica Indiana*. México:
1870.

Meyer, Hans Eberhard. *The Crusades*. Trans. John Gilligham. Oxford, 1972.

Meza Gutiérrez, Arturo. *Mosaico de turquesas*. México: Ed. Malinalli, 1994.

Minge, Ward Alan. *Frontier Problems in New Mexico Preceding the Mexican War, 1840-1846*. Albuquerque: University of New Mexico Press, 1965

(de) Molina, Alonso. *Vacabulario: Castellano-Nahuatl, Nahuatl-Castellano*. México: Ediciones Colofón, 1966.

Moquín, Wayne, Charles Van Doren and Feliciano Rivera, eds. *A Documentary History of Mexican Americans.* New York: Praeger, 1972.

Moreno, Wigberto Jiménez. "Diferentes principios del año, entre diversos pueblos del Valle de Mexico y sus consecuencias para la cronología prehispánica". In *Mexico Antiguo, Vol. 9.* 1961.

Morner, Magnus. *Race Mixture in the History of Latin America.* Boston: Little, Brown and Co,1967.

Montejano, David. *Anglos and Mexicanos in the Making of Texas 1836- 1986.* Austin: University of Texas Press, 1987.

Moore, Michael. *Medicinal Plants of the Southwest.* Santa Fe: Museum of New Mexico Press, 1977.

Murillo, Nathan. "The Mexican American Family" in *Chicanos: Social and Psychological Perspectives.* St. Louis: Mosby Company, 1971.

Noriega, Chon A. *Chicanos and Film: Representation and Resistance.* University of Minnesota Press, 1992.

Novoa, Juan Bruce. *Chicano Authors Inquiry by Interview.* Austin: University of Texas Press, 1980.

Orozco, Manuel y Berra. *Historia Antigua de la Conquista de Mexico, 4 vols.* Mexico: Porrúa, 1960.

Paredes, Américo. *Folklore and Culture on the Texas Mexican Border.* Austin: CMAS Books, 1993.

Paredes, Raymond. "The Origins of Anti-Mexican Sentiment in the United States" In *New Directions in Chicano Scholarship.* ed. Romo and Paredes. La Jolla: San Diego Chicano Monograph Series, 1978.

Paz, Octavio.. *Laberinto de la soledad.* Mexico: Fondo de Cultura Económica, 1959.

Perales, Alonzo. *Are We Good Neighbors?* Artes Gráficas, San Antonio, Texas 1948.

_____*En defensa de mi Raza.* San Antonio: Artes Gráficas, 1936.

Peña, Manuel. *The Texas-Mexican Conjunto: A History of Working Class People.* Austin: University of Texas Press, 1985.

Perigo, Lynn I. *The American Southwest.* New York: Holt, Rhinehart and Winston, 1971.

Potthast, A. *Bibliotheca Historica Medii Aevi (375-1500 A.D.),* 2 vols. Berlin: 1896.

Quezada, Noemí *Amor y magia amorosa entre los Aztecas.* Mexico: UNAM, 1977.

Rábago, Constantino. *Dioses, hombres y soles.* México: Metro, 1973.

Ramos, Samuel. *El perfil del hombre y la cultura de Mexico.* Mexico: Robredo, 1938.

Reisler, Mark. *By the Sweat of the Brow: Mexican Immigration in the United States, 1901-1940.* Connecticut: Greenwoods, 1976.

Rendón, Armando. *Chicano Manifesto.* New York: MacMillan Company, 1971.

Reyna, José. *Raza Humor: Chicano Joke Tradition in Texas.* San Antonio: Penca, N.D.

Riley Smith, Jonathan. *The First Crusade and the Idea of Crusading.* Trans. Marshall, Baldwin and Walter Goffort. London: Athlone, 1986.

Robelo, Cecilio. *Diccionario de la mitología Náhuatl.* Mexico: Ediciones Fuente Cultural, 1951.

Robertson, William. *History of America.* London, 1777.

_____*History of America.* New York: J. Harper, 1832 reprint.

Rodrigo, J.B. *Historia verdadera de la Inquisición.* Madrid. 1897.

Romerovargas Yturbide, Dr. Ignacio. *Moctezuma el magnífico.* México: Asociación Anhuacayotl de Tlaxcalancingo, A.C.,vols. 1-3, 1964.

Romo, Ricardo and Raymond Paredes ed. . *New Directions in Chicano Scholarship.* San Diego: Chicano Monograph Series, 1978.

(de) Sahagún, Fray Bernardino. *Historia general de las cosas de Nueva España.* Mexico: Editorial Pedro Robredo, 1938.

Sánchez, Ricardo. "The Clarion Sounded". In *S.A.* Summer, 1992.

Sanders, William, Jeffery Parsons, and Robert Santley. *The Basin Of Mexico :Ecological Process in the Evolution of Civilization* New York: Academic Press, c. 1979.

San Miguel, Guadalupe Jr. *Mexican-American and the Campaign for Educational Equality in Texas 1910-1981.* Austin: University of Texas Press, 1987.

Secrest, William B. *Juanita: The Only Woman Lynched in the Gold Rush Days.* Fresno, California: Saga West, 1967.

Sefchovich, Sara. *Mexico: País de ideas, país de novelas.* México: Editorial Grijalbo, 1987.

Siegal, Bernie M.D. . *Love, Medicine and Miracles.* New York: Harper and Row, 1986.

Seler, Edward. *Gesammte Abhandlungen zur Amerikanischen, Sprachund Altertumskunde.* Austria: Druck und Verlaysanstaldt, 1969.

Soustelle, Jacques. *Daily Life of the Aztecs: On the Eve of the Spanish Conquest.* trans. Patrick O'Brian. New York: The Macmillan Company, 1968.

Stambaugh, Lee J. and Lillian J. Stambaugh. *The Lower Rio Grande Valley of Texas.* San Antonio: Naylor and Company, 1954.

Sylvester, Mowrey. *Arizona and Sonora.* New York: Harper and Row, 1864.

Tatum, Charles "Contemporary Prose Fiction: His Ties to Mexican Literature". *The Identification and Analysis of Chicano Literature.* Ed. Francisco Jiménez. New York: Bilingual Press, 1079.

Taylor Paul S. *An American-Mexican Frontier.* New York: Russell and Russell, 1971.

Tezozomoc, Alvarado. *Crónica Mexicáyotl.* Mexico: Imprenta Universitaria, 1949.

Toben, Bob, Sarfetti Wolf, *Space, Time and Beyond.* New York: St. Martin's Press, 1976.

Torres, Eliseo. *Green Medicine. Traditional Mexican-American Herbal Remedies.* Kingsville, Texas: Nieves Press. N.D.

_____*The Folk Healer: The Mexican-American Tradition of Curanderismo.* Kingsville, Texas: Nieves Press. N.D.

Trotter, Robert T. and Juan Antonio Chavira. *Curanderismo.* Athenes: University of Georgia Press, 1981.

Uranga, Emilio. *Análisis del ser mexicano.* Mexico: Porrúa y Obregón S.A., 1952.

Valdez, Luis. *Pensamiento Serpentino, A Chicano Approach to the Theater of   Reality.* San Juan Bautista, California: Cucaracha Publications, 1973.

Van Alstyne, Richard. *The Rising American Empire* New York, Norton, 1974.

Vento, Adela Sloss. *Alonso S. Perales: His Struggle for the Rights of Mexican Americans.* Arnoldo Carlos Vento ed. Trans. Jean Lord Vento. San Antonio: Artes Gráficas, 1977.

Vento Arnoldo Carlos. Imágenes y Esencia del Mexicano y Chicano: Mestizaje y Mexicanidad." Paper presented at U.N.A.M., México, D.F., 1993.

_____*La Generación Hijo Pródigo: Renovación Y Modernidad.* Lanham: University Press of America, 1996.

_____*Tres civilizaciones del mundo medieval: crítica, análisis y crónicas de la primeras cruzadas.* Lewiston, N.Y.: The Edwin Mellen Press, 1998.

_____ and Octavio Romano eds. *Canto al Pueblo Anthology.* A Special Issue of *Grito del Sol.* Berkeley: Tonatiuh Publications, 1979.

_____and Luis Leal. *The Ricardo Sánchez Reader: Critical Essays and Poetry.* Vols. I-II. (unpublished work).

Vigil, James Diego. Barrio Gangs: *Street Life and Identity in Southern California.* Austin: University of Texas Press, 1988.

Vitalis, Oderic. *Historia Aecclesiastica.* Trans. E.M. Chibnall, vols. 111-VI. Oxford: 1969, 1972.

Veytia, Mariano. *Historia Antigua de Mexico.* 2 vols. Mexico: Editorial Leyenda , 1944.

Vigil, Antonio. *The Coming of the Gringo (Ay vienen los gringos) and the Mexican-American Revolt.* New York: Vintage Press, 1970.

Wagner, Nathaniel N. and Marsha J. Haug ed. *Chicanos: Social and Psychological Perspectives.* St. Louis: Mosby Company, 1971.

Walker, Evan Harris. "The Nature of Consciouness," in *Mathematical Biosciences,* vol. 7, 1970.

Weber, David, ed. *Northern Mexico on the Eve of the United States Invasion.* New York: Arno Press, 1976.

Witt, Shirley Hill, Stan Steiner, ed., *The Way: An Anthology of American Indian Literature.* Toronto: Vintage Books, 1972.

Wolf, Eric. *Sons of the Shaking Earth.* Chicago: University of Chicago Press, 1959.

Zea, Leopoldo. "En torno a una filosofía americana" in *Ensayos sobre filosofía.* México: Editorial Style, 1948.

(de) Zorita, Alonso. *Los Señores de la Nueva España.* México: Imprenta Universitaria, 1942.

INDEX